I0121120

Utopia of the Uniform

THEORY IN FORMS

Series Editors

Nancy Rose Hunt, Achille Mbembe, and Todd Meyers

TANJA PETROVIĆ

Utopia of the Uniform

Affective Afterlives of the Yugoslav People's Army

DUKE UNIVERSITY PRESS
Durham and London
2024

© 2024 DUKE UNIVERSITY PRESS
This work is licensed under a Creative Commons Attribution-
NonCommercial-NoDerivatives 4.0 International License, avail-
able at https://creativecommons.org/licenses/by-nc-nd/4.0/.

Project Editor: Ihsan Taylor
Designed by A. Mattson Gallagher
Typeset in Untitled Serif by Westchester Publishing Services

Library of Congress Cataloging-in-Publication Data
Names: Petrović, Tanja, author.
Title: Utopia of the uniform : affective afterlives of the Yugoslav People's
Army / Tanja Petrović.
Other titles: Theory in forms.
Description: Durham : Duke University Press, 2024. | Series: Theory in
forms | Includes bibliographical references and index.
Identifiers: LCCN 2023015291 (print)
LCCN 2023015292 (ebook)
ISBN 9781478025689 (paperback)
ISBN 9781478020943 (hardcover)
ISBN 9781478027805 (ebook)
ISBN 9781478093787 (ebook other)
Subjects: LCSH: Yugoslavia. Jugoslovenska narodna armija—History.
| Draft—Social aspects—Yugoslavia—History. | Draft—Yugoslavia—
History. | Yugoslavia—Armed Forces—Social aspects. | BISAC:
HISTORY / Europe / General | SOCIAL SCIENCE / Gender Studies
Classification: LCC UB345.Y8 P487 2024 (print) | LCC UB345.Y8 (ebook) |
DDC 355.2/2363094971—dc23/eng/20231023
LC record available at https://lccn.loc.gov/2023015291
LC ebook record available at https://lccn.loc.gov/2023015292

Cover art: Photograph of Yugoslav soldiers by Franci Virant.
Courtesy of the artist.

This book is a result of the research program Historical Interpretations
of the 20th Century (P6-0347), financed by the Slovenian Research and
Innovation Agency. It is freely available in an open access edition thanks
to the generous support of the Slovenian Research and Innovation Agency
and the Institute of Culture and Memory Studies ZRC SAZU.

IN MEMORY OF MY FATHER

Contents

Acknowledgments

I took the first steps in the research that led to this book when my son was on his way into this world. In the year that this book is published, he will have reached the age when young Yugoslav men were once called up to serve in the Yugoslav People's Army. Life over these years has been deeply marked by the generosity and comradeship of so many people and the support of several institutions, but most profoundly by former soldiers of the Yugoslav People's Army who shared selflessly with me their experiences, stories, memories, and feelings. I cannot thank them all enough for their trust, patience, and time. This book is theirs as much as it is mine, and my greatest reward will be if they see it as such. I am particularly indebted to those of my interlocutors who stuck with me all this time, were always ready for another conversation about their experience in the army, trusted me with their archives of photographs, artwork, and texts, and often invested a lot of effort to excavate bits of these archives for me: Franci Virant, Želimir Žilnik, Dušan Mandić, Jane Štravs, Milovan Milenković, Oto Luthar, Radosav Majdevac, Milorad Milenković, Elmaz Jonuzi, Jure Gombač, Svanibor Pettan, Nebojša Šerić, Hariz Halilovich, Božidar Lugarić, Vladimir Nešković, Dejan Dimitrijević, Mitja Velikonja, and Milan Todorović.

My fellowship at the Institute of Advanced Study in Sofia provided me with a much-needed initial intellectual and logistical boost to think seriously and systematically through the meanings of the collective experience of military service in the former Yugoslavia. I was able to shape the contours of this project and significantly advance it during my marvelous year at the Wissenschaftskolleg in Berlin, where I was given ideal conditions for work and life, and a chance to be part of the most inspiring intellectual community. My fellowships at the Netherlands Institute of Advanced Studies, the Graduate School for East and Southeast European Studies at the University of Regensburg, and the Centre for Women's Studies at Jawaharlal Nehru University in Delhi offered me temporary academic homes where I could continue with my writing and refine it though invaluable exchange with the amazing scholars and students I met there.

My own academic home, the Research Center of the Slovenian Academy of Sciences and Arts (ZRC SAZU) in Ljubljana, is a wonderful and stimulating place to work in. I am immensely thankful to my colleagues at the Institute of Culture and Memory Studies ZRC SAZU for the solidarity, friendship, and regular conversations that make it possible to preserve and maintain what really matters in our academic life, in particular to Ana Hofman, my writing companion, to Martin Pogačar, on whose help I could always count, and to Oto Luthar, a colleague, a friend, director, and one of the protagonists of this book—all this in one person—for his support during all these years.

This book is the result of continuing conversations with a great number of people over many years and across continents. I was lucky to share my days at the Wissenschaftskolleg in Berlin with Julie Livingston, Behrooz Ghamari-Tabrizi, Nancy Hunt, Kamran Ali, Syema Muzaffar, Karen Feldman, Niklaus Largier, Steven Feierman, Claire Messud, James Wood, Jane Burbank, Fred Cooper, Elias and Najla Khouri, Birgit Meyer, Jojada Verrips, Albrecht Koschorke, Krzysztof Pomian, Karl Schlögel, Thomas Pavel, Reinhart Meyer-Kalkus, and Kathrin Biegger. I am very grateful for their interest in the questions I was concerned with, their valuable insights that profoundly influenced my thinking and writing, but also for the friendship, care, love, and laughter that made my year in Berlin so remarkable and unforgettable, and that wove ties that matter to this date. Patricia Hayes, G. Arunima, Ivan Rajković, Irene Stengs, Larisa Kurtović, and Dijana Jelača read different parts and versions of this manuscript and generously shared their thoughts and ideas. I am very fortunate to have them as interlocutors and friends. Ulf Brunnbauer, Miranda Jakiša, Nikolay Karkov, Dejan Đokić, Kaja Širok, John Bailyn, Maša Kolanović, Heleen Touquet, Mateja Habinc, Theodora Dragostinova, Armina Galijaš, Igor Duda, Marlene Schäfers, Nikolai Ssorin-Chaikov, Kateřina Králová, Tereza Juhászová, and Dragan Markovina invited me for talks and to conferences where I profited immensely from the exchange with various audiences. The bright, interested, and engaged students who took my course at the 2021 winter edition of the New York–Saint Petersburg Institute showed me that the questions this book asks resonate in meaningful, relevant, and important ways with the young generation and in different parts of the world, and I am very grateful for this reassurance.

Many colleagues and friends were loyal and patient companions of this book over the long years during which it was taking shape. I am particularly grateful to Maria Todorova, Vladimir Lukić, Danijela Lugarić, Tanja Radež, Dejan Ilić, Ana Kolarić, Boris Buden, Tatjana Jukić, Jelena Ćalić, Polly Gannon, Ivana Momčilović, Simona Ognjanović, Eli Krasniqi, Ana Panić, Mary Neuberger, Franko Dota, Nataša Strlič, and Gezim Krasniqi for important conversations and their continuous faith and support, as well as for their help with contacts, information, translation of military terms and commands, and for opening some institutional doors for me. Samira Kentrić generously allowed me to publish her art and the story behind it, and Mateja Rihtaršič created a beautiful map of Yugoslavia for this book.

I am also indebted to the staff of the gallery of the Central Military Club in Belgrade, the Museum of Contemporary History of Slovenia, and the staff of the Historical Archives of Belgrade, who assisted me in looking for and finding material invaluable for my research, to the amazing staff of the libraries of the Wissenschaftskolleg in Berlin and the Institute of East and Southeast European Studies in Regensburg for all the books they provided me, as well as to Igor Lapajne and Marko Zaplatil of ZRC SAZU for scanning and processing photographs and other visuals for this book.

Mitch Cohen, a Berlin-based editor carefully read almost everything I wrote in English about the Yugoslav army, from the synopsis of my 2011 talk at the Wissenschaftskolleg to the final version of this manuscript. I am grateful for his thoughtful and gentle approach to my writing, for all the linguistic nuances I learned from him, and especially for the poems and memories of Yugoslavia he shared with me.

Nancy Hunt, the editor of the Theory in Forms series, believed in this project from its earliest days. Without her generosity, solidarity, genuine interest in my book, and confidence that this series is the right place for it, this book would probably not have materialized, or it would be a very different one.

Several people at Duke University Press made the work on this book a friendly, rewarding, and intellectually gratifying endeavor. It was great luck to have a chance to work with such an amazing editor as Elizabeth Ault is. Her insightful comments and suggestions greatly helped me rethink the story I was trying to tell and to choose the right perspective from which to narrate it. I was deeply impressed by two anonymous reviewers and amazed by their generosity, dedication, enormous investment in reading my manuscript, and the fantastic and thoughtful suggestions they gave me. Ben Kossak and Ihsan Taylor carefully and responsibly led the whole process of the production of the book and were always helpful and responsive.

I owe special gratitude to Đorđe Hubert, who has stood by me over all these years with a lot of understanding, patience, love, and pride. Our children Ivan and Olga understood from their early days how much this work mattered to me, and they supported me on every step in their beautiful and hilarious way.

This book is dedicated to the memory of my father, Živorad Petrović, who raised me by himself as a true feminist, in a time and place in which this was far from easy and ordinary. He belonged to a generation that lived some of the utopian promises of Yugoslav socialism and most tragically experienced the loss of these promises. My hope is that Olga and Ivan and their generation will find their way to make utopias imaginable again.

Introduction

A Silent Force That Unsettles Ruins

Through the large windows of the café in a newly built shopping mall in Kosovo's capital Pristina, Elmaz and I could see the city and the valley stretching
behind it. Elmaz pointed to an abandoned building of the factory where he
used to work before the war. Then he showed me a hill with newly built houses
where diplomats, representatives of international organizations, other for-
eigners, and wealthy locals live. "When we have electricity outage, the whole
city is in the dark, only this hill shines," he said, laughing. Farther up the valley is Gračanica, a Serbian enclave, where life runs in parallel to but separately
from the life of Kosovo's Albanian majority. In the youngest of the independent
states that emerged from socialist Yugoslavia, people live in ethnically defined,
segregated communities; and political and economic life is driven largely by
the logic of this segregation and the colonial-like relations resulting from the
presence of representatives of the "international community" to which Elmaz
was pointing. Not much is different in the rest of the post-Yugoslav societies.

Elmaz Jonuzi, a kind, energetic family man in his late forties, now earns his living as a taxi driver. He met me at Pristina's airport in October 2017 when I came to town for a conference. It was my first time in the city and my first time in Kosovo after the wars that left Yugoslavia disintegrated. As he was skillfully maneuvering his car through busy streets, we chatted, looking for references to things that made up life in the country we used to share before the wars of the 1990s. I asked him whether the beer produced in Kosovo's town of Peć (Peja) still exists. It was my favorite during my student years in Belgrade. The last day of my stay in Pristina, before taking me to the airport, Elmaz made sure I would not leave without trying Peja beer again. While we were looking out over the cityscape from the café where he took me for a beer, I asked him about his service in the Yugoslav People's Army (Jugoslovenska narodna armija, JNA).[1]

For me, it was not an easy question to ask. As a woman, I did not serve in the army, so Elmaz and I did not share the experience common to all Yugoslav men of generations born before 1972 or 1973. As a Serb, I was asking an ethnic Albanian man about his experience in an army that was transformed into a military force dominated by Serbs in the 1990s and whose members, together with paramilitary units and Serbian police, committed numerous crimes against ethnic Albanians in Kosovo. Between Elmaz and me, sitting across the table in a fancy café in Pristina on that sunny autumn day, and between the two moments when I enjoyed a beer brewed in Peja—my student time in Belgrade in the 1990s and my visit to Kosovo in 2017—there was a whole nightmarish world of killing, suffering, and expulsions, of freezer trucks that transported bodies of killed Albanians and clandestine graves scattered across the Serbian territory where these bodies were buried.[2] I was, moreover, asking an Albanian man about experience that he most probably remembers in terms of hardships caused by Serbs. After September 1987, when an Albanian soldier, Aziz Kelmendi, killed four soldiers, wounded five, and then committed suicide in the garrison in the central Serbian town of Paraćin, Albanian soldiers serving in the JNA often faced oppression and open hatred. Elmaz was no exception. He spent his service at a military base in Kragujevac, Serbia, in 1988–89, at the height of ethnic tensions between Serbs and Albanians, when the wheels of Yugoslavia's disintegration had already been put in motion. A Serb officer from Kosovo gave him a hard time. Elmaz was often put in prison on the army base and given the most difficult and least desirable tasks. During his military service, massive riots by Albanians against Milošević's repression in Kosovo and his stripping the province of autonomy led to the introduction of a state of emergency. Elmaz's service was prolonged, and he could not go home for another long, tense, and fearful 35 days.

For Elmaz, it might have not been an easy question to answer for other reasons. His days in the uniform of the Yugoslav army and that sunny October afternoon might have felt worlds apart, separated not only by the passage of time, but also by numerous discontinuities the last decades had brought to the lands that used to belong to socialist Yugoslavia and, above all, by the ethnic violence and disastrous wars in which it ended. The line that sharply defined Elmaz's life into "before" and "after" was drawn on April 27, 1999, during NATO intervention in Serbia and Kosovo, when he barely escaped being killed by a man from Serb paramilitary forces. His two friends and neighbors were not so lucky. I suspected that what he had experienced years earlier on a military base in Serbia, in the uniform of a now nonexistent army that largely aligned with the Serbian side in the violent conflicts of the 1990s, was likely irrelevant or traumatic to him, something buried deeply under the ruins of the vanished country, and certainly not a topic for a conversation over local beer with a Serb woman visiting Kosovo for the first time after the war.

But with slight hesitation and a tinge of uneasiness, Elmaz had a lot to say about his experience in the JNA and was willing to share it with me. He did speak of nasty officers, of army prison, drill, and some tensions with local Serbs in Kragujevac, but he spoke even more of nice people in the surrounding villages where he was on watch, of village parties where he was welcomed, of tasty Serbian *rakija* and good food. The most important of all the stories from the army was his friendship with other four JNA soldiers. With warmth and softness in his voice, he told me about Robert from Ljubljana, Robert from Slavonski Brod, Nermin from Novi Pazar, and Zoran from Vranje. He asked me to help him find his Slovenian friend Robert when I went back to Ljubljana, and I promised I would. I have never succeeded in fulfilling this promise. And I still owe him the bottle of Serbian plum brandy that my uncles make that I promised to bring when I return to Kosovo.

Elmaz is one of more than forty men who performed mandatory service in the Yugoslav military with whom I have spoken extensively since 2006, when I became interested in the meanings of the shared experience of military service in socialist Yugoslavia in the social space torn by wars and violence during the 1990s. From 1945 to 1991—the lifespan of the Yugoslav socialist state—military service was mandatory for all men after they turned eighteen and/or graduated from high school.[3] Those who enrolled in colleges that would give them an education considered useful for the military, such as in medicine or engineering, could postpone their military service in the JNA until after graduation, but not after they turned twenty-seven. For conscripts, the duration of military service varied depending on the period, the education of the soldiers, and the branch of the army, but the majority of people who served in the 1970s and 1980s and on whose stories and memories this book is based served either for a year, fifteen months, or a year and a half.

The men I talked to, from various parts of the former Yugoslavia and with different ethnic, social, educational, and professional backgrounds, generationally range from those born during or immediately after World War II to those born in the mid-1970s. They served in the JNA between the late 1960s and the early 1990s, but the majority of my interviewees served in the 1970s and 1980s. In Yugoslavia, that was the time encompassing economic growth and decline, the massive emigration of workers to Western European states in need of labor, a time of relative stability, burgeoning popular culture and alternatives, rising living standards, but also rising social tensions and inequalities.[4] Nevertheless, these decades, preceded by post-revolutionary enthusiasm, construction, and rigor, and followed by the nightmarish destruction of the civil war that tore Yugoslavia apart, are remembered as "Yugoslavia's good (or golden) times," when the majority of citizens could live a decent life and the future seemed possible and bright.[5]

Most of the men I spoke with—irrespective of their personal and professional trajectories, of where they came from and where they currently live, and of their ethnicity and education—regard their experience with the Yugoslav military as important and meaningful. Friendships made in the army, like Elmaz's, are crucial for the importance and meaningfulness of that experience. These friendships, made among young men in the confined space of a military base, outside the ordinary and everyday flows of time, recall a world structured on premises different from those governing life in the post-Yugoslav present, a world in which uniformed men recognized and befriended each other because of their moral qualities and irrespective of which ethnic group they belonged to. They point to the possibility of an alternative future irrevocably lost during the Yugoslav catastrophe, in which men who once served in the JNA together ended up killing each other because they belonged to different ethnic groups.

The friendships made in the JNA constitute the driving force of the affective afterlives of Yugoslav military service that I explore in this book. They discretely mark life paths of Yugoslav men and resiliently persist among the ruins of Yugoslavia, challenging and unsettling them. The ruins of the Yugoslav political project come in diverse shapes—as burnt houses, ethnically cleansed villages, devastated landscapes, clandestine graves, and ethnic enclaves, but also as newly built neighborhoods for the wealthy, private hospitals and medical facilities available to the few, modern shopping malls, and stratified cities in which the rich never suffer from electricity outages. They cannot be reduced to the physical remnants of the destroyed country, as these are ruins not only of what was, but also of what could have been. They are also reminders of alternative futures—those past and those lost.[6] In this book, I am interested in the capacity of the feelings that emerged from the experience of former Yugoslavs with mandatory service in the JNA to unsettle these ruins and question the givenness of the present. I ask about the forms of these feelings and about the modalities in which their agency unfolds. This agency does not come from continuity and presence, but rather from their opposites. Continuity does not go well with war, destruction, and uprooting. Elmaz lost track of most of his army friends and has sporadic contact only with Zoran, but the way he spoke about them made it clear to me that lack of contact or even knowing their destinies since they all left the army base in Kragujevac had no impact on how much these friendships still matter to him.

Nostalgia offers itself as a handy interpretive framework to explain the fragmentary but recurring presence of feelings, memories, and pieces of the JNA experience. It is intrinsic to afterness, "a particular figure of modernity, that of following, coming after, having survived, outlived, or succeeded something or someone."[7] I, however, rather opt for a different register, that of *afterlife*. Too often understood as a past-oriented, passive, paralyzing, and unproductive feeling, nostalgia tends to pacify one's relationship with the past, thus cementing the pastness of that past and how it is structured vis-à-vis the present and the future.[8] Afterlife, on the other hand, invites us to think about the temporality of "endings that are not over" and presupposes an agency capable of unsettling the stillness of the aftermath.[9] This agency resides in the archives of the past, both material and immaterial, revealing itself as an ability to transmit affects across time and space, and inviting us to recognize signs of alternatives and futures imagined outside the places where we usually expect them.[10]

Afterlife, a concept through which I explore the faculty of feelings related to military service in the JNA to unsettle, remind people of lost possibilities, and silently recall utopia, brings together *time* and *form* as structuring forces for the narrative of this book. The capacity of the affective afterlives of the Yugoslav military to restructure social time, recalling lost futures, emerges from a mandatory, forced collective experience, performed far away from home and "normal" life, in the confined space of barracks, bases, proving grounds, and training areas. That experience was composed of repetitive disciplinary routines, ritualized practices, and performative language protocols, often void of deeper meaning. This relationship between the monotony, standardization, and voidness of form on the one hand, and the meaningfulness of the experience of Yugoslav military service and its capacity to unsettle fixed temporal frames on the other, is what this book explores. It asks about the ways in which feelings that inhabit these monotonous forms challenge the givenness of the relationship between the past, present, and future in the aftermath of Yugoslavia, working through silence, hesitation, suspension, and impossibility. Discussing these feelings rooted in the heart of socialist state institution and the political meanings of their afterlives, this book also asks about the intersections of the collective utopian imagination with personal affects and feelings; and it explores the forms through which the Yugoslav military institution engaged in the production of collective utopia and its affective foundations.

ARCHIVES AND FEELINGS

Over the last few decades, "we have seen a marked diminution in the production of new utopias" and have been living in a present in which the future is not easily imaginable and comes in dystopian registers, rather than the utopian ones.[11] As a consequence, the future as a heuristic term "saturates—or oversaturates—today's humanities."[12] The past increasingly becomes a place where the imaginations of the future are sought and "a densely animated object of enchantment."[13] An "archive fever" comes as a result of this quest.[14]

The failed socialist projects of the twentieth century and their legacies, archives, and material ruins have become an object of fascination for many and also a focus of scholars and activists. As Larisa Kurtović argues, archivist-activists turn to the legacies of Yugoslav socialism as "a potential mine of insights and practical knowledge that could be reactivated in the difficult and often exasperating postwar political present" in the societies still torn by nationalism and exhausted by neoliberal politics at the European periphery.[15]

Their archiving efforts focus on the legacy of the anti-fascist struggle during World War II, women's role in that struggle, socialist companies, and cultural production and social relations made possible by specific frameworks and infrastructures such as local cultural centers, workers' universities, voluntary labor, self-management, amateurism, and the Non-Aligned Movement. These archiving activities are paralleled by increased artistic and academic interest in diverse aspects of Yugoslav socialism and in its heritage that serve as an inspiration or as a source of knowledge for today's political imaginaries, as well as in these new archives and their political potential.[16]

Recuperating an archive of Yugoslav military service would be an unlikely ambition of these contemporary archivists due to its involuntary and disciplinary character, but also because of the very forms through which the military institution has shaped the experience of serving in the Yugoslav army. However, as I argue in chapter 2, this institution's work went beyond militarizing and disciplining: the profoundly collective experience of military service was designed to bring into practice some of the central political ideas of Yugoslav socialism, such as collectivity, egalitarianism, education, and comradeship. The performative, repetitive, and ritualized practices military service consisted of built a framework for life and love in which class and ethnic and social backgrounds were not organizing principles. Military service was, therefore, an exercise in soldiering, but also an exercise in utopian living in which one's class, ethnicity, or place of origin mattered much less than one's moral virtues.

The JNA-related archives concern me importantly in this book. I find the concept of the archive helpful in grappling with the emotional, social, and political afterlife of structures, sensibilities, and things because the archive, inseparable from an afterlife, is a site of encounter and a mediation among experience, memory, and history.[17] Here, archives include my own archive of interviews, stories, newspaper articles, photographs, letters, postcards, and material objects that I have collected since 2006, as well as archival projects by former JNA soldiers created during their military service, such as Franci Virant's photographs or artworks by Dušan Mandić. They also extend to a myriad of photographs, letters, postcards, and objects former soldiers possessed and often kept once their military service was over. There is an intrinsic link between the experience of army service and its remembrance and thus—indirectly—both some sort of archiving and some futures imagined or anticipated. Many practices performed during military service were aimed at creating memories for a later time, such as taking photographs, writing inscriptions or dedications on the backs of photographs, and making souvenirs during the long army days such as tattoos, models of the Eiffel Tower made of match sticks, notebooks filled with names and addresses of army buddies, or souvenir photo albums. These activities of memory-making, in all their diversity, not only resulted in a personal archive, but were also preconditioned with an afterlife of that archive. They confirm that "memory and afterness are constitutive of each other," and manifoldly so.[18] At the moment these memories were made, they "counted" on a future that was imaginable, based on continuity and smooth transitions and devoid of tragic ruptures. The future that came was not the one that was anticipated. Photos taken in the army often became the only visual reminders of men killed during the wars of Yugoslav disintegration. Notebooks filled with names and addresses suddenly became unreliable, as houses were burnt and people ended up displaced, missing, gone, dead.

In the aftermath of Yugoslavia's and its military's demise, many former JNA soldiers act as "rogue archivists" who digitize parts of their private JNA archives and make them available on the internet.[19] With such archiving endeavors, they grapple with catastrophe, loss, and rupture, and seek to regain continuity and temporal orders in which their own biographies can stand as "normal" and legitimate.

The concept of the archive seems suitable for thinking about the legacy of the shared, collective experience of military service in socialist Yugoslavia, also beyond remaking individual biographies. Despite the "democratization" of archiving practices in the digital era, the archive still echoes the authority of creating a publicly recognized voice about the past and possesses a legitimizing capacity.[20] The official archive of the Yugoslav military was significantly damaged and partially destroyed when army headquarters in Belgrade were bombed during the NATO intervention in 1999. Two decades later, the remnants of this archive are still mostly unavailable to historians and other researchers. The archives discussed in this book, and the book as a whole, are not meant to fill the void resulting from the absence of an institutional archive, but to point to the necessity of acknowledging the vicissitudes of the shared past as a knowledge relevant and useful in the present and for the future. This understanding of memories from the socialist period is largely missing in Eastern Europe.[21] Here, the collapse of socialism triggered a "testimonial drive" that shifted from early concerns "with political repression, justice, and retribution" to seemingly apolitical "revivals of the social, cultural, and everyday experiences of socialism," but with a pervasive "authority of personal

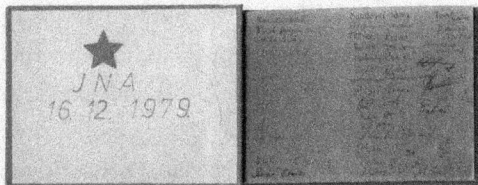

Figures I.1, I.2, and I.3 Memories from military service in the JNA. From the archive of Milorad Milenković.

experience."[22] The memories, objects, and sentiments relating to the JNA and the forms in which they persist in the aftermath of Yugoslavia, although very personal, evoke a specific collectivity due to their shared nature, and thus unfold as political and politically relevant.

As I bring together the archives, their forms, and feelings that persist through ruptures in time and space, my understanding of the archive comes close to what Ann Cvetkovich labels an "archive of feelings" in her study of multisided queer archives in the United States.[23] Cvetkovich strongly argues for the importance of what affective archives both store and evoke: the archive "must preserve not just knowledge, but feeling."[24] Broadly defined, in Cvetkovich's study, an archive is composed of both narratives (voice- and video-recorded testimonies, memoirs, letters, and/or diaries) and material objects (photographs and/or other objects that have emotional, even sentimental value). It is, moreover, composed of cultural texts "as repositories of feelings and emotions, which are encoded not only in the content of the texts themselves but in the practices that surround their production and reception."[25] While Cvetkovich approaches American "national trauma histories and their cultural memory from the unabashedly minoritarian perspective of lesbian cultures," my perspective is profoundly majoritarian.[26] I look at the archival material shaped by the experience shared by millions of former Yugoslavs. Just like the case of the gay and lesbian archives in the United States, however, the experiences, memories, and feelings of these men are contested and largely absent from the narrative regimes through which socialist Yugoslavia is remembered and historicized.

UNDERSTANDING SOCIALISM THROUGH FORMS

In spite of scholars' growing interest in the archives that emerged from the socialist experience and in the potential of these archives to contribute to shaping and reimagining future politics, not much has been written about the forms in which these archives have taken shape or about the forms through which feelings intrinsic to these archives live their afterlives, emerging in the present as a force that unsettles it and points to past futures. The forms that shaped these archives and feelings are inevitably associated with the predictability, routine, and consequent banality associated with this experience: with its standardized, performative, monotonous, and ritualized character.[27]

As such, they are not intuitively linked to any emancipatory potential of the socialist past, nor do they make a likely connection with deeply meaningful memories that keep coming back as a discreet but resilient force.

On the other hand, repetitive, performative, and ritualized forms have a very important place and interpretative value in scholars' attempts to understand socialism as a historical experience and its demise. They have also been recognized as an important means of extorting and maintaining power in colonial, late-capitalist, and totalitarian social contexts.[28] For the period usually described as late socialism, from the 1960s to the late 1980s, there is a seeming consensus that there was a "deep gap between ideology and reality, especially as that reality grew progressively consumerist and lifestyle-oriented."[29] This perception is familiar also in the post-Yugoslav context. There, the argument goes, a utopian imagination characteristic of an early period of socialist production became "ideologically ritualized, creatively stale."[30] Additionally, this ritualization and performativity eventually led to the exhaustion of the socialist project.[31] The ritualized forms lacked authenticity and made late socialism starkly contrast with "authentic" forms of resistance in World War II and the period immediately following the war.

The standardized, ritualized forms by which socialist ideology was maintained diverged from citizens' lives, so socialist subjects developed various strategies of making social meanings and positioning themselves through their use and appropriation. Concepts such as "imitative exaggeration," "subversive affirmation," "*stiob*," and Alf Lüdtke's concept of "Eigensinn" proliferated as a consequence of academic efforts to understand this self-positioning and meaning-making.[32] The influential work of Alexei Yurchak points to these forms' capacity to produce complex subjectivities, social relations, and meanings. According to Yurchak, "the performative reproduction of the form of rituals and speech acts actually *enabled* the emergence of diverse, multiple, and unpredictable meanings in everyday life, including those that did not correspond to the constative meanings of authoritative discourse."[33] Drawing on Sonja Luerhman, Anna Kruglova similarly argues, "The schism between ideology and life could have been accepted by people not as a reason to be 'cynical,' 'ironic,' or otherwise distanced, but instead as a challenge of creative interpretation and artistic execution."[34]

Thinking of ritualized, hyper-normalized forms and their relation to life, however, still remains within the framework of knowledge and interpretation, and their affective outcomes remain insufficiently addressed. The very concept of ideology, as Kruglova importantly observes, "continues to provide cognitive and affective tools for the objectification of one's own and others' social and historical conditions, for thinking about social and cultural aspects of life *as if they were separate from life*."[35] This does not mean that socialist ideology and its forms were detached from life and incapable of producing affect. In his study of the late socialism in the USSR, Alexei Yurchak emphasizes that citizens reproduced these forms while untethering or ignoring their constative meanings, which "enabled creative production of new meanings and forms of life."[36] He points to parades organized for major socialist holidays in May and November as massive rituals that provided ideological frameworks for the production of socialities and a public "nonidentical with how the addressed public was articulated in authoritative discourse, such as the 'Soviet people' or the 'Soviet toilers.'"[37] "With their massive scale," writes Yurchak, "parades were a powerful machinery for the cultural production of the publics of *svoi*, creating temporary collectivities of friends and strangers who marched together through the streets, carried the same portraits and slogans, shouted 'hurray' in response to the same appeals blaring from loudspeakers, and publicly displayed the same celebratory mood."[38] In addition, "millions sent greeting cards with good wishes on the occasion of these national holidays. The pictures on the postcards contained Soviet symbols: stars, banners, hammers and sickles, slogans, and Lenin portraits. On the postcards people typically wished each other health, happiness, success in work, and so on. They also used the occasion to exchange news with friends, relatives, and colleagues."[39]

These collective Soviet rituals and their ritualized discourses indeed resulted in affective communities, whereby ritualized forms (formulae written on the postcards and the symbols they displayed) were used as tools for affective connecting and exchange. This production of affective ties, however, was not intended by the authoritative power, but was rather a side effect of the ritualized forms' work, the unexpected and unpredictable result of that work. "Participating in these events reproduced the collectivity of belonging that was enabled by these slogans and portraits," Yurchak writes, "but no longer bound to their literal sense."[40]

The authoritative power of the socialist state used these same forms for the intentional production of affective communities. In the Yugoslav case, this production was related to the key concepts of brotherhood and unity (*bratstvo i jedinstvo*) and comradeship (*drugarstvo*), essentially oriented toward building solidarities and ties across ethnic, class, and gender divisions. The Yugoslav military was an institution explicitly engaged in this affective work. It brought together radically different people to serve together and made them the same (and equal) through the uniform they wore and exposure to standardized, repetitive, and ritualized procedures, discourses, and routines. Outside what normal and everyday life used to be and far away from it, young Yugoslav men spent a year or more on JNA bases, and their sharing a confined, isolated space resulted in friendships and meaningfulness that would hardly be possible outside it. As one of my interlocutors emphasized, one year of serving in the army is a substantial amount of time: it spans all four seasons and comprises one condensed life. Long-term exposure to ritualized, repetitive, predictable discourses and practices, very different from the temporariness of parades and other socialist rituals, made these discourses and practices, through which the authoritative institution exercises its power, forms of life. In the context in which the subject's position is not one of the distance and control necessary for interpretation and strategic use, but one of embracing a year or more of long, ritualized, performative experience of military service as life as such, these forms produced an emotional fabric, and this production of affect was not something the military institution did not intend, could not predict, or was not interested in, but was one of its most important aims.

This production of affects of friendship and solidarity through ritualized forms is what the Yugoslav army wanted, as a Yugoslav institution par excellence; these affects are simultaneously the primary reason why very diverse men still consider their military service important and meaningful. This accord between the authoritative institution of the military and the young men subjected to it was by no means absolute, as the ritualized nature of practices constituting military service also enabled soldiers to produce diverse meanings, take different positions, and use their protective capacity against the hegemonic power of the military institution, all of which I discuss in chapter 5. It nevertheless offers a helpful perspective for attempts to understand how anticipated futures and utopian imaginations could be nested at the heart of the total, compulsory, all-male, oppressive, and strictly hierarchical institution of military service, as well as to better understand how not only violence, destruction, and betrayal, but also love, loyalty, and friendship shape the present in the aftermath of Yugoslavia's political catastrophe.

As Walter Benjamin insisted, the afterlife is central to the historical object of interpretation.[41] It goes together with history and tends to complicate it.[42] The afterlife of military service in the Yugoslav army prompts us to rethink the forms in which the history of Yugoslavia and Yugoslav socialism is told. In the wake of the disastrous dissolution of Yugoslavia and its socialist project, the temporality of the aftermath keeps histories and memories caught in an event-aftermath straightjacket, bringing narratives that historicize Yugoslavia close to postcolonial histories: they are all reduced to single trajectories directed by violence and trauma.[43] This reduction not only shapes historiographic or artistic narratives, but also affects lives and bodies and flattens biographies, because a "trauma frame would congeal subjects into overwhelmed victims and survivors, effacing social action and practice."[44]

Sticking firmly to the event-aftermath pattern, the scholarship addressing the Yugoslav People's Army that has been published since the country fell apart has focused mainly on its role in Yugoslavia's dissolution.[45] Or, what is typical of scholarly production in the post-Yugoslav space, it describes the institutional history and technical characteristics of the Yugoslav military, offering a seemingly objective, disinterested narrative of the Yugoslav military's history, transforming it "into discrete units of time, and petrifying it within classificatory labels, all of which situate the past as an object of spectatorship."[46] This petrification works toward fixing the logic in which the ethnicity of individuals and groups is the only principle that governs political life and structures political time. It makes it possible for a revisionist historian with a key role in rehabilitating Nazi collaborators in Serbia in World War II to author a history of the socialist Yugoslav army, and to publish the book with a Croatian publisher, thanking in the introduction his Croatian colleague who is very active in rehabilitating Croatian fascists.[47] To work successfully, this logic needs to eliminate any reminder of a possibility of a different identification or of imagining a future based on different premises than the one that arrived after Yugoslavia fell apart. That is why it excludes from the institutional history of the Yugoslav military the generations of soldiers conscripted into the JNA, the multiple forms of their interactions with this institution, life within its institutional framework, and the modalities in which fragments of that life persist in the aftermath of the JNA and the country it was supposed to protect.

It is not the forms in which military service in the JNA was experienced per se that possess a capacity to unsettle fixity and the givenness of the temporality of the aftermath. For such a capacity, these forms had to be imbued with affect—they had to become a home of friendship, solidarity, and care. Only then could they have a capacity to silently, but persistently, recall alternatives to the reality of the aftermath of the Yugoslav catastrophe. Following the trajectory of these forms and the feelings they produced—from their creation on military bases across Yugoslavia to their afterlife amid its ruins—this book seeks to move away from narratives of "larger entities" and seamless histories in which the lives of Yugoslavia and its military are marked by a clearly defined beginning and end and whose pastness is absolute and thus incapable of making any intervention in the present.[48]

Yugoslav army service was performed by men, and Yugoslavia was destroyed in the catastrophe by men who killed each other—the same men who once wore the JNA uniform, shared dormitories in the barracks, made friends, and counted days left until the end of their army service. From the temporality of the aftermath, shaped by violence and defined by the catastrophic end of the Yugoslav socialist project, these men are observed through the prism of seemingly solid and "large" categories of (militarized) masculinity, violence, aggression, or patriarchy.[49] Such a view of men imposes problems already noted by scholars focusing on masculinity in (post-)conflict contexts. Donna Pankhurst notices that "the term femininity is not deployed in the same generalizing and deterministic manner as has been the case for masculinity; feminist scholars of militarism and peace-building have been careful to differentiate the 'various and contrasting roles, identities, sources of and constraints on power and control, access to and use of their own labor' for women, but they have neglected this task for men."[50] The link between men, soldiering, and violence is additionally essentialized in the case of the former Yugoslavia, because of both the supposedly totalitarian character of its socialist past and its violent dissolution in the 1990s.[51] But framing military service solely as a site of or pretext for male-initiated violence allows no scope for sentimental memories, unusual friendships, and their afterlives. They have remained largely outside the histories of Yugoslavia's disintegration and are absent both from nationalist narratives that venerate heroic masculine figures and from mainstream liberal, normative views on reconciliation in the former Yugoslavia that focus on men with marginal positions opposed to soldiering, violence, and war crimes: draft dodgers, conscientious objectors, peace activists, LGBT activists, and male victims of sexual violence.[52] What lies between these opposite poles of representation of men—the memories of the men who served in the JNA, from all corners of the former Yugoslavia, who performed army service together and found themselves on opposite sides once the war began—has no place in the heretofore standard narratives about masculinity in Yugoslavia, the violent dissolution of the country, and its aftermath. These accounts have no space for Elmaz's friendship with two Roberts, Zoran, and Nermin; for the pride with which my colleague, the sociology professor Mitja Velikonja, explains how, as an eighteen-year-old JNA soldier, he was able to cook for the whole of his unit of fellow conscripts in a remote post on the Austrian border; for Hariz's fond memories of Đurica, his army buddy from central Serbia who offered him shelter in his home once the war in Bosnia started; for the loss that Božidar is still struggling with, and which concerns Đura, his best friend from the army, with whom he maintained contact many years after his military service, but stopped talking to him once the conflict in the former Yugoslavia started. Nor do the standard framings provide space for the anxiety of the photographer Franci Virant, who displayed his photographs of army buddies at an exhibition in Ljubljana and asked me to locate the people in them. He himself did not dare do so, being too afraid of what he might learn about their fate in the time of violence and killing.

This book is about men in an all-male military institution and its homogenizing effects, but it strives to de-homogenize discourses on the history of Yugoslavia and socialism in general, attending to memories, friendships, and feelings generated during military service, their forms, and the modalities through which they manifest themselves in the present. This attention reveals men not as a homogeneous, solid collective, but as troubled and fragmented selves, whose social existence has been marked by contradictions and is irreducible to firmly defined categories. These forms and modalities, memories and emotions are recognizable and shared by very many, but they simultaneously decisively shape individual biographies in unique ways. In an attempt to acknowledge this simultaneous sharedness and uniqueness, I call the interviewees who feature prominently in this book by their actual names.

This book's narrative is also shaped by the complex ways I positioned myself vis-à-vis my interviewees and their stories and feelings. Just as life on JNA bases could not be separated from the ritualized forms in which it was lived, my research on experiences of military service among former JNA recruits cannot be separated from entangled lives of us all in the aftermath of the Yugoslav catastrophe. The encounters during which I collected the material for this book were more than typical ethnographic situations. While some of the men I talked with were entirely unknown to me, I came to a majority of them through people I knew: they were fathers or other relatives of my friends; some of them were also my own friends and relatives. My father served in the Yugoslav army, and many people who mean a lot to me were also JNA soldiers.

Some of them were my colleagues and friends—some scattered across the former Yugoslavia and some now living far away from it. Whether I already knew the men I interviewed or not, sharing memories made during military service—and their later struggle to incorporate this experience into the trajectories of their own lives and of broader histories characterized by rupture and loss—was an important aspect of our relationship. Through this ethnographic situation, I learned something new and different about my male relatives, friends, and acquaintances, something intimate and unrelatable to the selves they revealed in ordinary interactions. Many stories—about places in Serbia or Slovenia where men spent time as JNA soldiers or about friends from the army—were triggered by who I am, where I come from, where I live now, or what language I speak. For the men I did not know before, sharing army stories with me was often preceded by a subtle searching for common ground and mutual recognition and trust, and resulted in long-lasting friendships.

Many could not tell me stories about their time in the army without also telling me about the subsequent events that decisively marked their lives and their view of the past. For Elmaz, it was an event in April 1999, and for Hariz it was his confinement in the Trnopolje concentration camp and the massacre in Srebrenica, in which he lost most of the male members of his family at the hands of members of the Bosnian Serb Army units. For these two men and many others I talked to, offering army stories to a Serb woman was much more than sharing anecdotal memories about military service, all similar, funny, often banal, and sometimes bizarre. Nor was this just ethnographic work for me. The interviews were post-Yugoslav encounters, and often took place far from where my home and that of the man I was interviewing had been before Yugoslavia was torn apart by ethnic wars and violence. And there is the passage of time, a temporal dimension that importantly shaped my relationship both to these men and to this book: during the many years it took for this book to take shape, I carried their stories around with me—intimate, painful, unresolvable, unique.

STRUCTURE OF THE BOOK

After providing the sociopolitical context of the Yugoslav People's Army and the system of mandatory military service, which existed for four and half decades, in the first chapter I describe the main narrative threads about Yugoslav military service and the modalities in which they emerge and circulate in the aftermath of Yugoslavia. I focus on the tension between the ubiquity of army-related stories in the post-Yugoslav space and the difficulties of incorporating them into the biographies of actual men, a tension resulting in silence, hesitation and suspension, forms through which the feelings related to military service work as a force recalling a lost future in the aftermath of political catastrophe.

Chapter 2 explores the characteristics of the Yugoslav military institution that made it possible for the utopian imagination to be seeded in the total, oppressive, and ritualized experience of Yugoslav military service: its syncretic character, its link to Yugoslav supranational citizenship and the ideology of brotherhood and unity, and a combination of the sameness (and equality) of men and their radical diversity that marked this experience.

Chapter 3 offers a glimpse of the everyday reality of military service and the routines that structured it, everyday routines and protocols that filled almost every moment of a day in the JNA and had to be learned through repetition. Two parts of military service were structured through different perceptions of time. In the first part, soldiers were exposed to intense training, education, and drill, aimed at disciplining them, but also at enabling them to function as a collective in a synchronized and effective way. In the second part, time slowed down, but the experience remained structured by daily routines. This chapter discusses the working of these routines and highlights their role in providing a common ground for very different men gathered in JNA units. They not only made it possible for these men to act efficiently and harmoniously, but also gave them a common language, however stiff, monotonous, and performative, and enabled modalities of life that resulted in emotions, friendships, and meaningful experiences.

The following two chapters dwell on the dynamics between sameness and radical difference among the young men serving in the JNA, discussing the ways in which the forms that constituted the day-to-day reality of military service affected soldiers' subjectivities and (self-)perceptions, and how these forms were productive of affective and meaningful relationships. Chapter 4 discusses the uniform, its difference-erasing capacity, and the ways it structured life in the barracks and outside them. It looks at the concrete effects of the military uniform and its implications for relations among young Yugoslav men gathered on JNA bases, as well as for relations between men's uniformed and "ordinary" selves.

Chapter 5 focuses on the ritualization and standardization of life in the JNA and shows how they enabled the military institution to function and strengthen its power over soldiers, but also protected soldiers from that very same power. Ritualization's protective capacity stretched beyond life on the base, working against the ethnicizing forces that shape reality in the aftermath of Yugoslavia and its military. The uniform had the capacity to make everyone the same and equal, and ritualization's protective work moved the ethnic and class identities of these men into the background and their uniform to the fore. This worked together in pointing to a utopian possibility for these men to be recognized in universal and moral terms, as *humans* and *good men*, and to matter as such—a possibility largely lost in the disastrous events of the 1990s. The routine, the ritualized, the uniformed, in all their limitations and constraints, thus unfold as forms inhabited by lost (political) alternatives and emotions that still linger among the ruins of the socialist state and its military, based on the ideology of brotherhood and unity.

Chapter 6 retains the focus on form and observes the early signs of the process of Yugoslavia's tragic destruction through the loosening and dissolving of fixed ritualized and standardized forms of being and living in the JNA: the protective capacity of the ritualized forms subsided, ethnic belonging became decisive for soldiers' treatment and destiny, and prevailed over the uniform's difference-erasing capacity. With the end of Yugoslavia approaching, peaceful experience of military service began to fade away, and the Yugoslav military became associated with the usual notions attached to military institutions: violence, fear, humiliation, war, and killing.

An interlude between chapters 6 and 7 offers a glimpse into the terminal stage of the dissolution of forms through which the Yugoslav military created a framework for a specific sociality, ethicality, and futurity, all lost in the process of dissolution. I invite the reader to walk with me through a chronology of events in the time of the catastrophe that marked the lives of JNA soldiers whose memories feature in this book and of all of us in lands devastated by violence and destruction. This chronology of events is inevitably selective and incomplete, but even in this condensed form it offers a sense of the tragic intertwinement of people, places, events, and destructive forces that govern them, of landscapes, lives, and selves altered forever by the catastrophe.

After the catastrophe came the aftermath, motionless and with foreclosed horizons of the future. It brought new borders and normalized the ethnicized logic of life that dictates the flattening and remaking of biographies, squeezing people into narrow boxes of ethnic identity, dismantling known worlds and eradicating once imaginable futures. The JNA archives have also had to accommodate to this new logic, revealing the past as "a stable referent in the service of the present."[53] This accommodation is my main concern in chapter 7, which discusses how it affected bodies, biographies, post-Yugoslav cinematic narratives about the JNA, and the politics of remembering and forgetting in the aftermath of the Yugoslav wars.

Bits of the JNA archives and memories, however, are capable of questioning the current ethnonational logic and of pointing to alternatives to it. To understand this capability, in chapter 8 I explore the relationship between ritualized and monotonous forms of military service and affect, and focus on modalities through which these forms did not work as performative means, but became life, and temporalities that condition these forms to be loci of the utopian imagination and lost possible futures. My focus is particularly on male friendship and economies of solidarity and care as an extremely profound emotional fabric that has resulted from monotonous, ritualized, and performative patterns of life on JNA bases.

Chapter 9 sheds light on the capacity of memories from the JNA to work against the stillness of the aftermath and to question and destabilize it. The afterlife of military service in the JNA manifests in forms defined by a negative value—in silence, hesitation, suspension, and impossibility—but these are the forms through which that afterlife unsettles the past, questions fixed temporal frames, and discreetly but persistently points to alternatives to the present in the aftermath of the Yugoslav catastrophe.

In the epilogue I look back to the collective experience of serving in socialist Yugoslavia's military from the global moment shaped by the COVID-19 pandemic, war in Ukraine, burgeoning right-wing populism, and failing late capitalism. I ask about the political meanings of this experience and its afterlife for the citizens of former Yugoslav lands on the European periphery, but I also consider broader efforts to imagine the future and to practice collectivity and solidarity in the global political present.

Focusing on the form and its capacities throughout this book, I suggest a trajectory of the evolution of ritualized and standardized forms: they were solidified together with Yugoslav socialism and its army, had an important role in the army's work, but also enabled emotional ties and hosted the utopian imagination. As the end of socialism and of Yugoslavia neared, and the violent conflicts during which it disappeared approached, these fixed forms became looser and incapable of producing meaningful connections and affects, while their protective power subsided. As simplistic as it may be, this evolutionary arc provides a corrective perspective to dominant views on European socialisms, which see the solidifying of ritualized forms as an indication of the ideology's exhaustion and its emptying of content and meaning, and the ultimate dissolution of socialism. Such a trajectory of forms that made up the experience of socialism, as well as the fact that socialist institutions used these forms to enable the production of affective fabrics that still render that experience meaningful, important, and valuable, suggest a different reading of the relationship between monotonous, standardized, "ideological" forms and the failure of socialism. They invite us to consider the possibility that socialism has not failed because citizens could no longer relate to authoritative discourses and practices because their forms became too remote from their meanings, but because the infrastructure in which these discourses and practices made sense was weakened and ultimately destroyed, rendering Yugoslav socialism incapable of maintaining its own ideological values and future-oriented imaginaries of brotherhood and unity, solidarity, comradeship, self-management, and nonalignment. In such a reading, citizens did not reject socialism because its forms became too empty and too distanced from what made sense in life, but because the social and institutional infrastructures were altered in such a way that they could no longer meaningfully accommodate the forms productive of collective meanings, affects, and future-oriented imaginaries.

1

History, Stories, and Selves

The roots of socialist Yugoslavia and its military reach back to World War II
and the mass mobilization of citizens in the People's Liberation War that
united anti-fascist resistance with class struggle and social revolution. With
its formal foundation at the second assembly of the Antifascist Council for
the National Liberation of Yugoslavia in the Bosnian town of Jajce on November 29 and November 30, 1943, the Yugoslav federation emerged from the war
composed of six republics and two autonomous provinces: Slovenia, Croatia,
Bosnia and Herzegovina, Montenegro, Serbia (with the autonomous provinces
Vojvodina and Kosovo), and Macedonia (see map 1.1).

As a political project, socialist Yugoslavia gathered together several ethnic
groups, marked by different historical legacies, separate national identities,
and disparate past experiences of statehood. This project was closely and
complexly related to the political idea of Yugoslavism, which was a century
old when it was put into practice for the first time in the Kingdom of Serbs,
Croats, and Slovenes in 1918, renamed the Kingdom of Yugoslavia in 1929. As

Map 1.1 Map of socialist Yugoslavia and Yugoslavia's position in Europe. Created by Mateja Rihtaršič.

the historian Dennison Rusinow has pointed out, Yugoslavism had a different meaning for different South Slavic nations in the nineteenth century.[1] In the time of the Kingdom of Yugoslavia, two main understandings of Yugoslavism crystalized: the first "has been called 'integral Yugoslavism' or 'Yugoslavist unitarism.' It either denied the separate nationhoods of Slovenes, Croats, and Serbs alike, or sought to supersede these by positing the existence or potential (now called 'nation-building') of a single Yugoslav nation subdivided into historically formed 'tribes' or merely 'names.' The second acknowledged and approved enduring separate nationhoods and sought federal and other devices for a multinational state of related peoples with shared interests and aspirations."[2] The second version prevailed, particularly in post–World War II, socialist Yugoslavia. Yugoslav political authorities abandoned their insistence on an integral Yugoslav identity as an alternative to ethnic identities in the

1960s, and the state functioned as a "genuine federal state providing a great deal of regional autonomy to its member nationalities and ethnic groups."[3] The federalist, pluralistic approach was further institutionalized in the 1974 Constitution. However, the dynamics—and tensions—between particular national interests of republics and autonomous provinces on the one hand and the federal state on the other defined political life in Yugoslavia to its very end.

The official abandonment of integral Yugoslavism did not mean that the idea and the possibility of being and acting outside the frames set by ethnic belonging totally disappeared. This possibility never lost its importance and was intrinsically connected with Yugoslav identity. This connection became particularly strong as centrifugal and nationalist tendencies gained impetus, bringing Yugoslavia to its end. Likewise, Yugoslav socialist citizenship remained an important political concept, closely related to three important ideological pillars: anti-fascism, internationalism/nonalignment, and self-management, through which Yugoslavia strove to develop its own version of socialism.[4] It also shaped the intimate worlds of Yugoslav citizens and defined the horizons of their political imagination and self-perception well beyond the lifetime of the socialist state. For example, in the 1981 census, 5.6 percent of citizens declared themselves Yugoslavs, five times more than a decade before. In post-Yugoslav Serbia, in the 2002 census, 80,721 inhabitants of Serbia did so, while in the 2011 census the figure dropped to 23,303. The 2022 census registered a surprising rise of the number of Yugoslavs, to 27,143. Insisting on belonging to the nation that has not existed for three decades already, citizens of Serbia (and other post-Yugoslav states) individually and symbolically oppose the reality fixed through the violent wars in the 1990s "followed by the emergence of seven new nation-states and one ethnical state within a federative state: Slovenia, Croatia, Bosnia and Herzegovina (and within it, Republika Srpska), Montenegro, Serbia, Kosovo, and North Macedonia."[5] In that reality, "authoritarian capitalism within mono-ethnical and mono-religious communities became the indisputable horizon of their future."[6]

The Yugoslav People's Army (Jugoslovenska narodna armija) was established in 1945, when the People's Liberation Army rather rapidly transformed into the Yugoslav Army as a peacetime military force based on universal conscription, and it became a powerful symbol and key domestic factor in socialist Yugoslavia.[7] In 1948, it was renamed the Yugoslav People's Army (JNA).[8] As an institution, the JNA was one of the three pillars of political power in socialist Yugoslavia, together with the Communist Party of Yugoslavia (which in 1952 became the League of Yugoslav Communists) and the State Security Administration.[9]

The Yugoslav military, like other federal institutions, emphasized the "national cultures" of its soldiers and was very careful not to impose any unitary or hegemonic model on the organization of military life, but it was also sensitive to any manifestation of ethnonationalism. It simultaneously strove to strengthen the spirit of Yugoslavism among officers and soldiers and the coherence among them that would be indispensable for their efficient defense of the socialist country, if need be. To be able to create such coherence, the JNA was organized in accordance with an extraterritorial principle: the recruits were sent to perform their army service as far as possible from their homes, almost always to a different Yugoslav republic, and units were composed of young men who came from all corners of the country, and were very diverse in terms of ethnicity, education, social background, experience, cultural preference, and plans for the future. The network of barracks, garrisons, training grounds, border posts, and army cultural centers (*dom vojske*) covered the whole territory of the former Yugoslavia. Nevertheless, military service as an experience and the institutional life of the JNA were detached from wider society and its mores and structures to a significant extent. The life of JNA soldiers was shaped by isolation, discipline, drill, and routine, and as such was quite remote from the Yugoslav ideals of self-management, freedom, and self-realization.

In 1968, the Yugoslav military underwent significant transformations and was reconceptualized as Total National Defense (*opštenarodna odbrana*) to include all citizens in the nation's defense forces through nationwide campaigns, exercises, and training measures, thus coming closer to these socialist ideals. It introduced territorially organized units of the Territorial Defense Forces. The JNA became one element of this nationwide defense system, but these transformations did not affect it significantly: until Yugoslavia's demise, the JNA retained its universal conscription system and its strictly extraterritorial principle of organization. Ideologically, it kept insisting on the primacy of Yugoslav state interests and remained intolerant of any manifestations of ethnonationalism, which proliferated as the end of Yugoslavia approached. It made all young men don a uniform, except those with serious health issues or specific family situations, and never showed much understanding for requests for civil service and conscientious objection that emerged in the 1980s with the rise of civil society and social movements.[10] In the early 1990s, amid growing ethnic tensions and violence, JNA soldiers were still performing military service far away from home, in mixed units intended to embody Yugoslav ideals that had already been abandoned outside the isolated spaces of military bases. They also faced the impossible and tragic task of defending the federal socialist state that had been abandoned by all its constitutive parts. Sticking to the rhetoric of preserving Yugoslavia, the JNA aligned itself with the Serbian side in the ensuing ethnic conflicts. The JNA officially ceased to exist in 1992, when it was renamed the Army of Yugoslavia and became a military force of the Federal Republic of Yugoslavia, which comprised Serbia and Montenegro.

In the aftermath of socialist Yugoslavia, the JNA, and the violence in which the country and army both vanished, the image of the Yugoslav military as a conservative, rigid institution detached from the country's citizens had been firmly fixed in political and academic discourses. It was perceived as opposed to the emancipatory aspects of Yugoslav socialism as articulated in the politics of the sovereignty of nations and nationalities, self-management, and nonalignment. In 1988, Marko Milivojević, a researcher at the University of Bradford, described the JNA as "highly conventional and distinctly conservative," in stark contrast with both the World War II revolutionary National Liberation Army and the general ideological orientation of Yugoslavia, "well known for its radical ideological experimentation in all spheres of political, economic and social life." Unlike the wartime partisan army, "which was overtly multinational and totally socially integrated with the people," wrote Milivojević, "the Yugoslav Army (and later the Yugoslav People's Army) was exclusive, hermetically sealed off from Yugoslav society and allegedly endowed with supranational 'Yugoslav' identity."[11]

This understanding of the JNA echoes views on socialism as a political system in which ideological staleness, conventionality, rigid forms, conservativism, and consequential detachment from citizens' lives inevitably led to its demise. The idea that the Yugoslav army was totally detached from society, however, stands in an uneasy relationship not only with the abundance of references to JNA service in the popular culture of socialist Yugoslavia, but also with the ubiquity of narratives about, memories of, and references to the experience of serving in the JNA that circulate in the post-Yugoslav space. What do these "army stories" look like, what do their forms tell us about that experience, and how do they complicate our understanding of Yugoslav socialism, its military, and the men who served in it over decades? How do they relate to biographies and the specific temporality of afterness marked by loss and rupture?

In spite of huge differences among men who served in the Yugoslav military, the narrative fabrics of "army stories" fit few recognizable molds. The limited-ness and the sameness—of the material world of the army, of the language used, of the routines and protocols that made up everyday life—made the inventory of themes that emerge in these stories and memories rather limited. These themes result in three recognizable narrative threads: They are about the friendships men made during their army service. They are also about what they learned or gained in the army—exceptional experiences that would not be possible in other social contexts. Finally, they are about the skills and strategies they employed in engaging with the military institution—how they showed stamina in enduring drills and officers' caprices or were creative in inventing subversive strategies to make service easier or simply confront the authorities. Most of my interviewees touched upon these themes in one way or another when sharing their memories and sentiments with me. Highly intertextual, these themes also dominate JNA-related narratives mediated by popular culture products in socialism.[12] For example, the film *Vojnikova ljubav* (A soldier's love, 1976) is about a young Belgrade playboy, the spoiled child of a rich family, who changes for the better because of military service in the JNA.[13] *Nacionalna klasa* (The national class, 1979), a cult Yugoslav film about a spoiled, immature playboy and aficionado of automobile races nicknamed Floyd, ends with his departure for the JNA, which is supposed to make him a responsible man and future father.[14] Lastly, the TV series *Vojnici* (The soldiers, 1981, a sequel to the TV series *Kad sam bio vojnik* [When I was a soldier], 1969–70) is a eulogy to friendship in the Yugoslav army.[15] These story lines also have their visual counterparts: paintings, sculptures, and graphics made by soldier-artists picturing friendship and various activities of soldiers serving in different military branches; group photographs of army buddies taken in photo studios; snapshots taken in the barracks, in which young men in uniform stand in groups, often hugging each other in a comradely way; and snapshots of men posing with weapons or pretending to fight each other or documenting subversive behavior such as playing instruments on the table in the base library, posing half-naked with weapons or next to a sign warning that photographing is forbidden.

These three narrative threads may be read as "collective and culturally dependent narratives that make up the pillars upon which individuals build their own personal stories."[16] They are by no means unique to stories and memories about serving in the Yugoslav army. They are also often found in all-male conversations and memories of all-male institutions other than the army, such as prisons and boarding schools.[17] They generally shape all-male collective experiences of mandatory military service. Close, intimate friendships are common features of military experiences in different places and periods.[18] Recalling his own experience in a naval training camp in Greece, Nicos Mouzelis writes, "Very often recruits, or ex-recruits seem to exaggerate and boast about the hardships and punishments (*Kapsonia*) that they had to undergo during their basic training."[19] He also emphasizes that the belief that the army "makes a man out of you" is quite widespread in Greece. For upper-middle-class boys, army discipline is supposed to be a good antidote to the "spoiling" of their home environment and good training in democratic principles (equal treatment for all). For peasant boys who have rarely left their villages, military service is supposed to widen their limited horizons and to operate as a "civilizing" process, teaching them basic hygiene procedures (such as brushing their teeth) as well as elementary technical and social skills.[20]

As Tom Smith argues, "military institutions are closely connected to a society's ideals of masculinity," and that is certainly true of socialist Yugoslavia as well.[21] Fitting recognizable frames of typically men's narratives, the JNA stories and memories make it compelling to observe their authors in terms of two familiar, but polarized categories of masculinity: hegemonic or militarized masculinity; and marginal or alternative masculinity. Attempts to understand how men subjected to military institutions position themselves in relation to these institutions' are usually based on the assumption that there is a conflict "between societal norms, institutional practice, and personal values and ideals."[22] Everything that does not fit the solid concept of idealized masculinity—most prominently emotional ties among men—is seen as in opposition or an alternative to that (imposed) ideal and as a cause of tension between individuals and the institution. This rather consensual view is even stronger when it comes to socialist military institutions. Smith's analysis of film and literary works addressing the experience of military service in the German Democratic Republic seems to suggest that a conflictual and cynical attitude of individuals toward the military institution was intrinsic to socialism, although it may be found in Western societies, too.[23]

My ethnographic material, which reveals a great degree of uniformity of narratives about military service told by very diverse men, and which suggests that a large majority of these men see their service as a meaningful experience, calls for an interpretive framework that goes beyond understanding the relationship between military service and the individuals performing it as being regulated by socially predefined ideas of masculinity and as necessarily tense and conflictual. It reveals binary interpretive categories of hegemonic, military masculinity versus alternative masculinity, and cynical opposition to collective values versus uncritical identification with them, as inadequate for understanding the relationship between the individual and the ideological infrastructures of Yugoslav socialism in general, and military service as one of the central Yugoslav institutions in particular.

In contrast to dominant understandings of the JNA as detached from Yugoslav socialist society, its ideological core consisted of values and ideals that were of great relevance for that society, such as equality, multiculturalism, comradeship, collectivity, and solidarity. Insisting on these values and structuring life on military bases around them, the Yugoslav military institution did not provide a normative framework in which soldiers could either comply with the ideal of militarized masculinity or challenge it, but created broader axiological coordinates in which emotions, morality, and familial, social, and state values and ideologies were more in concert than in friction.

The uniformity of narratives about military service and the shared inventory of values attached to that experience point to a specific form of collectivity able to accommodate very different and diverse individuals, rather than to the JNA's efficiency in "militarizing Yugoslav men" and shaping them in the same mold of masculinity. As I demonstrate in chapter 4, the uniformity of the men whom the military institution made all the same and the individual characteristics of these men (which made them radically different from each other) were not mutually exclusive, but existed in a complex relationship—frequently tense, but simultaneously productive of meaningful content and attachments. The belief that opposition, distance, and cynicism are the only legitimate attitudes of an individual toward socialist collectivist ideology (on the military base and outside it) comes from a temporality defined by the afterness marked by the failure of the socialist political project. "The empowered entrenchment of an intolerant and fundamentalist version of liberalism," David Scott reminds us, made "cynicism an acceptable, if not always necessary, part of so-called transitions from illiberal rule."[24] Participation in the collective ideological schemes that did not unambiguously involve distance, opposition, and cynicism, as William Mazzarella argues, makes "an itch in the liberal imagination," destabilizing "basic psychological categories commonly attached to the liberal subject—categories like individuality, intention, and sincerity—through which we are wont to distinguish between autonomy and influence, reality and theater."[25]

The ritualized, monotonous, and predictable forms that made up military service served as the main vehicle of collectivity on Yugoslav military bases and the lowest common denominator that enabled all these diverse men to perform their army service: to respond to orders, follow protocols, form units, and fulfill tasks. They simultaneously enabled connections and exchange across class, ethnic, and linguistic barriers—rendering the shared experience of military service meaningful and important emotionally, but also politically—an aspect I discuss in detail in the next chapter. The experience of simultaneous radical diversity and intimate proximity resulted in kinds of friendship, solidarity, care, and mutual recognition that were intrinsic to the extraterritorial, isolated, and liminal spaces of military service and would not be possible in other social contexts. These meaningful relations, values, and affects were not accidental, but constitutive of the work of the military institution. They belonged to the inventory of "objectified social imaginaries" valued and maintained not only by the military, but also by other institutions and social domains of Yugoslav socialist society—by families, schools, youth organizations, working collectives, popular culture, and citizens as "vernacular ideologists" of Yugoslav socialism.[26] In this light, the JNA appears not as isolated from the Yugoslav people, society, and institutions, or in opposition to them, but rather in harmony with them.

Army stories, anecdotes, jokes, and references to military service are widely present in post-Yugoslav social, cultural, and virtual spaces, providing an important form of social glue among both strangers and friends. Military service in the JNA is still one of the most recognizable shared experiences that connect people in the former Yugoslavia across ethnic lines. When two men from different parts of the former Yugoslavia who belong to generations born in or before 1972 or 1973 meet for the first time, it is very probable that, in fewer than five minutes after they meet, the question "Where did you serve in the army?" will arise. Men who know each other well also very often engage in fond exchanges of army stories and anecdotes about places and people all around the former country. References to military service and episodes from army life are frequent ingredients of casual all-male conversations. They may be triggered by a plethora of geographical and personal names, objects, smells, and tastes: "You live in Ljubljana? I served in the army there in 1977." "I heard about Hanka Paldum for the first time while serving in the army in Kolašin."[27] "You are from Belgrade? My best friend from the army was from there." "This food reminds me of the days I spent serving in the JNA." "Each time I hear this song, I recall my JNA service." Characteristic army jargon and events constituting army life are still recognizable in the former Yugoslav space and are used as a common cultural reference and an inexhaustible source of humor. Those who did not serve in the socialist military due to their sex or age are by no means spared from participating in keeping the legacy of the Yugoslav army alive in the post-Yugoslav era: army memories are part of family histories that women and children hear hundreds of times. Although directly and essentially a male experience, service in the Yugoslav military was part of a much broader cultural imagination in the Yugoslav social(ist) world. The artist Tanja Radež has written that army stories and memories do not belong to men exclusively and that places all over the former Yugoslavia such as "Tuzla, Kikinda, Titov Veles, Mostar, Vipava, Postojna, Kragujevac" are important points in women's personal maps because their "boyfriends, schoolmates, neighbors, brothers, and cousins served there in the JNA."[28] The writer Goran Vojnović adds a generational perspective to this, writing how "our fathers bothered us with their stories from 'the famous' JNA, which led us throughout our whole childhood to avoid mentioning places such as Prizren, Kikinda, Vrbas, or in my case Vipava, places where they had so many funny, but also crucially important, experiences."[29]

Service in the JNA was also accessible to Yugoslavs from all walks of life though popular culture: many songs, films, and TV series had JNA service as their theme or setting. Not only in popular pop and neo-folk songs played on local radio stations at the request of parents, grandparents, and relatives for soldiers' send-offs, but also in socialist "high culture" and in songs for children, the Yugoslav military occupied a highly important place. Several generations grew up watching *Dozvolite da se obratimo* (Let us address you—an adaptation of a military phrase used to request permission to speak) every Sunday morning—a television program that brought details of life in the JNA to the broader Yugoslav public via their TV sets. Today, army stories live an intense life in virtual space, where men from all parts of Yugoslavia gather to share their army memories, exchange jokes and anecdotes, and eagerly try to locate soldiers who served alongside them. Not least, they became part of popular culture in post-Yugoslav societies through literary texts, films, and theater performances dwelling on the experience of service in the Yugoslav army.

The continued prominence of JNA-related memories, experiences, and references attests to their ongoing cultural relevance in the decades after the demise of Yugoslavia. Even more, they are still important and relevant for the individuals who served in the JNA. These former soldiers usually place them in a precisely defined temporal frame: most men remember the exact dates of the beginning and end of their service and other details—the names of all their army buddies and officers, the places these came from, the precise geography of the places where they served and completed training exercises, the meticulous terminology of the weapons and tools they used, and so on. Such precision and attention to detail has been recognized as a common characteristic of male stories and the way "the language of these stories accomplishes masculinity."[30] This attention to detail, Jennifer Coates writes, "constitutes an important strategy in men's conversation: it enables men to avoid talk of a more personal nature."[31] This is often a deliberate strategy, Coates notes, and she quotes from David Jackson's autobiographical study of masculinity, in which Jackson comments, "I often turn to the sports page in the daily newspaper, concerning myself with the raw material for endless non-emotional non-conversations with other men."[32]

In stories from the Yugoslav army, however, the insistence on details unfolds as more complex and not so exclusive of men's emotions. The experience of service in the JNA was dislocated from "normal life" and everything that life was made of: it would start after "an absolute (albeit temporary) disconnection from the old, known life that came without preparation and there was no logical building-up on the old, or a continuity with the previous life."[33] For this reason, military service is remembered differently from the chain of events that make up the "usual" biographical trajectory, in which some names and details are blended, blurred, or forgotten. This dislocation, however, does not unfold as a disruption and as psychological and emotional trauma—categories with which Tom Smith explains "the continued interest in East German military service in life-writing, both autobiographical and fictional, even after the institution was dissolved."[34]

Despite the notable presence of service in the JNA in popular culture, during casual table talk, in random encounters, and in virtual spaces and media, and despite the meticulousness with which it is remembered and the obvious relevance of that experience, incorporating the military service into biographical trajectories does not come naturally and easily to the men of the former Yugoslavia. Difficulties emerge on several levels. They stem from the essentially liminal nature of this service: far away from home, cut off from family, friends, and things they loved and that were important for them, and exposed to the disciplinary regimes of the military, the soldiers experienced military service as something very different from—and often unrelatable to—their "normal lives," despite its universality and the normative understanding of military service as a requirement of a "normal biography." Their time in the military was, in many ways, a time of exception from the everyday milieus of their lives.

Additional challenges come from the loss of the political imagination that made military service socially meaningful, but that disappeared in the Yugoslav catastrophe. So much has changed since these men served in the army—locally, in the societies the former JNA soldiers are now a part of, and in global geopolitical regimes. The army they served in is no more, and neither is the country that that army was established to defend. Mandatory army service was abolished and replaced with professional militaries in all Yugoslav successor states, with Serbia being the last to introduce a professional army on 1 January 2011. Because of that, sharing one's army stories cannot serve as a tool for intergenerational connection among men that would bridge the rupture of the 1990s. Writer Miljenko Jergović thus describes the anxieties that perceived outdatedness and inappropriateness of such sharing provokes among men:

> Sooner or later, every Croatian male feels the need to tell of his experience in the Yugoslav National Army. We mostly do that in the most inappropriate social situations. Then the ladies scold us and roll their eyes and those nice boys—who were released or have served their time recently by cleaning windows in dorms or bringing kindergarten teachers snacks from the shop—think that our stories are completely outdated. Fuck, perhaps they are right, those guys who object because of their conscience, but we cannot give up a year of our lives just like that, just because it is not trendy anymore.[35]

Above all, the violent dissolution of socialist Yugoslavia makes the experience of serving in the Yugoslav army difficult to incorporate into the trajectory of life and the flow of biographical time. In the fractured temporality of the aftermath of the catastrophe, continuity between one's past and present selves cannot be established, and they exist only as "bilocation"—"the residence of the body and soul in two different places at the same time," as two Slovenian artists have described it.[36] For Elmaz, Hariz, and too many other Yugoslav men, the time they spent in the JNA is irreparably divorced from their present by the violence, death, and destruction of the 1990s, when the world they knew disintegrated. Not knowing what happened during those years to the people who mattered to them—what they became and whether they survived—makes it additionally impossible for most men to reflect on their own biographies without hesitation, melancholy, or discomfort.

The dissolution of Yugoslavia not only brought ruptures, uncertainty, and discontinuities, it also eradicated ideological and institutional infrastructures that made specific modalities of life, forms of sociality, affects, and values livable within the confined space of military bases, thus destroying coordinates that would render references to the experience of military service legible in the aftermath of Yugoslavia. Consequently, men coming from all corners of the former Yugoslavia and having very different biographies insist on the importance and meaningfulness of their army service through modalities of silence, hesitation, and suspension. When I told her about my Yugoslav army project, a female Montenegrin friend shared with me the following story:

A friend of mine, a French woman who is married to a Slovenian guy, called me last summer from Žabljak when I was in Podgorica.[37] Her husband took her to this place because he served in the army there. Can you imagine—poor French woman. There is nothing in Žabljak, nothing at all. It probably looks the same as when he served in the JNA. He is a young, successful guy, but his service is so important to him that he had to show the place to his wife. I find that amazing.

An anthropologist colleague similarly told me that the high-ranking officers of the Kosovo Liberation Army whom she interviewed for her research, even though they would not speak very openly about serving in the JNA, considered that episode in their biography to be something "that must not be touched or laughed about." Most of my interviewees also let me know that what they experienced in the JNA mattered to them, but the reasons why service in the JNA is important for who they are today has largely remained in the realm of the untold and the inexplicable.

So many men's uncompromising insistence on the importance and meaningfulness of their army experience contradicts the general perception of time spent in isolation in total institutions such as the military as "wasted or destroyed or taken from one's life."[38] Moreover, this generally positive view of mandatory military service across ethnic, social, and educational divisions makes the Yugoslav case quite different from other countries' peaceful mandatory conscription. For example, Anders Ahlbäck describes the polarization among men in relation to their army service in interwar Finland as strongly dependent on these men's class identity. Finnish workers and peasants and generally men with little education saw their service as "simply time wasted," made up of meaningless drills and unfair punishments that "offended two basic elements of their self-esteem as men: personal autonomy and honest work."[39] The testimonies of educated men and intellectuals, on the other hand, depict military service "almost like a boy scout camp with an atmosphere of sporty playfulness and merry comradeship," "a last safe haven of adolescence before an adult life of demands, responsibilities and duties," and the place where boys "learned to submit themselves to a higher cause and thereby matured into the responsibilities of adult manhood."[40]

An unsettled relationship among the ubiquity of references to the JNA in the aftermath of Yugoslavia, difficulties in incorporating the experience of military service in biographies and in finding continuities, and a silent but persistent insistence on the importance of this experience results in an afterlife of military service manifesting in subtle, suspended registers and in moments of hesitation—in pauses and silences. This silent, troubled, hesitant afterlife destabilizes the present and points to lost horizons of the future, alternative to the one that became the present in the post-Yugoslav lands: it would be a future in which men, very different in ethnicity and all other ways, could live together, share, feel, and care for each other, and be friends; a future these men imagined to be ahead of them and that would come once they removed their JNA uniform; a future that looked bright and abundant with possibilities. But in the future that came, these men's biographies were reduced to a single trait: their ethnic identity and adjacent religious ones.

The possibility of this alternative future lost with Yugoslavia and the meaningfulness of the experience of military service were not seeded in the Yugoslav military institution in spite of what this institution was, with its repetitive routines and ritualized protocols, but were, to a significant extent, outcomes of precisely these workings. In the following chapter, I address the most important institutional aspects of the JNA that made it possible for military service to be seen as a locus of the utopian imagination in the aftermath of political catastrophe.

2

A Barbed-Wire Utopia

The Yugoslav People's Army (JNA) derived its legitimacy from its continuity with the partisan movement and the massive struggle for national liberation and emancipation during World War II. There were, however, major differences between the organization of the two armies. While the partisan movement in World War II was spontaneous and self-organized, the JNA was the opposite: military service was mandatory, highly structured, and composed of heavily prescribed, predictable, repetitive, and ritualized practices centered around forms, and often distanced from constative meanings. To a large extent, Yugoslav partisan units were organized territorially, while the JNA strictly followed the extraterritorial principle, sending recruits to perform their military service far away from home, in a different national and cultural setting, and creating mixed and diverse units.

Mandatory, detached from everyday life and based on orders, strict hierarchy, and lack of free will, the JNA appears to be in a stark contrast to the revolutionary partisan army of World War II as well as with the main projects of Yugoslav socialism—self-management and nonalignment—which are still subjects of interest and fascination because of their utopian, universalist character and the ambition to enable agency outside relations governed by power and domination. This contrast particularly stands out when the JNA is observed in terms of the political positions characteristic of our time—be it a distinctively liberal one that focuses on individual rights and freedoms and diminishes possibilities for collective political projects, or the position of leftist activists and radical movements that have abandoned the statist model of revolution, and see resistance to capitalism and an alternative to it only as anti-systemic and outside state structures.[1]

The JNA was an essentially syncretic institution that offered soldiers more than just military training, and was closely related to Yugoslav citizenship. The strong connection between the military and citizenship was by no means specific to the Yugoslav socialist state; the importance of the army for nation-building is well documented in scholarly literature, particularly in multinational and imperial contexts.[2] This connection is made particularly strong and relevant through military service based on universal conscription.[3] There are nevertheless specificities of mandatory military service in the JNA that make it close to and compatible with other emancipatory aspects of Yugoslav socialism. These aspects link JNA service to a collective imagination that unfolds as utopian in the aftermath of Yugoslavia, in which citizens' possibilities of being and acting are defined by the limits of organically understood ethnic communities, hostile states, and violent capitalism.

The JNA's project of universal conscription had a much broader aim than merely catering to the military needs of the Yugoslav state. Like the partisan army in World War II, it invested significant resources in cultural and educational activities that were considered a necessary adjunct to military training, aimed at creating conditions for JNA soldiers to realize themselves as autonomous, complete, and complex social subjects, which was also a way of creating a collectivity on qualitatively new grounds. As William J. Stover has argued, it is characteristic of military forces that develop out of revolutionary insurgent units to be "more broadly defined to include political, economic, social and cultural missions," and the way the JNA was organized resonates with the visions of socialist revolutionary theorists from Vietnam, Cuba, China, and Algeria.[4]

The Yugoslav socialist military had a distinctively "peaceful" character: except for the early post-World War II period, marked by the tensions of the

Trieste crisis and Yugoslavia's split from the USSR in 1948, up until the 1980s and early 1990s, when the country the JNA was supposed to protect disintegrated in violent conflicts and the military became largely associated with the Serbian side in the dissolution process, for most of its history it was not directly related to combat, warfare, and violence.[5] The Yugoslav military was frequently regarded and self-described as "the army of peace" (*armija mira*). This made the JNA different from most professional armies, which, "by framing the status, worthiness, and very humanity of the people who are killing and being killed, they shade all deeper notions of what war means and what it is for."[6] It also made it different from military systems in which conscription is closely related to war operations. Moreover, although former JNA soldiers mention hazing practices typical of all-male institutions, mostly directed at newly arrived recruits ("the rookies"), violence among soldiers did not play a prominent role in narratives related to the JNA. This suggests an important difference between the Yugoslav military and some other mandatory systems of military service, particularly if observed in relation to subsequent military conflicts.[7]

The obligation that all young men serve in the Yugoslav military for a year or more gave the experience of that service a temporary character, unlike professional armies, and made it a rather exceptional (albeit obligatory) episode in the biographical trajectories of Yugoslav men. Unlike some military institutions that employ universal conscription, such as the Israeli one, where "one can say without too much exaggeration that the Israeli army is the Israeli society and the Israeli society is the Israeli army," the experience of military service in the JNA was very detached from the ordinary world and social life.[8] But this detachment did not make it alien or opposed to the ideas of Yugoslav citizenship and the state's socialist ideology. In fact, quite the contrary. While the values of social equality, brotherhood, and unity, and the ideological premises of self-management and nonalignment, were intrinsically framed as Yugoslav and as such promoted by institutions, media, and culture, they largely remained abstract for the majority of Yugoslav citizens, whose everyday life was still bound to their traditional ethnic, linguistic, and social settings. And these settings significantly differed from each other. Mobility, cosmopolitanism, and the possibility of transcending the limits of one's social world were still reserved for intellectual elites.[9] An exception to this pattern, the aim of military service in the JNA was to make it possible for young Yugoslav men to experience these Yugoslav values and ideals by bringing them together, irrespective of ethnic, but also class and linguistic boundaries. The JNA based its conscription strategy on the belief that the unity and homogeneity of military units could stem only from the cultural diversity of the conscripts and officers who were brought together—any other approach would mean either imposing unitarism or catering to ethnonationalism.[10] This is why the JNA has been seen and saw itself as one of the most important pillars of Yugoslav unity, and why it was often referred to as "the forge of Yugoslavism" (*kovačnica jugoslovenstva*) and the "school of brotherhood and unity" (*škola bratstva i jedinstva*).[11] Warren Zimmermann, who witnessed the disintegration of the country as the last US ambassador to socialist Yugoslavia, stresses in his memoir that the JNA was the most Yugoslav of all institutions, since "people from all parts of Yugoslavia were meeting there."[12]

To be able to create a framework for a truly Yugoslav experience and a space in which young conscripts would live together in equality and sameness (produced by uniform, daily routines and protocols) and simultaneously in radical diversity (of ethnicity, language, class, experience), military service in the JNA somewhat paradoxically had to be radically different and removed from recruits' everyday and ordinary lives and familiar spaces and networks, and detached from the ordinary lives of Yugoslav citizens in which the Yugoslav, cosmopolitan dimension of their experience was only partial and more imagined than lived.

MILITARY SERVICE AND YUGOSLAV CITIZENSHIP

Being the most important pillar of Yugoslavism, the Yugoslav military was a distinctively inclusive institution that did not discriminate among citizen-conscripts: all men had to serve, regardless of their ethnicity, class background, education, or place of residence. Illiterate shepherds and college graduates, men from small, remote villages and those from large urban centers, Croats, Serbs, Albanians, Macedonians, Roma, Catholics, Muslims, Orthodox Christians, aspiring rock stars, alternative artists, rebellious sons, workers, philosophers, engineers, sons of *Gastarbeiter*—all were gathered in barracks, dressed in the same uniforms, assigned the same duties, and subjected to the same procedures.[13] The JNA never divided men by class or social background—unlike the pre-World War II Soviet army, where after 1925 all citizens were obliged "to participate in the defense of the USSR, but activities involving weapons were limited to workers."[14] There was also no structural way to differentiate men according to their ethnicity—all Yugoslavs had the full right (and obligation) to serve in the Yugoslav army, unlike many other national contexts in which mandatory conscription created hierarchies of citizenship. For example, Arab citizens are not required to serve in the Israeli army, and in socialist Bulgaria, nonethnic Bulgarian citizens served in special units (called "construction units") and were not obliged, or allowed, to bear weapons. In the USSR, "Russians were treated as the primary nation despite claims of multiethnic brotherhood," and this influenced relationships and the logic of violence within the military.[15] Service in the JNA was deeply linked to multiethnic Yugoslav citizenship and seen as one of its important vehicles. For this reason, the army never prioritized military efficiency over all-inclusivity, making universal conscription a citizenship project that transcended strictly military needs and interests. Soldiers perceived their service in the JNA as an egalitarian experience both socially (in terms of class) and politically (in terms of citizenship). Božidar Lugarić, a transport engineer from Zagreb, emphasized, "The biggest advantage of serving in the JNA was that everyone became equal. The uniform made everyone equal. No Saint Laurent suit, no Gucci—we were all equal and the same. It was individual ability, and not one's background, that really mattered." Albanians from Kosovo, the Serbian southern province, went to serve in the JNA with mixed feelings: this was one of the rare frameworks in which they could feel like equal citizens of socialist Yugoslavia, but at the same time, as an Albanian man I talked to in Ljubljana emphasized, they would leave for the JNA fearing mistreatment and mistrust. This fear became particularly profound in the 1980s as the oppression of Albanians by the Serbian authorities increased.

Military defense was never perceived as the only task of the Yugoslav army. It was also a space for citizenship-related actions and an essentially important factor in building the country's infrastructure: soldiers worked on large construction projects alongside volunteer labor brigades, and the JNA units were also important aid providers and rescuers during natural disasters, such as floods and earthquakes. In addition, the JNA put a strong emphasis on the educational aspects of military service. It not only taught young men military techniques and how to use weapons; it also taught them courses on history, world politics, the political functioning of Yugoslavia, and other aspects of the contemporary world. The education was also oriented toward practical, real-life skills, aimed at leveling drastic differences among young men

artiljerijski sistem lansiranja
PT mina na daljinu RAMS

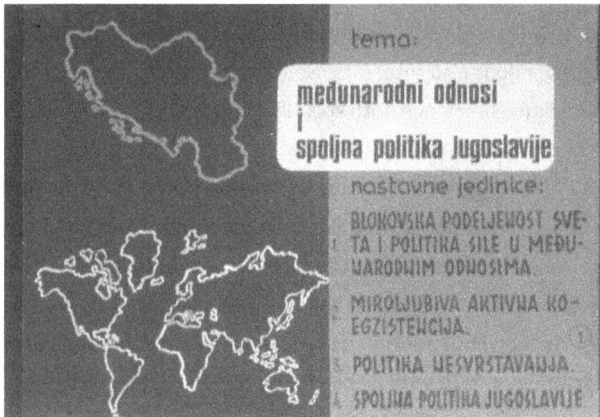

Figures 2.1 and 2.2
Slides used for
education classes
in the JNA.

gathered on army bases: many soldiers earned their driver's license in the army, others learned to cook or use a camera, while some learned to write and read.

Although strongly linked to Yugoslav citizenship and envisaged as a "cradle of Yugoslavism," the experience of military service was limited to only half of all Yugoslavs: male citizens only.[16] The JNA was almost exclusively a male institution: officers and conscripts were all men, and women were present on the base only in strictly defined and typical roles—as workers in canteens, shops, or the medical corps. The absence of women in Yugoslav army uniforms made the experience of army service distinctively gendered. The partisan movement of World War II was characterized by the massive participation of women, including a significant number of female combatants,

Figure 2.3 A uniformed woman at a General National Defense exercise.

so the postwar exclusion of women from the conscription system comes as a surprise, particularly considering the army's pivotal ideological role in constructing supranational Yugoslav citizenship.[17] The 1968 reform established a nationwide system of General National Defense and Social Self-Protection and Territorial Defense. Closely related to self-management, this system was "more universal" than conscription and, according to the 1974 Constitution, was not only an obligation, but also a right guaranteed to all citizens (*svi radni ljudi i građani*).[18]

Within the program of General National Defense, women and school-age youths were taught to use weapons and trained to act in case of attack or natural disasters. In addition, from 1948 onward, pre-military training was organized as part of the secondary education system.[19] Although females were able to play a full role in this training and the national defense program, these general self-defense activities were much less linked to building a Yugoslav spirit through experience than the JNA was because of the territorial logic of their organization.[20]

The JNA authorities were not entirely insensitive to this citizenship deficit and the tension between the ideological and symbolic role of the JNA and the absence of women among its ranks. In the 1980s, they tried to fill the void and open up the military to female citizens. Female students of defense were obliged to complete military training as part of their education. Lidija Pelc from Radgona, Slovenia, a fourth-year defense student at the University of Ljubljana, departed for Sarajevo in 1982 to complete such training on the JNA base there, where she spent almost five months together with sixteen other female colleagues from all over Yugoslavia. At the time, a woman dressed in the JNA uniform would attract a lot of curiosity, so the news about Lidija joining the army made it to a local newspaper.[21] This news item inspired Zoran Predin, the singer of the Slovenian rock group Lačni Franz, to write a song, "*Naša Lidija je pri vojakih*" (Our Lidija is in the army), which became widely popular after its release in 1984. The song's lyrics have the recognizable form of a letter sent to a soldier in the JNA. Here, Lidija's fiancé Franci writes to her from a village in Slovenia, saying that he misses her, encourages her to endure hard army days, and sends regards to her from others in the village: "father, mother, godfather Vinko, the priest, Šeka, and piglets." We learn from the letter that it was sent together with "a package" of goods Lidija asked for, including "three pairs of lined SMB nylons."[22] There is also a sentence familiar to most Yugoslavs of the time that resonated with the publicly promoted image of the JNA as a guardian that made it possible for citizens to have carefree lives and peaceful sleep: "We all sleep peacefully because we know that you protect us" (*Mi zdaj vsi mirno spimo, ker vemo, da čuvaš nas ti*). Inverting the usual context, in which girlfriends or wives would send this kind of letter to men in the army, the song effectively parodies the perceived inversion of gender roles entailed by the introduction of army service for women. The effectiveness of this parodic touch reveals much about the general sentiment about women entering the typically men's space of the military.[23] It also made the song popular among urban youth, who were not eager to wear the JNA uniform for a year or more. Interestingly, however, the song decisively contributed to the popularity of Lačni Franz in the local Slovenian context: as Petar Janjatović writes, only after the song was released did Lačni Franz start performing in smaller Slovenian towns—before it, their audience was primarily in urban Yugoslav centers such as Belgrade, Zagreb, and Ljubljana.[24] This is probably because of the very local (albeit ironic) coloration of the song: the extensive use of local expressions, picturing typical life in a local rural community, and singing in an exaggerated northeastern Slovenian dialect.

Female defense students' military service in the JNA was part of a broader, but short-lived attempt to introduce general army service for women that would make soldiering in Yugoslavia a truly inclusive citizenship project: in July 1983, the first female recruits were received in several barracks across Yugoslavia. They enlisted voluntarily for service that lasted two months and twenty-two days for female soldiers and six months for female officers. As a local newspaper reported, on one of the bases in the Slovenian capital, Ljubljana, the military authorities even built a new object "to meet the specific needs of female soldiers."[25] An issue of *Naša vojska* (Our army), a military newspaper, published just a day after International Women's Day, featured several articles and photographs illustrating the life of the new female units in the JNA. There is a short article about Gjylter Beqiri from the Macedonian capital Skopje, the only Albanian among women serving in the School of Reserve Officers. Gjylter said that the decision to serve in the JNA was her own, but strongly supported by her family members. The decision made her family very proud, especially her father, who had been a partisan fighter in World War II. There is also an interview with 22-year-old Svetlana Ćosić from Skopje, who completed the first three months of her training in Sarajevo and was then transferred to Ljubljana for the rest of her military service. Svetlana emphasized, "At the beginning, women in uniform were perceived as something very strange, which motivated us to prove that we are capable of being just as good JNA soldiers as men are." She also argued that the presence of women in the JNA uniform was more than a "mere step in women's emancipation in our society": it was also important as a mechanism of "training all our citizens to appropriately fulfill their role in the defense system and in the case of defensive war."[26]

Despite the obvious enthusiasm and determination of enlisted female soldiers, the practice of including women in the JNA was soon abandoned in 1985 since it faced numerous difficulties and women's interest in serving declined significantly.

Another uneasy and ambiguous realm for the military to navigate was the issue of homosexuality among men in the army. Although a large part of the communist elite still considered homosexuality irreconcilable with the morals of socialist society, it was decriminalized in Yugoslavia in the 1970s. As Franko Dota reveals, the Coordinative Commission for Realization of the Constitution formed by the Executive Committee of the Presidency of the Central Committee of the Communist League of Yugoslavia met in April 1977 to discuss possibilities of harmonizing penal legislation, as the law significantly diverged on the level of constituent republics. One of the topics discussed was the legal status of homosexuality. Most of the participants in the discussion advocated abandoning the criminal prosecution of homosexuals, and, interestingly, the representative of the Yugoslav army was a particularly fervent supporter of the proposal. He also welcomed efforts to harmonize legal policies, since differences among the constituent republics made the work of military courts and disciplinary commissions difficult and complicated. The representative emphasized that the JNA still considered homosexuals "inadequate and incompatible with the army," but also admitted that the JNA had not prosecuted them in military courts "for many years already," as it believed that "jail cannot correct them." The army would discreetly reprimand its officers and ask them to change their behavior, or, if there was no other solution, "simply dismiss them." According to data from the military courts presented at this meeting, JNA recruits whose homosexuality was revealed were sent to disciplinary trial and consequently dismissed or moved to another unit.[27] With such an approach, the JNA followed the general Yugoslav pattern, which associated homosexuality with criminal acts, decadence, and the influence of capitalism, but avoided public exposure of the issue and any extensive implementation of strict legal measures.[28] It seems that both the Yugoslav communists and the military quite early stopped treating homosexuality with ideological fierceness and rigidity and instead adopted a rather pragmatic approach. Franko Dota reports on the 1956 case of

> the clerk employed by the municipal court in Bjelovar [Croatia] who was caught in sexual intercourse with a recruit serving in the JNA. This clerk was a Communist Party member and the local prosecution office sent a plea to the republic prosecutor not to launch a criminal trial against him, because he is "an excellent and very reliable public servant" and the trial would "make this issue public and compromise him." His partner, the JNA

soldier, would also have to be prosecuted. The prosecutor office in Zagreb agreed with the Bjelovar local authorities and both men escaped jail, while the Communist Party was saved from public shame.[29]

Gender imbalance and exclusivity were not the only source of discomfort for the military, making its relation to Yugoslav citizenship based on diversity and inclusiveness ambiguous and somewhat paradoxical. There was also the issue of language use in the army. Linguistic plurality and equal treatment of the languages of all Yugoslav nations and nationalities was one of the central principles of the organization of the Yugoslav federation. This meant that "there was no national language, nor a generally accepted *koine* [a common dialect], but . . . Serbo-Croatian often served as an informal *lingua communis*."[30] Language policies thus followed the general view that unity at the Yugoslav level could be achieved only by a plurality and equality that enabled individuals to realize their full capacity as citizens, although in practice this approach faced some limitations.

On the legislative level, the Yugoslav military, as the main embodiment of socialist Yugoslavism, was no exception to this pluralistic principle. All the successive constitutions of the Socialist Federal Republic of Yugoslavia gave equal status to the languages of all Yugoslav nations and nationalities in the Yugoslav military. Article 42 of the 1963 constitution stated the nominal equality of the languages of all Yugoslav nations and nationalities in the military, but reserved a special status for Serbo-Croatian: commands, administrative communication, and training were to be carried out in Serbo-Croatian exclusively. The 1974 constitution gave equal status to the languages of all "nations and nationalities" (*narodi i narodnosti*) and made all of them administrative, though they were not all major languages. In this constitution, the exceptional status of the Serbo-Croatian language in the military was somewhat relativized: article 243 states that in commands, administrative communication, and training, one of the languages of the Yugoslav nations should be used. Throughout the existence of the JNA, only Serbo-Croatian held this role. All official communication was conducted in Serbo-Croatian, and all the soldiers had to learn it to some extent. Insisting on the extraterritorial principle as a way to provide space for contact and interaction among young men from all parts of the country, the JNA had to sacrifice another principle of inclusion—that of the equality of the languages of all Yugoslav nations and nationalities.

This choice was an object of substantial criticism, and Slovenian intellectuals and public figures were particularly sharp critics. One of them was Jaka Avšič, a Slovenian general and active officer both in the army of the Kingdom of Serbs, Croats, and Slovenes and in the Yugoslav People's Army. He joined partisan units in 1941 and had important functions in Slovenian partisan structures. After retirement in 1947, he fiercely advocated the equality of the Slovenian language within the JNA and published several articles on the topic.[31]

The Yugoslav military was not deaf to this criticism and tried to open spaces for other languages of Yugoslavia's nations and nationalities in certain domains of army life. The "language problem" was actively discussed at forums established by the military itself. In a volume published after a conference organized by the State Secretariat for National Defense in 1970, many contributors addressed the problem, pointing to ways to alleviate it. Increasing the number of officers who mastered constitutional languages other than Serbo-Croatian, more literature on military issues published in Slovenian and Macedonian, and more novels in languages other than Serbo-Croatian in libraries on military bases were some of the proposed solutions.[32] Army newspapers published in military regions featured texts in both Serbo-Croatian and the languages predominant in these regions. For example, *Naša vojska*, the periodical of the Ljubljana military region, featured articles in Serbo-Croatian and Slovenian. In 1977, the JNA awarded a special prize to a Slovenian military dictionary.[33] Strong emphasis was placed on cultural activities that were seen as a way to transcend language barriers.[34]

The language issue in the Yugoslav army became particularly relevant in Slovenia in the late 1980s, during the events that eventually led to Slovenia's independence and the breakdown of Yugoslavia. In 1988, four persons were arrested and accused of revealing a military secret. The decision to conduct the trial in Serbo-Croatian (and not in the Slovenian language) caused public protests and extensive intellectual dissent in Slovenia.[35] Avšič's views on the status of Slovenian within the JNA from the 1970s were brought to public attention. In 1986, the academic journal *Časopis za kritiko znanosti* published a letter that General Avšič had sent the Federal Parliament and the Federal Constitutive Commission in 1973. The letter addressed the issue of language hegemony within the JNA.[36] In the letter, Avšič stressed that each nation's formation required the use and development of its language, and if a language is excluded from some domain of communication, that nation's development and ability to maintain its genuine characteristics are endangered. Avšič saw the obligation to learn and actively use another language as being particularly problematic for recruits who belong to the working class and who "have difficulties even with their mother tongue."[37] He believed that the use of only one language for communication in the army produced a feeling of inequality, provoking conflicts among recruits and jeopardizing the brotherhood and unity of all Yugoslav peoples, which simultaneously weakened the institution of the army.

My own research among former Slovenian JNA soldiers did not confirm the assumptions of Avšič's. I conducted several interviews with Slovenians who performed military service between 1986 and 1990, in the period when discourse on the equality of languages in the JNA was most extensively present among the Slovenian public. None of these soldiers, regardless of their social and educational background, stated that they had any problem with the fact that the language used for official communication during their military service was not their mother tongue. The men I talked to saw this fact neither as being to their disadvantage, nor as a cause of any tension among recruits belonging to different Yugoslav nations. Most of them said that Serbo-Croatian was already familiar to them because they were accustomed to watching TV programs and reading comic books in the language.

The discrepancy between the public views framed through discourses of particular national interests or individual rights on the one hand, and the experience of serving in an isolated setting characterized by great degree of diversity and equality on the other, points to a particular logic of life on Yugoslav military bases and the specific nature of a collective formed within their fenced-in spaces. Conceived as an essentially citizenship-oriented project aimed at leveling and overcoming ethnic, linguistic, class, and cultural differences among citizens and at strengthening their Yugoslav belonging, military service in the JNA was to a large extent a heterotopian space with regulatory principles often in opposition to those in the "ordinary world" of socialist Yugoslavia: isolated and detached from that world, it insisted on monolingualism (as opposed to linguistic diversity as the Yugoslav ideal), excluded female citizens from its framework, and tended to ignore, but sometimes prosecuted, soldiers and officers whose sexuality did not fit traditional, patriarchal, and heteronormative forms.

Military service in the Yugoslav army was based on universal mandatory conscription and was thus imposed on all male individuals at a certain point in their lives. On the other hand, because it was universal and mandatory, going into the army was also a normal(ized) event in the biographies of Yugoslav men. According to Daniela Koleva, the characteristics of a normal biography include the following: they are widespread, largely predictable, and concern all or almost all.[38] Additionally, a normal biography is considered normal because it is predefined by institutionally set norms. Mandatory and universal, Yugoslav military service defined normality in normative terms (vis-à-vis pathological or deviant) and, as such, densely intertwined with the family values and notions of honor and shame.[39] Joining the army thus was an obligatory, common, and expected event, and a normal point in men's biographies.

This kind of relation between normal as common and normal as nondeviant was made possible because the figure of the Yugoslav soldier was a point where state ideology intersected with tradition, family values, and shared ideas of masculinity and self-value. Božidar, who graduated from the Faculty of Transport at the University of Zagreb and got married in February 1977, asked to be sent to serve in the JNA in May of the same year. This is how he explained his decision:

> What is important is that I really wanted to go. It was an issue of personal honor for me, a man's honor. I never wanted to be excused because my vision was not perfect. It never entered my mind to try to cheat by claiming an illness and thus avoid the service. And of course, I was lucky I was not ill and was capable of serving in the army. None of my friends ever tried to avoid conscription. We were all into sports, and once we graduated, we all said that we wanted to go.

Dejan Dimitrijević says that he "used connections" to promptly join the army: his neighbor worked in the municipal office for the registration of young recruits, and he asked her to send him as far as from his home town in Pančevo in Serbia as possible. She made his wish come true and assigned him to serve on the island of Lošinj in Croatia. In Dejan's words, he joined the army to clear his mind and distance himself from his parents, which would enable him make some important life decisions. One of the decisions he made during his military service was to enroll in Belgrade's art academy and become an artist.

The pattern of social relations that existed in the JNA followed those that have been noted for socialist states in twentieth-century Europe: "the communist establishment kept to some extent the directness of traditional social relations" and not only tolerated but also maintained a "quasi-patriarchalism" in which familial patriarchal authorities were replaced by the authority of the state.[40] Moreover, traditional gender roles were reproduced rather than questioned. In more traditional parts of Yugoslavia, army send-offs were celebrated in a manner similar to weddings; on local radio stations, one could greet a future soldier with an appropriate song—a practice that existed also for birthdays, the start of primary school, a wedding, the birth of a child, retirement, and other milestones in a person's life. The photographs taken during military service had their place in family albums next to those taken at other important points in life.

As an essentially Yugoslav experience, military service in the JNA was regarded as a way for young Yugoslavs to internalize the ideology of Yugoslav socialism. To achieve this goal and make military service a constitutive experience of normal biographies, the military made use of traditional, patriarchal networks and practices, sometimes making compromises that included giving up some of the strict principles on which a military is based. For security reasons, soldiers were not allowed to take photographs on army bases. At the same time, in garrison stores they could buy a photo album in which to place photographs taken during military service—many of which were taken despite the official restriction. Likewise, the widespread practice of tattooing in the army was officially illegal and always performed secretly, but officers and military authorities tolerated it. Once done, tattoos were not hidden but publicly displayed. Many of these tattoos bore the inscription "JNA" or symbols of various army branches. Although against strict military rules, they did not contradict army or state ideology, but actually worked to embody it.[41]

The Yugoslav military's exploitation of existing social values, networks, and relations based on family, kinship, patriarchy, and traditional masculinity accords with scholars' insights about the complex and subtle dynamics between the state and traditional social structures and practices in socialist societies.[42] Scholars' intense focus on kinship and family relations, discourses, and metaphors, as well as the fact that during socialism kinship and the state "were seen more as complementary or mutually constitutive than opposed," seems to suggest that these are also primary ideological domains for the social production of loyalty, solidarity, and unity as politically relevant affects.[43]

Socialist institutions, however, did not limit themselves to these traditional domains, but were engaged in the creation of frameworks and infrastructure for collective experiences that would be productive of such affects, generative of qualitatively new, transformative social relations, and oriented toward the future. Such infrastructures included Youth Labor Actions (Omladinska radna akcija, ORA), voluntary campaigns that gathered youth labor brigades from all parts of the country (and in the early period, also from abroad). They completed several critically important infrastructure projects in the aftermath of World War II, and their contribution to the reconstruction of the country was essential. The tradition of Youth Labor Actions was kept until the late 1980s, and under the program very diverse men and women organized in volunteer brigades were unified through the labor they performed together. This unity in labor not only leveled significant differences among them, but also enabled the creation of a community on radically new grounds, different from all traditional relations and models of exchange. One of the outcomes of this common experience and unity in labor was a qualitatively new mode of friendship (*drugarstvo*), which transcended the limits of communities defined by language, origin, or class.[44]

These Youth Labor Actions forged unity and equality as foundations for qualitatively new relations, affects, and the imagination of the future through common labor, while in the case of military service in the JNA, the unifying and difference-erasing power inhered in ritualized, repetitive, and uniform patterns and practices. The two experiences were very different in nature: the former was voluntary, and its capacity to produce collective emotions was governed by purposeful labor whose material results pointed toward the future.[45] The latter was mandatory, composed of collective and individual repetitive routines whose purpose was not always easily discernible and often produced a sense of bizarreness and surrealness. Nevertheless, these routines worked as a great equalizer, able to unify young men from different parts of the country, men of different professions, radically different social status, and different ethnic and social backgrounds, who spoke different languages and dialects.

Some of these young men went into the army eagerly, like Božidar, who followed friends of his generation, or Dejan, who saw military service as a welcome escape from parental pressure and a place to be on one's own and sort out things in life. For many men, military service offered a unique opportunity of exposure to experiences that were beyond the reach of "ordinary" life. They saw towns and parts of the country, met people, and encountered a variety of cultural and linguistic patterns. Moreover, the infrastructure of the JNA enabled soldiers to participate in practices that were outside the horizons of their ordinary lives. Nebojša Šerić Šoba, a Sarajevo-born artist, used free time at the JNA base on the island of Lošinj and later in Sinj in 1987–88 to play guitar. Šoba belonged to the vibrant alternative scene of Sarajevo before joining the JNA, so at first he could play only rock and the other kinds of alternative music he knew and liked before he joined up. "As the end of my service was approaching, I was able to play more than 300 folk songs that I learned at the request of my army buddies," he remembers. Milovan Milenković, a worker from the village Majur in central Serbia, got a "007" inscription tattooed on his forearm after he saw a James Bond movie in a cinema in Sarajevo, where he served in 1972. Dejan Simčić, a young peasant from Šumadija in Serbia, wrote a poem: "My house is like an island / confined by a stream on the one side / and a path on the other" (*Moja kuća je kao otok / s jedne strane je potok / a s druge strane put*) for a wall newspaper in the cultural club which Oto Luthar, a historian from Ljubljana, and his army buddies improvised in a storage room on Titograd army base in 1987.

For others, however, military service rather appears as a radical narrowing of horizons. Many were not so keen to leave their accustomed life and postpone plans for the future to spend a year or more on remote, fenced-in army bases, dressed in the JNA uniform. A popular urban legend is that the careers of several promising punk bands ended after their front men were forced to cut their hair and go serve in the Yugoslav army. "I detested the idea of going to the army," confesses Mitko Panov, a Macedonian-Swiss film director. "At eighteen, all I dreamt of was leaving the country and pursuing the life of an artist. Spending the whole year in a barbed-wire compound and wearing the green uniform was the last thing I wanted to do."[46]

Regardless of their initial positions toward the "debt" they had to pay to the country in the form of military service, the majority of former Yugoslav men do not dismiss the experience as pointless and "a waste of time." The important aspect of military service that most of the former soldiers value and point to is an immediate experience of diversity that was not possible in any other domain of social life. "When I went to the West for the first time, I was shocked by the great diversity of people there. It was the same when I went to serve in the JNA," said Šoba about his service on Lošinj in 1987. The renowned Yugoslav film director Želimir Žilnik went to the Croatian town of Bjelovar to serve in the JNA in 1969, arriving directly from New York, where

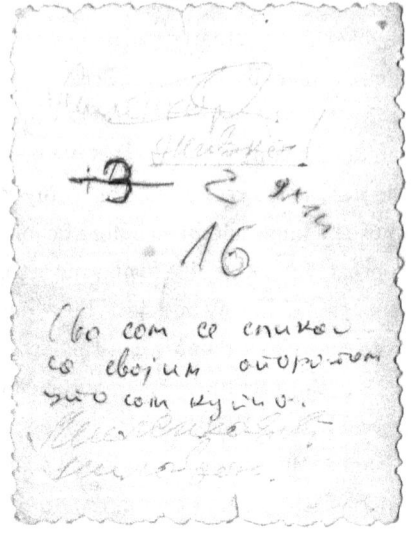

Figures 2.4 and 2.5 A photograph of Živko Milenković, a worker from a village in central Serbia, taken in the city where he served in the JNA. The inscription on the reverse reads, "This photograph was taken with my own camera, which I bought."

his films had been screened as part of the New Yugoslav Films retrospective at the Museum of Modern Art, and he had had a chance to meet people like Andy Warhol and Miloš Forman. His film *Rani radovi/Early Works*, vehemently criticized and forbidden by the state authorities in Yugoslavia, won a Golden Bear in Berlin that same year.[47] In spite of the dramatic contrast between the world he left and the one he entered when he put on the JNA uniform in a small and remote Croatian town, Želimir does not see his service in JNA as a radical reduction of his social space, but as an experience that enabled him to know and befriend people whom he would never have met had it not been for military service:

> My service in the JNA was overall an irritating experience, but when I was done with it, I went home with awareness that, for a great number of young men, this service was a kind of school they do not have in their villages. Furthermore, many friendships were made there. And finally—and this is most important—some men who came from places I would never go to myself became my friends and we remain friends to this day. There is one

from faraway Surdulica who calls me each time he comes to Vojvodina. And then, there are my friends from Zagreb—I still go and visit them.

Many former JNA soldiers remember their encounters with very diverse men on army bases as eye-opening and as making them aware of what kind of society Yugoslavia was—a very diverse one with tremendous economic, social, educational, and cultural differences. Dejan and Šoba, two artists who met in the barracks in Mali Lošinj, in Croatia, stress these various aspects of the experience of diversity that military service brought. Dejan says that he was shocked by this diversity—Muslim Montenegrins particularly impressed him. For Šoba, the most important aspect of his JNA experience was that he "got to know Yugoslavia for the first time in the army. I never had any contact with an Albanian, and had never met a Slovenian before I went to the JNA," and he went on to emphasize that he would feel deprived if he had not spent that year in the army. Oto, who served in the Montenegrin capital Titograd (now Podgorica) in 1986–87, similarly stresses the encounter with tremendous differences and diversity that could not have been experienced outside army bases as the most relevant aspects of his military service:

> In the army, I met a "real" Slovak, a Yugoslav citizen from Vojvodina, as well as a man who called himself a Turk. In my unit, there was a man whose profession was swineherd. At first, I thought it was a joke. But it turned out that he had been working as a shepherd with pigs for ten years already and that it was something usual where he came from, even considered a good job. There were also men who were illiterate. There were literacy courses organized in the JNA.

The infrastructural frame provided by military service offered more than learning about these tremendous differences: with its ritualized, repetitive forms and practices that functioned as an equalizer, the JNA unified a dramatically diverse group of men and, like the unity in labor of Youth Labor Actions, enabled the production of new affective relations—of friendship, solidarity, care, and mutual recognition that was not concerned with ethnic, class, or linguistic sameness or difference, but with the ethical qualities. These affective ties that were possible in the limited and ritualized space of JNA bases provided a hint of the possibility of a different social order, outside traditional frames of kinship, ethnicity, locality, cultural taste, or language. These infrastructural

Figure 2.6 A JNA soldier on watch. Photo by Franci Virant.

frames not only enabled recognition and affects regardless of class boundaries, they also made it possible to transcend these boundaries, enabling young men from remote villages to write poems, take photographs, go to the cinema, or learn to use a typewriter. Creating the infrastructures that enabled people to transcend the confines of their social background, class, and ethnicity was a defining principle of Yugoslav socialism. Living in modernist neighborhoods such as New Belgrade, Split III, Ruski Car in Ljubljana, and Alipašino Polje in Sarajevo were citizens with differing educations, professions, ethnicities, and mother tongues. They all shared living space, and their children played together and went to the same kindergartens and schools. Factories were not only spaces of production but also of cultural activities, education, and self-management. Infrastructures such as workers' universities, cultural centers in rural areas, amateur clubs, reading rooms, and libraries provided a space for the encounter, coexistence, and intertwining of very different cultural and artistic activities.[48]

Military service in the JNA was an involuntary experience abounding with ritualized, repetitive, and sometimes torturous routines and protocols with little meaning and devoid of purpose; it was a life lived in a confined, barbed-wired space, where soldiers counted the long days until they left the army and dreamt about the moment they could go back to their normal lives. Small calendars on which they would cross out day after day were an "obligatory" element of every soldier's equipment. They would invest all necessary efforts to make military service shorter: donate blood, behave well, and excel in competitions in order to be awarded additional days of leave and be allowed to shed their uniform weeks before their period of service officially ended. And yet the infrastructures of military service could orient this collective experience toward the future—the future that would be forever lost in Yugoslavia's disastrous ethnic wars and made unthinkable by the ethnicized logic of post-Yugoslav societies. This capacity connects military service with other future-oriented projects of Yugoslav socialism, such as nonalignment, self-management, and amateurism, although its mandatory nature and rigid organization does not make this connection obvious.

Observed from the vantage point of the aftermath of Yugoslavia and the limited horizons of the present, the barbed-wired space of military bases unfolds as a locus of utopian imagination. The utopian qualities inherent in military service in the JNA were not so much a result of a forward-looking agenda of the socialist military institution; they rather emerged from a retrospective recognition of the possibility of both a different collective and a different relationship between the individual and the collective. To open a space for collective life, self-perception, and mutual recognition outside the set frames of ethnic or class identities, the experience of military service had to be heterotopian in character and divided from the other streams of Yugoslav life. This not only sheds a painfully ambivalent light on the very nature of the Yugoslav project, but also on the uneasy relationship between the meaningfulness and the importance of the affective ties among the JNA soldiers woven during military service on the one hand and, on the other, the dramatic and total failure of the Yugoslav project that unfolded in unthinkable violence, in which the same men who served together in the JNA were, voluntarily or involuntarily, involved.

UTOPIA'S UNLIKELY HOME

In a book written with the philosopher Boris Buden, Želimir Žilnik describes the utopian character of collective life and the experience of diversity on Yugoslav army bases:

In retrospect, the Yugoslav People's Army can be understood as a historically unique form of collective life, a kind of military equivalent to the factory floor's collectivity in the time of industrial modernity and national sovereignty. Nowadays, that kind of collectivity is extinct, an endemic rarity. It exists only in memories with an approaching expiry date. In some fifty years, all of those who served in the JNA will be dead. But even now, it seems that young generations find it difficult to believe. From the present-day perspective, it seems impossible that people drastically different from each other—culturally, linguistically, ethnically, nationally, religiously, politically—lived together in a limited space in intense, almost bodily contact. Common life in the army was normal, self-evident, routine, almost natural, without significant tensions.[49]

This is a utopia of a different kind from the notions of utopia usually attached to the material leftovers of Yugoslavia and other socialist societies: unlike the forms that linger in the present as ruins of modernity and can be easily abstracted, de-territorialized, Orientalized, and "reconstituted anew," the utopia emerging from collective life in the JNA was more concrete and less prone to abstraction.[50] Bound to a lived experience of army service and its monotonous, ritualized, and repetitive forms, as well as to feelings of estrangement, oppression, entrapment, and surreality, the JNA bases scattered across socialist Yugoslavia may not seem likely places for a utopia. Nevertheless, the utopian conception of the military as a model for an (ideal) organization of society has a long history, extending from Plato's *Republic* to Fredric Jameson's essay "An American Utopia."[51] For Jameson, who advocates universal conscription as the model for the communist reorganization of American society, universal military service is a subsystem "which can function in so truly revolutionary a fashion."[52] In his view, the association of new utopian states with the army and army organization would "cut both ways: it can serve as a new form of social articulation, as the modern army begins to translate hierarchy into differentiation of functions, or it can aim at democratizing the army itself and inventing some new relationship between civilian society and this foreign body."[53] Jameson sees the utopian character of universal conscription in its capacity to offer a new socioeconomic structure and thus an alternative to the existing order of neoliberal capitalism and to provide a system of welfare (particularly in the spheres of healthcare and education) that avoids the limitations of the federal organization of the state. The universal conscription he proposes would encompass "everyone from sixteen to fifty, or, if you prefer, sixty years of age: that is, virtually the entire adult population." The universal draft would, he emphasizes, find a position within the system also for the handicapped, and "pacifists and conscientious objectors would be placed in control of arms development, arms storage, and the like."[54]

Although a future-oriented, utopian agenda was probably not in the minds of the Yugoslav officers responsible for the logistically, psychologically, and operationally highly demanding project of military service in the JNA, Jameson's utopian vision of the universal army shares several characteristics with the socialist Yugoslav military based on the draft: the design of both focuses on those aspects of the military that go beyond military efficiency, such as social cohesion and education, and both are imagined as "peaceful armies."[55] In addition, both aim to avoid the logic of federal organization and to transcend the fragmentation of interests, and both are based on the universal draft (limited to men, in the case of the JNA), which provides the basis for the utopian imagination. The experience of radical difference was crucial for how the JNA was experienced and remembered. Jameson ascribes equally important meaning to the fact that "the army is virtually the only institution in modern society whose members are obligated to associate with all kinds of people on an involuntary, nonelective basis, beginning with social class as such."[56]

However, in these two instances, utopia unfolds very differently through the relationship between the army and broader society, as well as through different temporalities. Jameson's universal army is a future utopian project bearing the promise of a classless society and an alternative to the dominant capitalist paradigm. His project's utopian character, as well as other visions of a universal army as a model for society that have been shaped through history, are significantly defined by an ambition to translate the structure, morals, and functioning of the army as a collective institution into other, broader social structures and spheres. But the JNA's utopian moment is located in the past, the time before political and social tragedy, as a promise of a future based on the possibility of radically diverse, but equal and unified people living together, and a promise of a society in which the individual and the collective are not in collision and the state functions in accordance with its citizens' aspirations. As such, it is largely and firmly connected to real experience, to something that existed, that was possible and real, however ambiguous it was and however impossible it seems today from a temporal distance and for the generations that have grown up in the aftermath of the Yugoslav tragedy. Furthermore, this utopian moment was made possible not by the Yugoslav military's ambition to intertwine with civil society and the social world outside the barracks. On the contrary, what makes military service in the JNA a locus of utopia for former Yugoslavs is the military's opposite characteristics and its heterotopian character: its remoteness from the ordinary, its dependence on routine, and its existence through uniform, ritual, repetitive forms. To become a site of the practical realization of ideals of radical difference, equality, and classlessness, the Yugoslav military had to detach its world from the ordinary world, and this detachment inevitably made the experience of army service oppressive and limiting, placing young Yugoslav men in an uneasy, often ambiguous relationship with their uniformed selves.[57] This uneasy relationship is my concern in the following chapters, but before I turn to them, I provide an insight into day-to-day life on JNA bases and the routines constitutive of that life. The repetitive routines and ritualized forms of army life worked toward harmonizing extremely diverse collectives of soldiers dressed in the JNA uniform and placed in the isolated, limited, and limiting space of army bases. But that was not all that the routines and forms effected: they also resulted in meaningful affective outcomes—in friendships, care, and solidarity among men so different from you that you would probably never meet them in "ordinary life." In the present, these affective outcomes function as a reminder of the possibility of living together outside ethnic, class, or linguistic divisions, a possibility created in the heterotopian space of army bases but now forever lost, together with the many lives, houses, families, hopes, and friendships that vanished during Yugoslav wars. The capacity of these affective outcomes to keep pointing to this lost possibility is where the utopian character of the collective life of military service in the JNA unfolds.

3

The Routine

Spontaneous organization, authentic forms of interaction, and nonhierarchical relations are often stressed as characteristics of the Yugoslav partisan units in World War II. Many therefore see them in stark opposition to their successor, the Yugoslav People's Army (JNA)—an isolated, conservative institution relying strongly upon discipline, drill, and strict hierarchy. "The wartime National Liberation Army," wrote Marko Milivojević, "was a revolutionary army, in which ranks, for example, were only introduced in 1943. It was an army that prided itself as being of and for and by the people, which would certainly have been approved of by Marx, who favoured a People's Militia (based on the one that existed in the 1870 Paris Commune) as being the most suitable form of military organisation in a communist society. After the war, however, Marx's preference and the whole revolutionary ethos of the NLA were quickly forgotten, as the new regime created a highly conventional army and military establishment."[1]

A glance at the wartime notes of the famous partisan commander Konstantin Koča Popović contradicts this dichotomous view of two military formations, questioning the romanticized idea of the partisan forces as entirely spontaneous, self-organized, and nonhierarchical. Popović came from a wealthy Belgrade family. He was a Sorbonne student of law and philosophy, a poet, and a prominent member of both French and Serbian Surrealist circles. He became involved with the Yugoslav Communist Party and fought in the Spanish Civil War on the Republican side. In 1941, Popović joined the Yugoslav partisans and, when the legendary First Proletarian Brigade (later First Proletarian Division) was founded in December 1941, became its commander. An experienced soldier who had "a touch of military genius and hatred of war," Popović's role was crucial in many major battles against the Axis powers and Chetniks, most notably in the battle of Sutjeska in May and June 1943.[2]

The Historical Archives of Belgrade keeps several small notebooks and sheets of paper with his dense, hard to decipher notes written after these battles. In a note titled "Intervention impérative" from December 27, 1944, Popović writes: "Our units have significantly grown in both men and weaponry. The majority of soldiers are young, the officer cadre is sparse, and our weapons diverse. All of this requires a change in the way we lead our army." He emphasizes that the transformation needs to start from below, "from the basic duties and rules," and provides a long list of practices to be changed or introduced. Among them are: lining up for roll call every morning; constant exercises and training (strictly scheduled watch shifts, familiarization with weapons and practicing with their use); collective and mandatory morning hygiene (*zajedničko i obavezno umivanje*); inspection of weapons at least once a week; maintaining order during marches and in camps; strict fulfillment of orders and commands. He further stresses that "apart from the intense work with soldiers, the style of giving orders needs to change: individual initiative can be allowed only within strictly defined tasks."[3] In the notebook titled "Operations," Popović wrote remarks related to partisan military operations in Bosnia on March 28 and 29, 1945. He points out several shortcomings, among them a too familiar style of giving orders, loose protocols, and illiterate, arbitrary, and unclear reports that lead to incorrect decisions during battle.[4]

After the end of World War II, Koča Popović was appointed chief commander of the General Staff of the Yugoslav army from 1945 to 1953. His notes from this period show that military discipline, solidifying the army, "reality and practicalities of training," commands, and protocols remained his important concerns.[5]

The insistence on strict discipline, repetition, routine, and hierarchy may seem out of kilter with the Surrealist poetics and theory and practice of experimental art that preoccupied Popović in the prewar years, but it can be understood as the outcome of necessity, just as the decision by the educated, well-off, young Yugoslav artist to join the communists and go and fight was the result of necessity and urgency. Popović describes this decision as follows:

> I was engaged with literature, and at some point, I understood how useless it was. I quickly realized that the only possibility left was a direct conflict with the enemy . . . I need to add that I made this unsolicited decision in France. I became a communist and opted for action on the eve of World War II. I understood the obvious advance of fascism as a challenge to which there was only one way to respond: we have to fight. I saw that the danger was approaching and that I had to resist to it. There was no sense in writing some half-intelligible poems. I had to act.[6]

A skillful, talented, and devoted commander, Koča Popović saw discipline, hierarchy, strict protocols, and repetitive practices as necessary to secure the victory of the Yugoslav partisan units in World War II. After the war, his views on the Yugoslav "regular" army and the concerns he had as chief of the General Staff were still informed by Yugoslavia's precarious position in the international arena, and particularly by the looming threat of military conflict with the USSR after Yugoslavia rejected Soviet influence in 1948.

In the 1970s and 1980s, the period that concerns me most in this book, military service in the JNA was no longer associated with an immediate threat of war and military conflict, but by then it had perfected the principles Popović insisted on in World War II and its aftermath. Rituals, routines, strict hierarchy, and elaborated protocols became the spine of the JNA's organization and the fabric of everyday military service. At the same time, the nature of the Yugoslav military was the reason for growing criticism of it as Yugoslavia approached its end.[7]

Military service in the JNA was a life strictly defined and constrained by the "rules of service" (*pravila službe*) that thoroughly prescribed every aspect of it. The ambition to make everything subject to highly controlled and organized processes went as far as encompassing rather ordinary and everyday objects. For example, the entrances to army bases (*kapija*) were referred to with the abbreviation KPS, which stands for *kontrolno-propusna stanica* (control-admittance station), while a towel was not just a mundane accessory for daily hygiene, but a technically understood object that, according to the rules of service, consisted of two parts: the towel's body and its hanging loop.

Subjecting young men coming from all parts of the country to these highly structured, elaborate, repetitive, and regular protocols was a way to make them JNA soldiers and to make the units in which they were grouped able to act in a coordinated, harmonious way. Efficient acting is a priority in any military, be it in wartime or in peace. But routines constituting military service in the JNA mattered beyond purely military reasons. In a broader temporal frame, the JNA itself became increasingly routinized during the years and decades of Yugoslav socialism—its organizational structures solidified, minimizing improvisation and enabling the harmonious functioning of heterogeneous collectives of young recruits. And within the period of an individual's military service, these routines served to structure, but also constitute, life. However far the experience of military service was from the ordinary life young soldiers left behind, these routines made it not only ordinary in its own microcosm, but also meaningful beyond it.

LEARNING

The repetition, regularity, density, and intensity of practices gave a shape to a specific economy of time that was differently structured in two parts of military service in the JNA: *obuka* (training) and the time that followed *preko-manda* (assignment to another unit, typically on another military base). *Obuka* lasted between three and seven months, depending on the military branch, and was dedicated to educating conscripts. This was also the period in which they were expected to achieve a high level of physical fitness. At the end of *obuka*, they were expected to have mastered the use of weapons, learned all the protocols of commands and reporting, and perfected everyday operations such as making their bed, packing clothes and other belongings in a prescribed way, and performing physically demanding tasks on the base and during field exercises. The intense drill and repetition of operations was expected to have led JNA soldiers to internalize the world of the army. In the second part of military service, these already formed soldiers joined units in which they would perform daily tasks. The main difference between the two periods of military service was in the amount of free time and consequently in the velocity at which time would pass. During training, every moment was well planned and the army's main concern was not leaving a soldier alone or doing nothing. The second part of military service abounded in free time and lazy afternoons. If soldiers' priority during *obuka* was accommodating and finding a way to get through intense drill as smoothly as possible, a significant part of their efforts after *prekomanda* can be described as the art of speeding time up.

Variations in the intensity and velocity of time passing notwithstanding, the structure that defined days in the JNA remained firm throughout. "Every day is the same as any other day," Oto Luthar said, describing his military service in Titograd in 1986–87. Milan Todorović, an IT expert from Valjevo, Serbia, who served in the JNA in Jakovo and Bela Crkva in northern Serbia in 1987–88, similarly stressed, "Day after day everything is absolutely the same, with minimal variations."

Throughout military service, the soldiers would have to get up in the early morning, at 5 a.m. or 6 a.m., woken up by an officer on duty who would enter the room shouting "*Ustaj, vojsko!*" ("Get up, the army!"), or on some military bases by the sound of a bugle. That was the case in Jakovo near Belgrade, where Milan performed the first part of his military service. After beds were made and hygiene done, including mandatory daily shaving, soldiers would run to the training ground to perform twenty minutes of physical exercise. The time after breakfast and before lunch was dedicated to structured activities—training, work with weapons, and classes. Each morning, the daily order (*dnevna za-povest*) was read, announcing the activities for that day. In the evening, there was dinner, followed by collectively watching the daily news, after which it was time to retreat to the dormitories for sleep (*povečerje*). Before the beginning of most of these daily activities, the soldiers would have to line up (*postrojavanje*).

These daily operations were expected to be performed seamlessly and harmoniously. The tiniest deviation was followed by the command "*Ostav!*" (repeat/resume), after which the operation had to be repeated, sometimes many times, before the officer was satisfied by the performance.

As soon as the military base woke up in the morning, music would start from the loudspeakers. It was a sonic companion of most daily activities. The choice of music was rarely "ideological," but a result of the preferences of the soldier in charge of the music on the particular day. Oto vividly remembered one morning when exercises were performed to the soundtrack of To- maso Albinoni's *Adagio in D Minor*, and many soldiers heard particular songs and bands from these loudspeakers for the first time. Hariz Halilovich, whose training started in 1988 in the firefighters' unit in Senta before he was moved to the infirmary, remembered his first days as something he barely survived. "Every morning, before the flag ceremony, the song "Kako je dobro vidjeti te opet" (How good is seeing you again) by the Novi Fosili band was played, and it touched me because I had to leave my girlfriend to go into the army (and she left me before I came back)," he recalled.

Day-to-day life on military bases was full of strictly defined and performative communication protocols. The officers and superiors had to be addressed in a prescribed way, and soldiers had to ask for permission to speak. Technical names and abbreviations were used for all sorts of things, including weapons (such as the PAP M59 semiautomatic rifle), meals (SDO and GG9), colors (SMB), tools (RAP), cleansers (DRNČ), and roles (*požarni*, *četni evidentičar*).[8]

To be successfully socialized into the military, young conscripts had to master these prescribed scripts. This required a certain effort and investment by every soldier. However different they were among themselves, the routines and rituals that constituted military service in the JNA were equally remote from what they were used to in their "normal," everyday lives. All JNA soldiers—those who graduated from university and illiterate ones, those who came from remote villages and those who grew up in urban centers—learned these official protocols. They also acquired slang terms that were used to wittily address predictable aspects of the limited reality of military life: words for food included *cigla* ("brick," for a solid, hard piece of bread from a field ration), *drnč* (a dish made of a variety of vegetables and meat), and *dečja radost* ("children's joy" for bread and marmalade); different military branches included *prašinari* ("dusters," for the infantry) and *plavci* ("blues," for antiaircraft units); and terms for hierarchies based on the time spent in the army included *gušteri* ("lizards") and *fazani* ("pheasants") for rookies, and *džombe* and *stare kuke* ("old hooks") for soldiers who were approaching the end of their military service.

EMBODIMENT

The transition from civilian to army life was abrupt and rather dramatic for young Yugoslav men. There was much to get used to: uncomfortable uniforms and beds; being far away from home and loved ones; the snoring of a dozen or several dozen young men sleeping in the same room; waking up at dawn to an officer's shouts. For some men, adapting to this new reality was not easy or smooth; for others, who were already used to hard work and harsh life conditions, this could even be a more comfortable life. For all of them, however, life in the barracks was very different and detached from what they knew as normal, everyday, and ordinary. To get used to this new life—and even more, to experience it as normal, everyday, and ordinary—newly conscripted JNA soldiers were exposed to intense training that combined demanding physical activities and a learning process that relied heavily on repetition.

Morning exercises, drill, marches, and field training were supposed to equalize soldiers' capability and make units act in an efficient and coordinated way. Želimir, who served in the JNA in a tank unit, also points to this link between the strict organization of army life, the emphasis on physical work and fitness, and the functioning of the collective. In his words, "Army life was organized in such a way that the collective could function in a relatively rational way." Remembering the first months of his military service, Želimir said "After a couple of months, the units which comprised fresh recruits consolidated entirely physically. In the tank unit, apart from cleaning the tank and learning all the complicated procedures of driving and fueling the tank, we would also receive the order to entrench the tank. That meant as much digging as if you were making foundations for a house."

Field shooting exercises, boot camps, and participation in wider military or civil-military campaigns aimed at strengthening the self-defense capacities of the country and its citizens were also important events (such as "Nothing should surprise us" and military maneuvers in which JNA units were divided into "red" and "blue"). Here, what was learned on the army bases was practiced in circumstances close to real ones. Military shooting grounds such as Pasuljanske Livade, Krivolak, Bubanj Potok, Manjača, and Slunj are still important points on the memory maps of former JNA soldiers.

"Technical training" during the first months of military service was oriented to getting familiar with and mastering the use of the weapons young soldiers were responsible for. They learned how they worked and endlessly repeated procedures of cleaning, assembling, and disassembling them. "We disassembled and assembled the automatic rifle so many times that we could do it with our eyes closed," Oto remembers of his training in Titograd. The repetition of actions embodied and internalized these procedures. Oto adds that he would dream of assembling and disassembling his firearm for

Figure 3.1 A locker containing clothes folded and arranged according to the rules of service. Photo by Franci Virant.

many nights, including after his training was over. "Comrade lieutenant commander! Soldier Milan Todorović, semiautomatic rifle M59/66, 7.62 millimeter, weapon number 243789, ready for inspection!" (*Druže poručniče! Vojnik Milan Todorović, poluautomatska puška M59/66, 7,62 mm, broj puške 243789, spremna na pregled*) was the sentence Milan repeated so many times that he says he will never forget it. Making his bed so that its edges were as sharp as a blade and arranging clothes in the locker in a precise order were also skills acquired through endless repetition. This was also the period in which soldiers learned to answer to commands, understand the meanings of technical terms and abbreviations, and acquired specific slang that recruits used among themselves.

Filling in every moment of daily life with physical drill, repetitive procedures, and tasks was aimed at accelerating the process of internalizing the world of the army for young recruits. During the first weeks of service, the only free time they had was when waiting in line for a meal or going to the store on the base. Keeping fresh soldiers busy all the time, occupying their bodies and minds with constant repetitive tasks, and taking care that they were never left alone, had another purpose as well, as many of my interlocutors pointed out: it was meant to prevent these young men from "thinking too much" and surrendering to despair and depression amid the profound transition from civilian to military life and to eliminate possibilities for conflict, aggression, and provocation. Young recruits reacted differently to the new situation and the radical change from what they were used to before entering a military base, depending on their psychological profiles, but also on their previous life experiences. To handle these differences, the JNA relied not only on intense disciplinary routines, but also on the dynamic among soldiers themselves, governed by care for one's fellow soldiers, mutual help, and support. The age difference between recruits enlisted when turning eighteen or immediately after graduating from high school on the one hand, and those who performed military service after graduating from college on the other, seemed to play an important role in this dynamic. Želimir recalls: "It was all organized in such a way that if a problem or a provocation emerged, there would be someone to react and neutralize it. For example, I was twenty-seven-years old and there were all these soldiers who were younger than me and were suffering from the separation from their families . . . I tried to be like an older brother to them." Similarly, Oto remembers that apart from all the challenges the intense training imposed at the beginning of his military service, he "suddenly found himself in a position to take care of someone."

Young urban men used to a comfortable life, to whom a harsh regime of hard physical work was alien, faced challenges different from those faced by illiterate peasants, Albanians or Hungarians lacking a command of Serbo-Croatian, or young men from *Gastarbeiter* families who came to serve in the JNA from Western Europe. Despite the differences among them, all newly conscripted JNA soldiers were in the same position: they were all "starting from scratch," as Oto put it—they had to learn the same protocols, embody routines, master various marches, bring bed-making to perfection. All these repetitive operations, ritualized practices, physically exhaustive drills, and restricted and performative communication codes were aimed at organizing life on an army base and securing harmonious and efficient actions. The military institution orchestrated all these dramatically diverse men through such forms, organizing them into a manageable whole. But as Oto's observation suggests, the meaning of these routines exceeded purely organizational purposes: they also provided a common basis for these men. Thus, these repetitive, restricted forms not only organized and harmonized, they also constituted life inside the fences of JNA bases—they provided a common language. The young soldiers could learn about and interact with each other and care about and help each other through participation in clearly prescribed operations, tasks, and drills, since the early days of army service did not leave much time for other kinds of interaction anyway.

HABITUATION

The passage of time brought a slight relaxation in life on army bases. The soldiers could feel the first signs of the loosening of the tight and intense daily regime after the oath-taking ceremony, which also symbolically made them "proper" JNA soldiers. The ceremony was a moment when they met their parents, siblings, and girlfriends for the first time since they had donned their JNA uniforms, as family members were invited to attend it. For soldiers, this loosening meant that they could spend some additional time in the canteen in the afternoons and were exempt from lining up on Sundays. After taking the oath, the soldiers were allowed periodic afternoon outings to the cities in which they served. Day-to-day life became slightly easier and less physically demanding, which resulted not only from a gradual lessening of the intensity of drill and training, but also from the soldiers' internalization of and familiarization with the procedures they were exposed to. As Oto described this process of internalization: "You get used to all of that, and start doing what is expected without even being told what to do. You are in, and everything seems easier."

Going through the first months of training, JNA soldiers not only learned daily routines and accustomed their bodies and minds to the logic of military life. They also figured out how to find their way around and make arrangements that would make their army days bearable. They learned to protect their clothes and shoes from theft or to find a way to replace a piece of equipment if it got lost or stolen; making friends with soldiers responsible for distributing equipment was a valuable thing to do and helped a lot in such situations. At the beginning, they ate whatever they got for breakfast, lunch, or dinner, but with time, the quality of food became closely related to who was responsible for cooking and for food distribution in the canteen. Soldiers in charge of the kitchen would provide better portions to their friends. Making phone calls from the base was virtually impossible in the early days of military service, but with time, many would find a way to call their parents, friends, or a girlfriend: they would learn where phones were located, when the officers were not around, and how to make it through the blockade set on military phones. This learning process was dependent on knowing and being on good terms with the right people on the base. Getting better food or more comfortable shoes or making a phone call would often cost a young soldier a couple of Spam cans or beers.

In the period that followed the first months of training, the soldiers would usually be assigned to a different base and a different unit, where they would use the knowledge they had acquired. They were given tasks of greater complexity, often based on their personal skills and preferences. Some became corporals and were responsible for men in their unit. Some, particularly those with higher degrees of education, were unit secretaries and record keepers, writing daily reports and records and creating schedules for cleaning dormitories, hallways, and toilets, for watch shifts, and for going out to the city, as well as for longer periods of leave to go home. These schedules were Oto's responsibility, and he was very careful to make equal and just distributions.

Such responsibilities importantly shaped relations among soldiers—their friendships as well as the affective economy of care, solidarity, and mutual help. These roles also brought privileges and were of huge significance in the internal economy of the base and soldiers' everyday life. As Hariz described to me: "Those of us with important roles—those working in the infirmary, administrators, those in charge of equipment, those working in the kitchen, couriers—we functioned in a manner that could be compared with a criminal union. We had control. We cared for and supported each other. For example, I never had to clean my shoes—I would take new ones every few days."

Relations among soldiers were additionally fostered by a specific temporal regime shaping the second part of their service, with its free afternoons and weekends and a lot of time left to soldiers to fill. "This was the time when you learn to do nothing," Oto recalled. It was important to look busy; otherwise the officers would assign soldiers something to do—mow the grass, collect leaves, or clean weapons. The daily rhythm remained defined by strictly scheduled practices—morning hygiene, exercises, daily meals, and orders—but the density and intensity of these practices subsided, leaving time for the soldiers to use on their own terms. There was a lot of soccer and chess playing, joking, and hanging out together. Some soldiers would use this time to write letters to their girlfriends, family members, or friends. The army itself also provided the infrastructure for the meaningful use of this free time. It encouraged cultural activities such as organizing an orchestra or producing a wall newspaper: on a designated wall in a common room, soldiers would display their own texts and artwork, information on life on the base, and clippings from printed newspapers dedicated to important holidays, personalities, or events from Yugoslav and global politics. Each military base had its own library, and many soldiers remember their army service as a time when they read more than ever. The library on the base in Titograd, where Oto spent his military service, contained books from a wide range of authors, from Dostoyevsky to Karl May. Želimir remembers that he read some amazing books in the library on the JNA base in Bjelovar: "For example, in the middle of the Yugoslav military, I could read the memoirs of the German World War II generals Guderian and Rommel, published in Serbo-Croatian by the military publisher Vojno Delo. Phenomenal, very thick books." Oto and his fellow soldiers were also allowed to remake a storage room into a cultural club. They hung up a portrait of the World War II hero Ivo Lola Ribar and regularly made wall newspapers for their unit. On a proving ground near Osijek where the photographer Franci Virant spent his time after *prekomanda*, soldiers even arranged a photography exhibition in the common space and, following the JNA propensity to label and classify, named it "canteen and gallery."

The chunks of uncontrolled time, unstructured by assigned tasks and activities, allowed for minor subversions of imposed orders, as photographs from the era suggest (see figures 3.2 and 3.3).

Franci captured many moments of life beyond the strict routines and protocols of the training ground Polygon C near Osijek. One of his photographs shows "the beach scene"—a group of soldiers enjoying the sun under a beach umbrella within the base (figure 3.4). At first glance, these men could be anywhere, enjoying a sunny summer day, but a soldier in the background, armed and fully dressed in uniform, in such stark contrast with their almost naked bodies and relaxed poses, suggests that this is not the "ordinary" world.

The life of military service was lived within the barbed-wired confines of JNA military bases. What constituted its fabric was limited and limiting: repetitive routines, ritualized protocols, orders, technical labels, abbreviations, commands, and strictly structured activities. Even when acting outside these firmly defined structures—when creating and using their own slang, engaging in slightly subversive behavior, celebrating New Year's and other holidays, organizing their free time, and arranging spaces where they spent these free hours—they could do so only using the same monotonous, perfor-

Figure 3.2 Soldiers entertaining themselves in their free time. From the archive of Svanibor Pettan.

Figure 3.3 Soldiers photographed next to a sign that forbids taking photographs, Mali Lošinj, 1987. From the archive of Nebojša Šerić Šoba and Dejan Dimitrijević.

Figure 3.4 Soldiers sunbathing in their free time, Osijek, 1981. Photo by Franci Virant.

mative components, bound to the reality of military service and the ideology at its foundations, choosing from the existing, limited inventory of words, relations, labels, and images.

But it would be wrong to assume that limited and monotonous forms that constituted life on JNA bases made that life inauthentic or devoid of meaning. The embodiment of repetitive tasks and routines during military service in the JNA did not lead to desensitization and disaffection.[9] Nor did they work toward a normalization of war and violence, as in the case of the US military base described by Kenneth MacLeish. There, he writes, "the spectacular violence of a foreign battlefield and the routinized violence of the military apparatus bleed by various, complex routes into one another and into the everyday lives of soldiers and those close to them. There is not just the violence of meeting the enemy to consider: how that violence is anticipated, accommodated, forestalled, or aggravated by the Army itself, the lives that surround that violence, the prerogatives that drive it, and the discourses that make it intelligible all determine the sum and shape of living in and with war."[10] Daily routines of military service in the JNA were productive of something quite different: they had an important role in creating conditions for affect to emerge within the confined world of JNA bases. These forms—repetitive routines, strict protocols, and a limited repertoire of words, objects, and images—worked as a great equalizer, creating structures, nets, and means for very different men gathered on the base and dressed in the same uniform to interact, live and laugh together, and help, befriend, and care about each other. As I argued in the previous chapter, the affective outcomes of these forms' workings were not a side effect of militarizing Yugoslav men, but clearly part of the agenda of the Yugoslav military institution, which invested tremendous effort, resources, and infrastructure in bringing together young men from all parts of the country and all walks of life to expose them to the experience of radical diversity and simultaneous equality. In chapters 4 and 5, I explore complex and multifaceted ways in which these forms—routines, uniforms, and rituals—and the subjectivities of young men in the JNA uniform encountered each other.

4

The Uniform

On the first day of their military service in the Yugoslav People's Army (JNA), as soon as the young men went through the gates of the army base, they were exposed to disciplinary and difference-erasing mechanisms that made them all alike, equally subordinated to the institution they had just entered, but also equal among themselves. Long before Erving Goffman labeled it "mortification," as early as the eve of World War II, the Bulgarian political philosopher Ivan Hajiyski effectively described this difference-erasing mechanism in the army in Bulgaria.[1] In an essay on the psychology of military discipline, Hajiyski stressed that one of the basic characteristics of a military system is its attack on each person's individuality, the first step of which is accomplished through the "elimination of the person's particular physical characteristics; soldiers are deprived of their old social and physical worlds, their clothes are changed, and hair cut off."[2]

Similarly in the JNA, the set of procedures that marked their first day in the army turned young men who arrived at the base from all parts of Yugoslavia into JNA soldiers. The first step, the one everyone remembers so well, was having their hair cut off. "I experienced that as a most dehumanizing procedure," remembers one of my interlocutors. At the end of the day, a new soldier was dressed in a uniform, hardly recognizable to himself or to his new acquaintances that he had met that day. As one person wrote about his first day in the JNA on an online forum: "In the evening, we got our hair cut, took a shower, and got uniforms. When we got dressed, we could not recognize each other, with our hair cut short and in navy uniforms. Although we spent the whole first day getting to know each other, at the end we were all checking: 'Are you the one from Zagreb?' 'Are you from Belgrade?'"

Photographs made for soldiers' identity cards and their personnel files resulted from this procedure of making young men all the same and estranged. For young men who had just completed high school and left the chaotic world of adolescence or who had recently graduated from college, it was not always easy to establish a link between who they were and these freshly shaved and short-haired men in uniform gazing out from small-format photos on their army ID cards. The step from one reality to the other was experienced as dramatic and radical by most JNA soldiers, regardless of who they had been in their "ordinary" lives. "It was as if someone kidnapped me from Hawaii and put me into a dark well," one of them wrote on an online forum. Radosav Majdevac, an artist and musician from Globoder near Kruševac in central Serbia, never got used to his new self without the long beard he had been growing for years before joining the JNA. A talented performer, before New Year in 1984, he was "hired" to act as Santa Claus at the kindergarten for officers' children. For him, these were the best moments of his military service in Maribor, Slovenia, in 1986–87, because he could have a beard again.

It is in this different, detached reality where young men lived the collective life of military service. The uniform made them all the same, and often not easily relatable to whom they had been before they joined the army. The military uniform, Tom Smith argues, "appears to present a clear and unambiguous narrative that fixes the individual in a specific military identity and replaces any existing civilian traits."[3] However, the relationship between the military and civilian selves and worlds was far from fixed and unambiguous for JNA soldiers. The ambiguity of this relationship, moreover, was ingrained in the very functioning logic of the institution of military service: the uniform and repetitive, standardized routines, practices, and language were used as equalizers for drastically different men gathered on the bases, but the military

Figure 4.1 The army identity card (*vojna knjižica*) of the musician Antonije Pušić, aka Rambo Amadeus.

simultaneously counted on differences among them and made use of who they were in their civilian lives. This complex dynamic between sameness and difference is at the heart of this chapter.

IN THE CITY

Soldiers in the JNA regularly left their barracks to go into the towns where they were situated, usually in groups, for a drink at the weekend or when someone—parents, relatives, or a friend or girlfriend—came for a visit. These brief excursions to towns exposed the ambiguity of the relationship between the self from before and the self in army uniform. Karpo Aćimović Godina's short film *O ljubavnim veštinama ili film sa 14,441 kvadratom* poignantly points to this ambiguity.[4] Godina, a Slovenian film director and one of the prominent representatives of the Yugoslav Black Wave film movement of the 1960s and 1970s, served in the JNA in the early 1970s in Ajdovščina, a small town in western Slovenia. Yugoslav army authorities learned about his filmmaking skills, and after six months of training in the infantry, he was transferred to a new post with Zastava Film in Belgrade, where he helped produce propaganda films for the military.[5] After reading a short article published in the army newspaper *Front* about the town of Štip in Macedonia, where there was a large textile factory and a JNA base, so that thousands of young women and thousands of young soldiers performing military service were in the same town but without contact between them, Godina asked for permission to make a film on his own in which he would poetically tackle this issue.[6] Although already known as a "troublemaking" director who worked with Želimir Žilnik on Želimir's *Early Works*, and who himself had produced "subversive" films such as *Zdravi ljudi za razonodu*, Godina was given carte blanche by the military authorities, always eager to showcase the positive effects of the presence of the JNA in Yugoslav cities.[7] This was the first—and last—film he made as a JNA soldier for Zastava Film. The film was banned, and he was threatened with jail.[8]

Presented with the script, Yugoslav military officials expected a film that would stress the importance of cohabitation and interaction between the military and "civilians" and how the presence of the JNA benefitted the city of Štip, but instead, Godina's images spoke of separation and loneliness in a small, faraway town in socialist Yugoslavia, with the sung refrain "A thousand soldiers and a thousand women, but no children" (*Hiljadu vojnika na hiljadu žena, a dece nema*) as a sonic backdrop.[9]

The film opens with a massive group portrait of young women employed at the textile factory. One of them says, in Macedonian, "In our factory there are more than 2,000 women, who very rarely have contact with soldiers." Another continues: "There is no contact between us girls of this town and soldiers, because this is a small town, there are gossips, and it is considered inappropriate to talk to a man in uniform. Also, the soldiers' attitude toward girls is rude; they do not know how to treat a girl. Not all soldiers are like that, but most of them are cruel and rude."

These words summarize what every Yugoslav soldier must have felt in precious moments when they were allowed to leave their military base and enjoy some free time in towns where they served: that the uniform he wore defined and separated him from the world outside the barracks, making contact with people in that world difficult, often impossible, and always limited. The young men looked forward to time off their bases. Their excursions gave

Figure 4.2 Soldiers in the city of Osijek, 1981. Photo by Franci Virant.

them a freedom they longed for while on the base, but the towns they walked through were alien and unknown, and the uniform made their step into the "ordinary" only partial. In the outside world, the soldiers were reduced to the uniform that made them all the same (and "cruel and rude") and trapped in the liminal space it defined. That limited and liminal space encompassed the base, but also extended beyond its gates.

"The city I never got to know" is how a former soldier on Facebook described Pula, a town on the Croatian coast where he served in the JNA. Dressed in uniforms and thus sharply distinguished from "ordinary citizens," soldiers would stick together, walking around the town or having drinks in restaurants. Or they would go to a local cinema to kill their free time. The places that uniformed soldiers would frequent were usually marked and avoided by "ordinary citizens." "You see that lane?" a friend of mine once pointed out as we were walking in Ljubljana's Tivoli Park. "Back then in the eighties, it was reserved for JNA soldiers only. The rest of us would use the other lane. We never mixed with them." The historian Darko Dukovski similarly writes about Pula, a town characterized by the massive presence of the Yugoslav military: "The Istra cinema was a bit away from the city's center, near Arena

Figure 4.3 Soldiers in front of the Papuk cinema in Osijek, 1981. Photo by Franci Virant.

[the Roman amphitheater]. It belonged to Pula less than any other cinema in the city, because it was mainly visited by soldiers, and its repertoire had been adjusted accordingly."[10]

The spaces inhabited by soldiers—barracks, training grounds, cinemas, restaurants—were often incorporated into the urban networks of Yugoslav towns, but also excluded from the ordinary paths of the people living there. Some of the towns, like Postojna in Slovenia, Pula in Croatia, Bitola in Macedonia, and Bileća in Bosnia and Herzegovina, which had a significant number of bases and soldiers serving on them, would become alienated on the days when soldiers had leave.[11] An inhabitant of Postojna told me that people who lived there would not go out on Sundays, because all the restaurants were occupied by soldiers and their families, who would come for a visit. "The town did not belong to us on these days," he said. In Pula, the massive presence of the army frequently made citizens feel that their city belonged only partially and intermittently to them. That was particularly true on Wednesdays and weekends—when the soldiers would receive permission to leave their base. One of them remembers, "When soldiers would go out, the citizens of Pula would slowly withdraw from public spaces."

Such statements, however, do not indicate that young soldiers were perceived as alien intruders in the local setting. Universal conscription meant that most of locals knew someone who had served, was serving, or soon would be serving in the JNA. This generated empathy and motivated many of them to buy drinks for soldiers in restaurants and bars. At the same time, they saw these uniformed young men as being outside "their" ordinary world. This double gaze may be best illustrated with two recognizable details from the cities where the JNA had its bases: in cinema halls, there was often a separate entrance, with a label "for children and soldiers only" (*samo za d(j)ecu i vojnike*). In Vipava, one such town in Slovenia, people still retell the following anecdote: when the director of the city cinema called a lady in the box office to check how many people came to watch a movie, she answered, "There are only three people, the rest are soldiers."

The army and the city cohabitated in complex and often difficult ways, but they were never two completely separate worlds. The most important feature of the presence of the army in a town was a "domain," a territory physically separate from the rest of the city, to which access was restricted. Cartographically, on cadastral maps, the presence of the military was designated by blank, empty areas, out of reach and beyond the control of the public and civilians.[12] The army, however, was present in the city in manifold ways that cannot be clearly presented on a map: there were apartment buildings occupied by JNA officers and their families and other buildings used by the military. And soldiers went to the city's restaurants, beaches, walking areas, bars, and cinemas, and were present in the streets and city squares. Soldiers sang together with locals in mixed civilian-military choirs and regularly visited local primary schools on important state holidays. Some spaces belonging to the military, such as army cultural centers, enabled interactions between a city's inhabitants and the military. These interactions were encouraged by both military and civilian authorities. Every Saturday, there were parties in the canteen of Pula's Arena textile factory, organized in cooperation with the JNA and its orchestra, and "at least a hundred Arena workers married local army officers" who came to the city from all over Yugoslavia.[13] Sometimes, the civilian and military worlds intersected in rather unexpected ways. For example, in 1980, the cult hard-rock band Atomsko Sklonište from Pula recorded a live album in the military cultural center, because it had the best acoustics and recording conditions in the town.

There were also rare possibilities for the soldiers to briefly experience "ordinary" city life or some chunks of it, and these moments are remembered and narrated as particularly important memories of service in the army: "I served on Katarina base in Pula in 1983 and 1984. It was on the coast, at the very entrance to the harbor. I went to the film festival in Arena and watched the premiere screening of 'Variola Vera.'"[14] "I also sang in the mixed military-civilian choir and we performed all around Istria." Another JNA soldier who served in Pula remembers: "I was twice at the film festival in Pula's Arena and, as a soccer aficionado, I attended soccer games of the Istria football club. Swimming was forbidden, but I remember Verudela Beach; I was there only once. Once the officers sent us to Arena to arrange seats for the film festival. Ljubiša Samardžić bought us beer then."[15]

Nebojša Šerić Šoba, an artist from Sarajevo, served the second part of his military service in the Croatian town of Sinj, and spent most of his time in the local JNA cultural center. His most important and memorable moment related to this place was when he was assigned the task of organizing a concert by the rock band Azra. The officers from whom the order came had no idea who Azra were, but for Šoba, this was a priceless opportunity to hear one of the most important Yugoslav music groups live—an opportunity he would have appreciated very much in "ordinary" life as well.

The uniform distinguished young men from the mass of a town's inhabitants and visitors, giving them some prerogatives stemming from the ideologically high value of the military in Yugoslavia, such as cheaper tickets, a separate entrance to cinemas, and using the city's public transport free of charge.[16] At the same time, however, it excluded them from some areas in the urban structure, limited and governed their movement and access to some places, and thus made it impossible for them to fully be who they were. There were places, especially those for young people's entertainment, such as discotheques, where entrance was denied to uniformed soldiers: "In Pula, there were the discotheques Piramida and Uljanik, but we could go there only if dressed as civilians. It was June-September 1988; the Piramida discotheque was very popular, but soldiers had no access to it." In the small town of Sinj where Šoba served that same year, there were only two places where the soldiers could go out, "a local bar and a pizza place owned by an Albanian."

The uniformed young men, walking in groups along the promenades in Ljubljana or on the Corso in Pula, sitting together in restaurants in towns across Yugoslavia, and watching movies in local cinemas, were gathered from all parts of the country. Under the uniforms were men with different experiences, skills, and tastes in music and books, men who came from very different worlds.

Figure 4.4 Soldiers in a restaurant in Osijek, 1981. From the archive of Franci Virant.

But the uniform made these worlds and the young men to whom they belonged invisible; in the towns where they served, exposed to the gaze of passers-by, they were seen just as soldiers, all the same. They could not be anonymous in the city, could not do the things they would if they were not in uniform. They could not swim in coastal towns where they served (swimming was forbidden to soldiers unless organized) and could not go to see bands they liked or to other events that were important to them. One former soldier remembers: "One of my first army memories in Pula was the death of Atomsko Sklonište's singer Sergio Blažić. I asked for permission to go to the funeral, but was rudely denied. I was very sad and upset about it."

The uniform often was like heavy armor for the young men serving in the JNA, preventing them from being who they were and thus causing frustration. It could not be removed, as the civilian clothes of JNA soldiers were sent to their homes by mail as soon as they had dressed in their uniform, with shipping costs covered by the JNA. But the uniform brought a certain freedom, too. "Locals did not like the soldiers, because the soldiers drank a lot, would become aggressive, with all that the combination of alcohol and nostalgia implies," recalls one of them. In the liminal time and space of military service, soldiers could afford to behave in a way that would otherwise be inappropriate:

observing young women passing by, whistling, making obscene comments—behavior that a young woman working in the textile factory mentions in Karpo Godina's film as the main reason why the women did not "mix" with soldiers.

The uniform that soldiers wore when they left their bases made them representatives of the Yugoslav military, and according to army authorities, it was a source of pride but also required responsibility. In the TV series *Kad sam bio vojnik*, on the first day of military service the officer tells the newly arrived recruits that when they go into the city, it is recommended that they do not drink alcohol, because "seeing you in the city, the citizens (civilians) would not see, say, Vukotić, but a JNA soldier."[17] Toward the end of Yugoslavia and the onset of the country's various violent conflicts, many young men felt the consequences of this unified, non-differentiating gaze they were exposed to because of the JNA uniform in a more immediate and a literally painful way. Jure Gombač, a Slovenian who served in Split in 1991 in the midst of the tensions between the JNA and the local Croatian population, told me that locals would regularly attack uniformed soldiers when the latter went into the city just because of the uniform they wore: "They did not ask and did not care if you were a Croat, a Slovenian, a Bosnian, or a Serb—they would beat you up because of the uniform." On the other hand, the uniform's difference-erasing capacity could also provide shelter, security, and much needed anonymity in the tense times on the eve of the catastrophe. In Serbian cities largely hostile to them in the late 1980s, Albanians felt safer in the JNA uniform. The uniform not only concealed differences, it had a protective power stemming from the still lingering authority of the military institution. Elmaz remembers how he was once sitting in a bar with another soldier when some local men started provoking and insulting him as soon as they realized that he was an Albanian. The bar owner called the police, who immediately came and arrested the locals, and even the local council president came to apologize to Elmaz.

ON THE BASE

In the reality in which they found themselves once they went through the base gates, exposed to the disciplinary mechanisms of the military institution and subjected to the power of officers, young men's principal goal was to get through their army service, to let time pass with as few complications and as little effort, trouble, and torment as possible. Here, the difference-erasing power of the uniform worked in their favor, since it was good to be one among many, indistinguishable, not standing out, not exposing oneself, and not attracting attention. Mario, a soldier from Istria, served in the town of Senta in Vojvodina in the mid-1970s. On October 24, 1974, he sent a letter to Pula, where I found it more than forty years later, hidden among old postcards at a Saturday flea market. In the letter addressed to his older colleague, friend, and namesake Mario, he points to the importance of not standing out as one of the key strategies for getting through military service without much trouble:

> Today we came back to the base from a 54-kilometer march and military exercise. We slept in tents and it was raining every day, so for the twelve days we were totally wet, but luckily, this is now behind me. When we practiced marksmanship, I was careful not to stand out either as the best or as the worst shooter, but to be in the middle. That is the best strategy because no one notices you and it is easy to move to another place. I almost made a mistake: in the first round of shooting, I achieved very good results, so in the second round I had to miss the target intentionally. In a moment when the officer was not paying attention, I shot two bullets into the air, so I moved down on the list of best shooters. That was much better.

Želimir Žilnik, already known for his critical films when he started his military service in Bjelovar in 1969, took the same strategy of not attracting attention: "I—naturally—tried to stay completely aside, and not to stand out in anything I did. I started the training and thought of it as a kind of jogging—a lot of stepping, marching, and running around," he remembers.

The uniform and ritualized routines of everyday life in military service worked to efface individual features and reduce differences among JNA soldiers. This effacement was beneficial for all the actors involved. It helped soldiers avoid exposure to the oppressive work of the military. On the other hand, it enabled the military to mold a collective that could act harmoniously when performing military tasks. But differences under the JNA uniform by no means disappeared, and they were, again, important and beneficial for all involved actors.

As an institution, the JNA was not blind to the "baggage" young men brought with them to the army. The different profiles and levels and kinds of knowledge of these men were essential for the operational capacity of army bases, which were self-sustaining to a significant extent, and most duties and tasks—from cleaning, cooking, washing dishes and clothes, to construction and maintenance—were performed by soldiers themselves. For this reason, soldiers educated to be bakers, cooks, cabinetmakers, builders, drivers, or medical technicians and doctors would often go through shortened basic training and be quickly assigned to units to perform tasks essential for everyday life on military bases. The variety of skills soldiers brought with them to their military service also contributed to the JNA's syncretic nature, which mirrored the tradition of the partisan movement in World War II and resonated with the value of self-realization central to the Yugoslav socialist modernization project. After completion of training, many artists and cultural workers had the opportunity to continue with what they knew and loved to do before they donned the army uniform. They were also in charge of cultural activities on the base. Journalists and those with writing talent would prepare their unit's wall newspaper. Musicians and those fond of singing would join orchestras and choirs. Soldier-artists could resume their work and participate in exhibitions.

From 1966 to 1986, yearly exhibitions titled *Vojnici—likovni umetnici* (Soldiers—fine artists) were organized in the gallery of the JNA cultural center in Belgrade. The following lines were repeated in several exhibition catalogs, serving as a motto of these exhibitions: "He is not a smelter, a sower, a student anymore—not since the moment he became a soldier. However, if he is an artist, he will remain an artist even after he becomes a soldier."[18] These lines reveal the interest of the military institution in the soldiers subjected to it, exposing the dynamics between their civilian and uniformed selves. The 1967 exhibition catalog varies these lines in the following way: "They were artillerymen, signalmen, infantrymen, engineers, radio operators. But they remained artists." Soldiers—painters, sculptors, graphic designers—who graduated from art academies across the country, but also some amateur artists, were allowed to "go back to the work they left when they donned the uniform" once they completed basic training.[19] The military provided the artists with the materials necessary for their work, and their main task was "to create artworks addressing life in the army" and "to provide artistic testimonies to soldiers and their army days."[20] Reproductions of paintings and graphics and photographs of sculptures published in this series of catalogs—some realistic, almost naive, some abstract and modernist—depict various aspects of everyday life in the JNA, but also reflect on major events in the "outside world." There is a painting of a soldier in navy uniform reading a book; a soldier writing a letter; a soldier helping the wounded after a catastrophic earthquake in Skopje in 1963; a group portrait of three soldiers in uniforms,

Figure 4.5 Danijel Butala, *Drugovi* (Comrades), 1968. Reproduced from GDJNA, *Vojnici— likovni umetnici* 1968, exhibition catalog.

labeled *Drugovi*, or "Comrades" (figure 4.5); a painting picturing the interior of a restaurant in a city, with soldiers sitting at tables; a sculpture of a soldier; a sculpture of a couple (a woman and a man in navy uniform) hugging each other; a painting of a soldier and his parents who have come to visit him; a print depicting a military orchestra; images of soldiers belonging to various military branches exercising in training. There are also artworks referring to the partisan struggle and the values of anti-fascism, as well as to global events: in the 1969 exhibition catalog, a majority of works refer to the war in Vietnam.

The text at the beginning of the 1966 catalog states that the exhibited soldiers' artworks "should help us understand the young men in uniform better and in a more humane way," acknowledging the erasure of individual characteristics by the uniform.[21] This interest in who the young men in uniform were is often mentioned in the catalogs' introductory texts. According to one of them, by offering soldiers the opportunity to work as artists during their military service, "the Yugoslav army confirmed once more its openness to the human personality and its creativity."[22] In the 1972 catalog, a rather poetic vignette expresses this interest: "A soldier—a human and a young person. . . . A human unconstrained by the monotonous color of his clothes. A young person unconstrained by the barracks walls and the watch guarding the entrance. A soldier—an intertwined and unconfined humanness of youth. He comes to the new setting, bringing his habits, knowledge, fascinations, and memories—everything that a young heart can take."[23]

Other artists found their place on JNA bases, too. Radosav Majdevac played an instrument in the army orchestra. Franci Virant continued photographing as a "unit photographer" in Osijek, while the Slovenian artist Dušan Mandić was a "garrison painter" in Niš, where he served in the JNA in 1981 and 1982. Both Dušan and Franci were allowed to go home and take the equipment they needed for their work. At the training ground Polygon C near Osijek, where he spent most of his military service, Franci was allowed to set up a dark room to develop the photographs he was taking. In the army cultural center in Osijek, he even had an exhibition of his pre-JNA works.

All the kinds of knowledge, craft, and skill that young Yugoslav men brought to JNA bases mattered inside their fences and generated valuable social capital. Hariz Halilovich worked in the infirmary in the Senta garrison because he had completed medical school. Karpo Aćimović Godina and Želimir Žilnik both got a chance to make films while they were in the army. Želimir remembers that, after his rather long training in the tank unit, he was summoned by the deputy brigade commander, who asked him whether he would make a film about the role of the military in the history of Bjelovar. Želimir said he could make a movie, but he needed a script. He instructed the deputy commander to write it: "Just close your eyes and imagine what would you like to see in the film." They had two eight-hour sessions in which the commander dictated one scene after another and Želimir wrote them down. Once the screenplay was written, Želimir asked for six fellow soldiers to help him, as filmmaking is a collective work. The officer at first rejected his request, but the next day assigned six soldiers to assist with the film, each belonging to a different Yugoslav nation. Želimir also got the equipment he requested and spent two months working on the movie. When it was completed, Želimir attributed authorship to his officers and described his and his army mates' role in the credits as "technical support." The officers were very happy with the

Figure 4.6 Franci Virant, soldier and photographer, 1981. From the archive of Franci Virant.

final product and proudly congratulated each other. "Soldier Žilnik, report in my office tomorrow at 8 a.m.," ordered the deputy commander. Želimir was concerned that the deputy commander was dissatisfied with some aspects of the film and would demand alterations, but it was quite the contrary. "Žilnik, the civilians lie," the deputy commander said, and pulled out from his desk a thick dossier. "These are all lies. They say in these documents that you are unreliable and a dangerous element. But we can see that you are a diligent soldier. What do you want as a reward?" "Comrade colonel," Želimir answered, "I would like to go home." After a short pause, the deputy commander pronounced the following command in a firm voice: "Soldier Žilnik! Halt! I order you to leave the base tomorrow at 8 a.m.!"

Often, the soldiers would use the status and position acquired within the unit hierarchy to achieve their own goals and for their own purposes. Making a documentary on Bjelovar allowed Želimir to go to Zagreb several times to edit the film and to spend time with his colleagues and friends from the cinema world. The Slovenian philosopher Slavoj Žižek served in the JNA in Karlovac in the 1970s. He was assigned to work in the library, but also had to teach other soldiers courses on politics. During these classes, he showed a series of Hollywood movies, justifying this to his officers as the best way to expose the "rotten nature of American capitalism."[24] The ethnomusicologist Svanibor Pettan was assigned the role of instructor for cultural activities on the army base in Prizren in Kosovo, where he served in the JNA. This position allowed him to regularly go out and perform fieldwork among the Roma and even use army equipment to record Roma music. After completing a training course in the communications and telephone unit in Niš, Dušan Mandić was put in charge of a soldiers' cultural club. This left him plenty of time for reading, writing, and producing artwork that was later included in the exhibition *Die Welt ist schön: Private D. M.*

Allowing such activities and supporting or at least tolerating them, the JNA made it possible for the young men in uniform to come close to their non-uniformed selves, albeit through the subtle subversion of the strict order of military life. There were men, on the other hand, who were not ready to accept the uniformed reality imposed on them in the military. Borut Telban, a pharmacy graduate from Ljubljana, never tried to normalize or find meaning in his forced presence on the base in Topčider, Belgrade. In his own words, throughout his military service he kept looking over the fence that surrounded the base. He would go to the theater, concerts, and movies whenever he got a chance. Several times, he escaped home to Ljubljana. He claims that in the years that followed there was nothing valuable, memorable, or useful he could take with him from a year spent in the army. Zoran Predin, the front man of Lačni Franz and the author of the popular song about the female soldier Lidija, mentioned in chapter 2, served in Zagreb in the early 1980s. After three months of training he got bored and decided he would do anything necessary to get released from the army. He finally succeeded after faking problems with his sight and psychological difficulties, and forging a doctor's report that enabled him to spend weeks at home in Slovenia while his officers believed he was hospitalized in Zagreb. With the diagnosis *psychoneurosis nuclearis*, Zoran was "dishonorably discharged from JNA service," but, as he puts it, he was "endlessly happy because he managed to steal seven months from destiny."[25] One of Radosav's army buddies in Maribor in 1983 was similarly determined to get away from the army base by "playing nuts." From his first day of service, he would climb a tree in the evening and refuse to come down. At the end, he "won" and was sent home.

Unlike Borut, Zoran, and those who took many risks to find a way to be released from military service or to never turn up for it in the first place, and those who had to dress in uniform but never really engaged with the reality of the JNA base, the majority of JNA soldiers invested time, energy, and emotional labor in making their existence within the confined space of the military base, their relationship to other men, and the relationship between who they had been and who they became once they entered the base acceptable and meaningful. This investment resulted in ties, memories, and sentiments that are hesitantly revealed in the aftermath of both army service and the rupture that marked the violent dissolution of the country that that army was supposed to protect.

Life in uniform, abounding with repetitive, physically demanding, and not always purposeful routines and ritualized practices, often felt surreal to the young men. The feeling of surrealness was amplified when some aspects of "ordinary" life, incompatible with the daily reality of military service, unexpectedly disrupted its firm structure, such as the sound of Albinoni's *Adagio* during morning physical exercises or Dostoyevsky's books and biographies of German World War II generals discovered in libraries on JNA bases. The surrealness also stemmed from the impossibility of relating one's uniformed self to the life one lived before military service and from the difficulty of recalling the reality left behind. Nebojša Šerić Šoba describes the estrangement resulting from these impossibilities: "At some point, my mother came for a visit from Sarajevo to Mali Lošinj and brought *burek* and *sirnica*.[26] Looking at this food, I realized how far I had become distanced from myself in the army—from what I used to be, to eat, to wear. The pastry from my hometown reminded me of that."

Although Šoba's description might suggest that serving in the military resulted in bifurcations of the self and the existence of two selves distanced from and almost unrelatable to each other, the self in uniform and the "earlier" self, we know from the rich literature on performativity and subject formation that the subject does not stand before the ritualized experience, nor is it fully given in advance, but is rather constituted in novel and not always predictable ways.[27] Moreover, the strong feeling of estrangement that marked days in uniform for Šoba and other soldiers did not lead them to assign categories of authenticity/realness versus fakeness to these two selves and the realities they occupy. The ritualized, standardized, performative practices that composed life in uniform did not diminish its realness and authenticity. The uniform did not work as a mask conditioning polarization between young men's personal and social selves, between what they did and what they believed.[28] Life in uniform *was* life; although lived through monotonous, repetitive, ritualized forms, that life lasted for a year or more, it was real and full, productive of meaningful social ties, of feelings, and of everything else life is made of.

A series of Franci Virant's portraits of young soldiers taken during long afternoons at the Polygon C training ground reveals this complex relationship between the uniformed life of JNA service and soldiers' subjectivities in a particularly poignant way (see figures 4.7, 4.8, and 4.9). In these photos, the soldiers, lacking part or all of their uniforms, break the military routines and protocols that governed everyday life on an army base. The photographs were taken at the young men's request, to show how they wanted to be seen, and aimed to express *who they really are* under the uniform they usually wore. But this desire for a representation of the self unconstrained by the uniform could not be entirely fulfilled because the photos were still being taken within the fenced-in space of the base, which inevitably gives the acts of newspaper reading, chilling out, and drinking coffee a somewhat staged effect, making them slightly abnormal in their normality and extraordinary in their ordinariness. These characteristics, on the other hand, do not make soldiers' desires entirely unfulfilled, either: the camera depicts them as cheerful, playful, serious, and neat, revealing about them what they want to be seen, but also what their army buddies see and recognize when they are all fully uniformed. The implicit staginess of these photographs does not prevent us from seeing the people in them as who they are; and neither did the uniform, which actually made this recognition possible, working as an equalizer among very different men, together with the ritualized, repetitive, and standardized forms that made up everyday life of military service.

As a form, the uniform is usually seen as the opposite of being different. The life on JNA bases described in this chapter suggests, however, that the relation of the two is one of complex dialectics and mutual constitution, rather than exclusion. François Jullien warns that what is uniform should not be confused with what is universal; it is about the production of the form, not the reason or content. In its most favorable case, standardization, the uniform is about functionality, he argues further.[29] In the case of the Yugoslav military, the uniformization of men and patterns of life did indeed have a standardizing role: it enabled an institution that gathered socially, linguistically, and culturally different men from all parts of the Yugoslav federation to function efficiently. At the same time, it was strongly connected to what is universal

Figures 4.7, 4.8, and 4.9 JNA soldiers, Osijek, 1981. Photos by Franci Virant.

in a very important way. It was the uniform and its equalizing, difference-erasing capacity that enabled mutual recognition, solidarity, friendship, and care to follow the universal, ethical logic in which what mattered was to be *a good man* and be recognized as such. This possibility to recognize and be recognized as (good) men that the uniform enabled, no matter how strong were the feelings of estrangement it simultaneously produced, made this temporary uniformed existence of former Yugoslavs very important for who they are and how they look back on their service in the Yugoslav People's Army.[30] The processes that led to the Yugoslav tragedy effaced options for identification transcending ethnic categories, but the main work that the limited forms constituting military service in the JNA perform in the aftermath of Yugoslavia is their subtle reminder of the possibility of an order based on universal, ethical grounds and of the future it promised.

5

The Ritual

Ritualization, understood as "the interaction of the social body with a structured and structuring environment," resonates with the experience of military
service in the Yugoslav People's Army (JNA) in manifold ways.[1] A year away
from ordinary, normal life, which was simultaneously necessary for maintaining the order of the normal and the ordinary, military service functioned
and was widely understood as a rite of passage that enabled boys to enter the
world of adults and become family men, intertwining socialist state ideology with traditional, family, and patriarchal values. It was "surrounded" by
a number of practices that were themselves ritual in character: army send-
offs, songs played on local radio stations at the request of parents and grandparents, being photographed in a local photo studio once the youths became
JNA soldiers, and sending photos to their family members, friends, and relatives. Young men participated in these rituals without necessarily fully engaging with their meaning and without completely internalizing them and
the messages they could convey. As MacDougall puts it, following Bourdieu,

what the soldiers did by participating in these practices "may have, strictly speaking, neither meaning nor function, other than the function implied by their very existence."[2]

As "a strategy for the construction of certain types of power relationships effective within particular social organizations," ritual was also constitutive of the military and its strictly defined power relations and interactions, and its highly ordered organization of life.[3] As a total institution, the military extensively employs formalized, routinized, and supervised practices. In military discipline, Foucault writes, a "plethora of signs indicates, to the point of redundancy, tightly knit power relations calculated with care to produce a certain number of technical effects."[4] Military life displays many of the features that Stephan Feuchtwang associates with ritual: it is characterized by repetition, standardization, and "orthopraxy"; it is a prescribed and thus deliberately learned discipline separate from everyday life; it is also essentially an expression of power that always involves the negotiation of authority.[5]

On JNA military bases, repetitive, standardized, and formalized practices described in detail in chapter 3 were used to impose and maintain certain types of power relations. The everyday reality of men serving in the JNA consisted of highly organized and structured practices and abounded with situations in which "a certain form is appropriate" and highly predictable.[6] This predictive power of forms regulated hierarchical relations between men on the army base, as it directed actions without leaving much (or any) choice to those in subordinate positions.

Ritualization and formalization inevitably made these forms stiff, reduced, impoverished, and restricted.[7] The restrictedness of codes used on JNA bases not only regulated official relations between superiors and their subordinates, and was not only a means of construing and maintaining frames for power relationships of domination and control in which ritualized agents "see themselves as only acting in a socially instinctive response to how the things are."[8] In a context such as military service in the JNA, where radically different men were brought together, the restricted code generated within the reality of army service was a necessary medium for communication among them.[9] Moreover, ritualized practices, a limited range of forms, and restricted codes also governed the micro-politics of everyday life on the base and power relations among soldiers themselves, based on seniority on the base or the duties they fulfilled (discussed in chapter 3).[10] They were also used in communication with the outside world, as these forms simultaneously reflected the reality of military life and the fabric that reality was made of. In a long-lasting temporality of the ritualized reality of JNA service, which brought very diverse people together in close, intimate proximity for a year or more, life was not only structured by standardized forms with little content, it also produced such forms in everyday interactions among uniformed men. These forms were threads with which meaningful ties among these men were woven: using these forms and living through them, they made friendships and memories, shared jokes, and expressed affection and solidarity.

The routinization, formalization, and repetitiveness that constituted life on military bases might have been a source of frustration for many soldiers, especially those to whom more expressive means of behavior and communication were central in their pre-uniformed lives. Dušan Mandić, an artist from Ljubljana, strongly felt the limits of forms in which life was lived on the JNA base in Niš, where he served in 1981–82. When he had to head off to the town in southern Serbia and dress in military uniform, Dušan was a director of Ljubljana's gallery ŠKUC (Student Cultural Center) and already a prominent member of the flourishing alternative art scene in Slovenia. "Having to go to the JNA was quite traumatic for me. In 1981, I was in the middle of a very intense cultural life in Ljubljana as an independent artist and manager of an alternative gallery. And that autumn, I was forced to go to the army, and I went to Niš and spent a year there," is how Dušan explains the situation when he was drafted into the JNA.

He was determined to continue his work as an artist during military service. However, the highly structured and standardized nature of life in the military posed serious challenges to his artistic creativity. In a lecture he gave in Ljubljana in February 1982, when he was on regular leave from the base, he stressed that his views on painting were strongly informed by his "current social position, marked this year by the olive drab of a military uniform." For Dušan, art and what is artistic were by definition "a perversion of the system. Of course, not just any perversion, but one so conceived that it introduces a new order through disorder. This is virtually impossible to do in the army, because everything therein is subject to the ROS (Rules of Service)."[11]

Dušan nevertheless found a way to make art while serving in the JNA by subverting the strict order, rigid rules, and laws of the military. As a "garrison painter," he got a studio on the military base and a huge canvas, on which he was supposed to paint a monument composed of three concrete obelisks that symbolize raised, clenched fists. Created by sculptor Ivan Sabolić, the monument, in Bubanj Memorial Park, commemorates the more than 10,000 citizens of Niš whom the Nazis executed during World War II. Uninterested in the realistic reproduction of an anti-fascist monument—an aspect of art production from which young, alternative artists in the 1980s were eager to distance themselves—Dušan never completed the painting. Instead, he used his status of soldier-artist and the available space and equipment on the base for a very different artistic project, in which his aim was to expose the oppressive character of the Yugoslav military and his own traumatic experience of it. Doing this, he focused exactly on the very structured and ritualized circumstances and patterns of military life that he saw as the main obstacle to pursuing his artistic practice. He chose the predictable and repetitive visual and linguistic components and the limited range that he could find in this limited and limiting living space, reframing these elements through his own artistic intervention. In one of his works, he uses a newspaper illustration, adding the labels "socialism" and "fascism," a row of crosses that became a recognizable symbol of his art (and of the art of the Slovenian artist collectives IRWIN and NSK, to which he belonged), and the sentences "Death to fascism, freedom to the people" and "'Loves' you and 'guards' you from the enemies, soldier D" (see figure 5.1). In these two sentences, Dušan made use of the familiar repertoire of highly present and recognizable phrases and slogans: the first was one of the central slogans of the Yugoslav anti-fascist struggle in World War II, and the second was a combination of a typical concluding epistolary formula and normalized ideological discourse about JNA soldiers as guardians of the country and its citizens, a trope that appears also in the song about Lidija's military service, discussed in chapter 2.

In another artwork, Dušan used a similar technique of putting together different, often irreconcilable, but familiar and recognizable texts, mediated images, and fragments of cultural and ideological repertoires to expose the performativity, ritualization, and limited range of expressive means that made up life in army barracks. In a short letter written to a girlfriend, Marija, by Dušan's army buddy, whom he taught how to use a typewriter, Dušan changed one letter (changing Marija to Marina) and pasted on it a copy of an iconic World War II photograph of the young female partisan Lepa Radić under a tree just prior to her hanging by fascists on February 8, 1943, in Bosanska Krupa; he also added a pornographic detail from a Yugoslav erotic magazine, and printed a cross over this scene. He then sent this modified letter to his own girlfriend (Marina) in Ljubljana. Written by an uneducated soldier who had

Figure 5.1 Artwork made by Dušan Mandić during his military service.

never used a typewriter before, the letter is short, limited in content, and full of typos, orthographic mistakes, and formulaic expressions that have a banalizing effect on the longing, love, and affection he tries to communicate to his faraway girlfriend.

Dušan also bought a series of postcards with pictures of attractive women, idyllic domestic scenes, young couples, children, and babies with mothers—the only ones that were available from the newsstand on the base and at kiosks in Niš—and transformed them "with a forceful painterly gesture, sometimes physically interfering with the material substance."[12] He placed crosses "over

Figure 5.2 A post-card from Dušan Mandić's exhibition *Die Welt ist schön: Private D. M.*

the provocative parts of female bodies, sometimes satanically piercing mouths and guts, covering the faces of young couples, children, etc." and thus created "a pervasive air of unease."[13]

Exposing ritualized, repetitive, expressively limited, ideologically (over) used or banalized patterns and forms that constituted life during military service through his artworks made on the Niš military base in 1981, Dušan anticipated what would become a very prominent thread of critique of state socialism in its last decade. With the art that he produced during his time in the JNA, exhibited in Ljubljana after he completed his service under the title *Die Welt ist schön: Private D. M.*, Dušan offers his own view of the reality of military service in the JNA, defined by the lack of freedom and the oppressive mechanisms to which he was exposed as a soldier. With its intertextual ref-erence to the title of the 1928 photography book by Albert Renger-Patzsch,

Dušan's exhibition, like Walter Benjamin's critique of Renger-Patzsch's naive realism that obscures social realities, aimed at pointing to the gap between the oppressive, traumatic reality of military service and official representations of the JNA. In this way, starting from own subjective experience of military service, Dušan indirectly adheres to the view that ritualization and the (hyper)normalization of discourses and practices were defining characteristics of both the military and the crumbling socialist system, as well as of totalitarian structures in general. Such a view established an interpretive frame in which the JNA has been perceived as the epitome of the oppressive character of Yugoslav socialism.[14]

Dušan's artistic appropriation of ritualized and standardized forms and patterns was based on a strategy of overidentification that became extensively employed in late socialism.[15] Labeled imitative exaggeration, subversive affirmation, or *stiob*, these strategic uses of ritualized discourses and practices require "such a degree of overidentification with the object, person, or idea at which [they were] . . . directed that it was often impossible to tell whether [they were] . . . a form of sincere support, subtle ridicule, or a peculiar mixture of the two."[16] They imply simultaneous identification and distance, presupposing incongruity, slippage, and a gap between form and content that generated ambiguity, thus making it impossible to judge unambiguously the intentions, positions, and beliefs of those participating in ritualized practices and giving them a certain autonomy and control over what goes on in the highly structured context characterized by relations of domination and subordination.[17] This capacity of overidentification points to an important feature of ritualization in general: On the one hand, "the power relations constituted by ritualization empower those who may at first appear to be controlled by them."[18] On the other, ritualization sets limits and constraints on those to whom it gives power and control.[19]

For the (former) Yugoslav army's soldiers and the afterlife of their military service, power relations and their destabilization, which were simultaneously enabled by ritualization, had profound consequences, reaching beyond the maintenance of ambiguity that blurs boundaries between domination, subordination, appropriation, and resistance. On the base, to soldiers faced with the regulatory force of army authority, ritualization offered tools to actively negotiate with that authority, using personal skills, histories, and views. In the aftermath of the army and of the country it was supposed to protect, ritualization and uniformization with their difference-erasing capacities unfold as forces opposed to narrowing the possibilities of identification and recognition of men who served in the JNA and to reducing who they are to their ethnic belonging—processes accompanying Yugoslavia's dissolution in catastrophic wars and violence. Ritualization, therefore, has a twofold protective capacity: on the one hand, mastery of ritualized forms protected JNA soldiers from the workings of the oppressive military institution, giving them a certain autonomy; and on the other, ritualization and uniformization worked as difference-erasing mechanisms that prevented the men in JNA uniforms from being too easily placed in dominant frames of ethnicity, class, or their combination, thus resisting the logic that structures life in the aftermath of Yugoslavia.

RITUALIZATION'S PROTECTIVE WORK

On a postcard sent in 1988 from the Montenegrin coastal town of Herceg Novi, a JNA soldier, signed as Laci, wrote the following to a couple in Kranj, Slovenia, most probably his parents: "How are you, civilians? You just keep implementing the action 'Nothing Should Surprise Us,' because it is better not to rely on me. Laci" (*Kako ste, civili? Samo vi sprovodite akciju 'Ništa nas ne sme iznenaditi,' jer ja baš i nisam neka garancija. Laci*).

In this slightly ironic text, the young man playfully (over)identifies with his role as a JNA soldier, adopting the performative language of the army and referring to his parents as "civilians," who are supposed to participate in the nationwide exercise "Nothing Should Surprise Us," aimed at preparing all citizens for self-defense and protection in case of war or natural disasters in the framework of the General National Defense program; he simultaneously self-mockingly questions his own ability to appropriately perform his role of nation's guardian as a soldier of the JNA.

Despite playful irony, the way the postcard was written does not offer us much about Laci and his attitude toward the experience of military service he was going through. Resorting to intertextual, recognizable chunks of discourse that were made available to him in the army and were familiar and readable to his addressees enables Laci to maintain ambiguity and leave the question about his own positions, feelings, beliefs, and values unresolved.

The same was true of the deployment of any pattern from the repertoire of ritualized practices and discourses that made up the reality of military service in the JNA. For example, young men who had themselves tattooed while in the JNA did not reveal much about their attitude toward the military through this practice. For many of them, this was an integral part of military service, a socially accepted behavior, something done without deep consideration of the reasons for or consequences of such action. The repertoire of images and texts that young men could choose to have inscribed on their skin was rather limited, mainly to those belonging to the dominant socialist and army imagery, depicting particular military branches or indicating dates and places of military service. So, we cannot confidently interpret these tattoos as very personal or firm expressions of an individuals' views and beliefs.[20] Nor can we exclude the possibility that many of Yugoslav men actually believed in the ideology of brotherhood and unity and embraced its symbols to the extent that they tattooed them on their bodies without hesitation. Whatever meaning and function these ritualized and performative practices had for those participating in them, we are unable to judge these meanings and functions unambiguously—just as with Laci's postcard message. We can never be sure about the men's attitude toward these practices—whether they took them for granted, were serious and sincere about them, approached them with subtle ridicule, or a combination of all these attitudes.

The uncertainty of how to interpret a person's deeds and words gave JNA soldiers a certain autonomy and provided them with a protective shield while they were in uniform and exposed to the oppressive workings of authority and hierarchy. The very ritualized, limited, formalized, and repetitive patterns that enabled control and domination by the military authority simultaneously destabilized that authority. This working of ritualized practices can be illustrated by the following excerpt from the 2006 film *Karaula/The Border Post*.[21] In the excerpt, a soldier, well known for his problematic behavior, approaches his superior, a lieutenant, with an unusual request to go to Belgrade on foot to visit the grave of Yugoslavia's late president, Josip Broz Tito:

> Soldier: Comrade lieutenant, Sir. Request permission to climb down.
> Lieutenant: Go on, climb down.
> Soldier: Comrade lieutenant, Sir. Request permission to speak.
> Lieutenant: What's up?
> Soldier: Comrade lieutenant, I would like to go to Dedinje to pay my respects to Tito's immortal legacy.
> Lieutenant: Really? Well, I'd like to fuck Vesna Zmijanac, but it won't happen . . .[22]

Soldier: Comrade lieutenant, I don't think you understood me. In honor of our late president Tito's birthday, I would like to go to Belgrade on foot to visit his grave.

Lieutenant: There you go again . . .

Soldier: Comrade lieutenant . . . am I to understand this as your refusal to allow me, a soldier of the Yugoslav People's Army, to go to Belgrade and pay my respects to beloved President Tito and express my gratitude for all he did for the brotherhood and unity of our nations and nationalities and our socialist self-managing community as a whole?

Lieutenant: What are you talking about, you idiot? What are you talking about?

Soldier: Comrade lieutenant, in honor of our late president Tito's birthday, I'd like to go to his grave in Belgrade on foot, to express my gratitude for all he did for brotherhood and unity of our nations and nationalities and our socialist self-governing community . . .

Lieutenant: As a whole?

Soldier: As a whole.

Lieutenant: Are you bullshitting me? Tell me that you are bullshitting me. Do not joke with this, Paunović.

Soldier: Comrade lieutenant, request permission to leave.

Expressing his request, the soldier, otherwise notorious as someone who breaks the rules and disobeys authority, strictly sticks to formal expressions and the prescribed use of language when addressing a superior officer. The officer, on the other hand, constantly tries to break the set language protocol—by informal responses to very formal addresses, by ironic comments, and by insulting qualifications. Deviating from clearly defined communication rules is a privilege of a collocutor who is superior in rank, but this practice can be fully understood only if related to the interpretational uncertainty caused by the use of ritualized forms and the autonomy these forms granted to the subordinate soldier addressing the officer. Breaking the fixity and ritualized character of formal and highly performative communication, the lieutenant hopes that he will succeed in provoking his interlocutor to do the same and thus step out from the shelter provided by the fixed forms. That would make it possible for the officer to decide about the sincerity and seriousness of the soldier's words. As long as the soldier remains in the domain of the fixed, ritualized, and performative forms and canon, the lieutenant cannot know whether the soldier really means what he says.

In contrast to the soldier, who could strategically use ritualization to leave the relationship between his non-uniformed self and his structural position defined by the military uniform unresolved, the JNA officer experiences what Maurice Bloch pointed to as a consequence of extorting control and power through ritualized forms: "This is done at the cost to the superior of losing *his own* freedom of manipulation."[23] The officer cannot afford any uncertainty and ambiguity in his acting, because his authority and power are depersonalized, lodged not in his person but in his rank and formal status.[24] As Bloch observed, such authority established through ritualization is disconnected from the real world.[25] Film director Želimir Žilnik remembers an episode that is a good illustration of Bloch's observation:

> Once they took us to practice tank firing on proving grounds near the Plitvice Lakes. It was a very hot day. When my unit finished the training, we sat down to play cards, since we had to wait for others for more than five hours. We were bathed in sweat and took our uniforms off and put them on the ground to dry. One of the officers came then—he was a perfect soldier, but totally obsessed. He started shouting to us: "You threw away the JNA uniforms! Are you normal?! Spies are now looking at satellite photos and they are seeing naked soldiers! Are you protesting against the JNA?" We responded: "It is no protest, you can see that we are all wet." But he did not listen to us. He told us: "What you did is an influence of hippieism! Only hippies undress themselves!" He took us all to where the commander of the proving grounds was, to show him what kind of provocations we had committed. We had to walk more than three kilometers with our uniforms in our hands. But the commander was not there, nor were other officers. He then ordered me to take a camera and take a photograph of the naked soldiers. So, I took about ten photos of him, dressed in a uniform, with a gun, and of thirty naked soldiers. After that he let us dress, and we went back to the base. A couple days later there was a huge scandal—the whole brigade, more than one thousand soldiers, were gathered on the proving grounds. A general from Zagreb came and announced to us: "Comrades, a diversion happened in this brigade. Major Furčić made soldiers undress and photographed himself with naked soldiers. These photographs are now probably in our enemies' hands and newspapers around the world— the *New York Times*, *Le Monde*, and others—will publish them to show how Yugoslav officers perversely undress soldiers." We were dying of

laughter. This poor major tried to explain that we took off the uniforms and he wanted to show his superiors what we did, but the general interrupted him: "All intelligence services around the world saw them already!" Major Furčić, who was a really dedicated soldier, was demoted and punished because of this episode.

Although the episode of Major Furčić poignantly exposes the extent to which JNA officers were detached from the "real world," it is important to emphasize that the JNA officer cadre, handling very different young men on army bases, was connected to the social reality of Yugoslavia in a very profound way. They needed to develop great proficiency in what modern-day parlance would call multicultural communication. Želimir also pointed to their skills: "The majority of officers were fools, but they knew how to communicate with soldiers, to make a coherent collective out of them, and to make everything function well. Some of them were uneducated and primitive, but not socially unskilled. They were able to assess soldiers' qualities and strong points, to notice who had skills to repair something and who, on the other hand, was soft and emotional."

The case of Major Furčić illustrates how ritualization lends authority to those with control over ritualized life, but simultaneously poses limits and constraints on such authority. On the other hand, the structured practices and defined procedures that constituted military service, which by their nature strengthened the hierarchy and kept soldiers subordinate to officers, simultaneously "protected" soldiers by providing them with the possibility of strategically keeping their own position ambiguous.

The protective capacity of ritualization did not cease with the end of military service. It keeps protecting former JNA soldiers in the aftermath of the Yugoslav project, preventing the flattening of their biographies and the reduction of who they are to a single trait and reminding us of the intrinsic link between restricted and ritualized forms and the utopian imagination.

Photographs taken in local studios in the towns where soldiers served in the JNA are one part of the JNA archives in which this protective capacity is particularly visible. Today, there is probably not a single photo album or box with old family photographs in homes in the former Yugoslavia that does not contain a portrait of a young man in the uniform of the JNA. These photographs depict male family members, but also relatives and friends, since soldiers used to mail them home to their relatives, family, friends, and

Figures 5.3 and 5.4 Studio portraits of JNA soldiers Milan Milenković and Dragan Josijević.

girlfriends. They were often stylized as postcards, with the inscription "A souvenir (memory) from the JNA" (*Uspomena iz JNA*) or "Greetings from the JNA" (*Pozdrav iz JNA*) (see figures 5.3 and 5.4).

Studio portraits of men in uniform are hardly unique to Yugoslav soldiers, nor are they a "socialist invention."[26] However, while portraits of this kind were usually taken during periods of war and sent by soldiers to their family members with the message that they were alive and well, in socialist Yugoslavia such studio portraits were products of a cultural practice that was characteristic of peaceful times.[27] These portraits had their meaning within the networks of family and kinship. They mark a milestone in men's life trajectories, signaling that young men were successfully completing their initiation into adulthood by realizing themselves in the role of Yugoslav army soldiers. As such, they were part of the ritualized practices through which both the reality and the social meanings of military service were constituted. Numerous soldiers would use the occasion of their first visit to an unknown city near their base to go to a photo studio, have photos taken, and send them in an envelope together with a letter to their families, friends, or relatives. As in the case of any ritualized practice, they did not necessarily identify fully with all semantic and ideological aspects of that practice.

Like most of the practices making up military service in the JNA, this one was characterized by fixity of form and very limited variation, by standardization and repetitiveness. Still, there was some space for an individual's subtle intervention in the standardized image. It could, for instance, consist of a lifted coat collar to suggest "coolness." The stage is neutral and does not provide any particular background. The only distinct and recognizable element of the photograph is the JNA uniform, which serves as a backdrop. Men photographed in dress uniform perform and stage the identity of the socialist Yugoslav soldier, just as Auschwitz inmates performed or staged the identity of concentration camp inmate on photographs they could have taken at a photo studio that had a camp uniform—"a new and clean one—to make souvenir photos."[28] While in the latter case, the mere performance of the identity of a concentration camp inmate makes the photographs particularly disturbing, the performance of identity by JNA soldiers is distinctly different in character. The JNA uniform as a backdrop, the neutral background, and the fixed posture and photographic conventions and protocols make the practice of taking studio portraits of JNA soldiers highly ritualized and the results of that practice uniform.

In spite of the uniformity of the photographs, it is nevertheless possible to follow the development of their formality, which increased over the course of time, but then started dissolving as Yugoslavia's end was approaching. Early portraits of JNA soldiers draw heavily on the partisan imagery of World War II, which had just ended (see figures 5.5 and 5.6). The soldiers depicted can be most easily placed in time by their still non-standardized uniforms, and the dividing line between partisan fighters and early JNA soldiers is often blurred. On one website dedicated to military memorabilia, one can follow several discussions about whether some photographs depict Yugoslav partisans or early-period JNA soldiers. For collectors, the most reliable way to distinguish partisans from early JNA soldiers is by the look of their uniforms. As one discussant wrote, with reference to a photo depicting a group of six men in uniform: "In the early Yugoslav army, soldiers would wear parts of German uniforms, but they were 'de-Nazified.' I have some photographs where this is visible. . . . But in this [particular] photo they are partisans for sure, because they wear uniforms of the Allies and some still have stars sewn on their caps— that was quite rare after 1946."[29]

Figures 5.5 and 5.6 Early portraits of men in JNA uniforms.

Studio portraits of JNA soldiers from the early period are also recognizable by the posture and decoration that were common to all studio portraits of the time: typical elements of studio decoration, such as artificial flowers, curtains, or armchairs provided a scene for all kinds of portraits—of individuals, families, marrying couples, and soldiers alike, usually portrayed in a full-body shot. Although the reasons for using these elements were often technical, they nevertheless (albeit inadvertently) further contributed to securing for early JNA portraits a firm place among other family photos. A full-body portrait and a posture of the photographed soldier that enables eye contact are important characteristics of these early photos (see figure 5.7).

While the partisan imagery was a fundamental ideological element of the JNA throughout its existence, in the case of studio photography it is nevertheless possible to claim that the image of a JNA soldier gradually gained a certain degree of autonomy from this imagery—not by a radical break from the partisan tradition, but with the formalization and increased fixity of the portraits and the ritualization of photographic practice that went hand in hand with technological development. The posture, expression, and design of the

Figure 5.7 An early studio portrait of a JNA soldier.

portrait as a whole were fixed in the period roughly between the early 1960s and the early 1980s. Apart from the absence of direct eye contact, the most salient visual characteristic of these portraits is the standardized, well-kept, and tight uniform (see figures 5.8, 5.9, and 5.10).

Portrayed on their own initiative, but still participating in a standardized, ritualized practice, set within a defined familial and broadly social framework in which this initiative could, to a large extent, be the fulfillment of set expectations, soldiers did not necessarily reflect on the act. The subjects of

Figures 5.8, 5.9, and 5.10 Studio portraits of JNA soldiers (*from left*) Milovan Milenković, Vladan Todorović, and Milorad Milenković.

these photographs did not have much choice about how and where their studio portrait was taken, but were placed in a staged setting. The very act of being photographed was powerfully predefined by the conventions and fixed protocols of the time, which minimized the photographer's role in deciding about the result of photographing. The minimized role of the photographer is nicely illustrated in a scene from *Svečana obaveza* (The solemn oath), a

TV film from the 1980s: a large sign shaped like the letter X is drawn on the studio wall, and the photographer does nothing but instruct the soldier to look at this sign.[30]

Although highly conventional, uniform, and defined by a repertoire of recognizable ideological symbols, the practice of studio photography offered JNA soldiers a certain means of cultural positioning. The symbolism of studio portraits was connected not only to partisan imagery and the ideology of Yugoslav socialism, but also to various aspects of popular culture, such as the Hollywood world of celebrities, whereby these cultural imageries did not necessarily stand in hierarchical or oppositional order. In *Svečana obaveza*, there is a scene in which, after the oath-taking ceremony, a soldier goes to a local photo studio called Hollywood. There, the photographer asks him whether he wants to pose as Marlon Brando or have a "Greetings from JNA" inscription. He chooses the former, for which he has to pay more. Even these highly standardized portraits, strictly defined by the JNA uniform, show what Raphael Samuel draws attention to: people "draw models for personal portraits from other media, including cinema."[31]

This photographic practice, moreover, sometimes provided a basis for cultural differentiation among soldiers: not all of them would create this kind of souvenir—urban young men often considered it kitschy and a sign of (rural) backwardness. But this division was never clear-cut, and the ritualized nature of this practice makes it impossible to be confident about its interpretation. "Taking a studio photo was a must. Someone would say 'Let's take a photo,' and we would just do it," Oto said, describing the context in which he was photographed with four army mates with whom he spent a lot of time during his army service—a lawyer from Ruma, an engineer from Sremska Mitrovica, a law student, and a peasant from central Serbia, Dejan Simčić. Dejan Kršić, a known artist and designer from Zagreb, and important actor in the alternative scene of the 1980s, shared his own studio photo from the JNA on his Facebook profile. From the vantage point of the present day, we cannot judge his or any JNA soldiers' motives to have a studio portrait taken in JNA uniform. It could result from a genuine desire to have a memento from days in the army; or it could be a response to expectations of parents at home, who impatiently waited to receive a photo of this kind, or to peer pressure; it could be an expression of solidarity with army buddies who wanted to have such photos taken, a consequence of too many beers, or just a joke, a result of curiosity, of having nothing to do during time out in the city, or much more.

The most radically formalized studio portraits of JNA soldiers are those called "photos with memory" (*slike sa uspomenom*) in JNA jargon. Here, the photographed person with his individual characteristics, attitudes, and beliefs is pushed even more into the background. In these portraits, the backdrop, already defined by the JNA uniform, comes to the foreground and becomes materialized as a frame within which individuals with their particularities are exchangeable. The frame is real, made of cardboard or wood, with the inscription *Uspomena iz JNA* (Memory from the JNA—hence the name) and drawings from the repertoire of recognizable symbols—the Yugoslav flag, a red star, tanks and other weapons, a portrait of Tito, or other images with which young men in uniform were expected to identify. Sometimes, such photographs were produced by placing a printed frame over an already taken "ordinary" studio photo.

A photograph made with this kind of frame (typically available at such sites as amusement parks, tourist sites, fairs, and festivals) usually suggests a ludic atmosphere and implies "ideas of humor, irony, or play" and the inherent ambiguity of the word "pose," "with its double implications of posture as deception and posture as stance."[32] The photographs serve as a tool for "resistance to the realist pretensions of photography, by distorting or escaping quotidian contexts and predicaments."[33] The frames in which JNA soldiers were portrayed, however, are devoid of any ironic, humorous, or playful pretext (which does not necessarily imply that such meanings could not be attached to them). They did not signal deception but stress and bring to the fore the backdrop already defined by the JNA uniform (see figures 5.11 and 5.12).

Veselin Gatalo, a writer from Mostar in Bosnia and Herzegovina, described his military service in Sarajevo in an autobiographic novel titled *Slika sa uspomenom* (A photo with memory). The meaning of the title is revealed in one of the chapters. One day, his army buddy Nazif, from Sandžak, leaves the base and goes to town.[34] The next day, he shows the author/narrator, with pride and delight, a photograph taken in a local studio. The narrator ironically describes what he saw: "It was him, Nazif, on the photo. Around him, Nazif, was some green heart-like wreath, with a red star on the top of it. Under the wreath were the letters JNA."[35] Nazif enthusiastically explains how the photo was made. "See, this is painted, and you need to stand here. The photographer takes a photo and, after one week, you can pick it up. . . . [The price] is nothing. I had three photos taken—one for my parents, one for my sister, and one for myself . . . It's called a *photo with memory*. When you go to the photo

Figures 5.11 and 5.12 Photos "with memory."

studio, that is what you need to ask for."[36] For the narrator, an urban guy from Mostar, ironic and distanced from most aspects of the JNA experience, these photos are ridiculous, while for Nazif they are important and a source of pride. For the young man from the underdeveloped region of Sandžak, this would probably be one of a very few photographs of himself.

The TV film *Svečana obaveza*, too, features a humorous and ironic scene of taking a "photo with memory." Zoran is a geography teacher from Belgrade who joins the army at a mature age, looking for a break from his prospectless life. He befriends Ranko, a farmer from Vojvodina. Ranko's father, who abandoned and rejected his son many years ago, now wants to reconnect, proud that his son is a JNA soldier, but Ranko is not ready and willing to meet him. At Ranko's request, Zoran meets Ranko's father and pretends to be his son. The father cannot recognize the deception. Having been drinking a lot already, the two of them go to a local studio to have a photo taken. The photographer instructs Zoran how to hold "the memory," a cardboard frame with the inscription "Memory from the JNA," pronouncing the sentences, "Lift the memory! Put it down a little . . . Even up the memory!" which are logically absurd, but necessary to produce the desired result: the photo of the "son," a JNA soldier, with which the "father" proudly leaves. During the photo session, Zoran is visibly confused because of the combination of his fake identity and his strange relationship with a man who believes himself to be Zoran's father, as well as of being drunk and involved in a photographic practice he would probably avoid himself. However, the outcome of photographing "with memory" is not affected by the confusion and estrangement of its protagonist, or by the original deception and identity switch: it is a romanticized photo of a forward-looking young man in uniform, framed with improvised decoration that is meant to transform the photo into an object of memory, a souvenir, the very instant it is created, adding a patina of pastness to it much earlier than it would actually attain through time's passage.[37] Countless very similar images can be found in family albums across the former Yugoslavia, at flea markets, in internet collections of "old photographs," and at auction sites where they are offered at low prices as "antiques."

Or to put it differently: it is precisely the highly ritualized nature of studio photography practices, due to which the meaning of the practice need not be important or available to those who practice it (detachment of the meaning from the practice is further strengthened by detachment of *memory* from *the photo* in this photographic practice), that enabled persons with such different backgrounds, personal stories, and worldviews as Zoran and Nazif to "fit" the improvised cardboard frames without any problem. Consequently, these uniform, standardized images allow for very different readings and meanings. Their explicit staginess warns us that plain, one-layered or self-confident interpretations cannot prove satisfactory for these images—and the same is true of the other ritualized aspects of the experience of JNA service. Like JNA uniforms, these photos provided a frame that could accommodate men radically different from each other, as well as a variety of meaningful relations, because their explicit staginess never stood in opposition to the realness and importance of the experience of military service and of the feelings, solidarity, and friendships that were constitutive of that experience.

In the aftermath of Yugoslavia, photographs from the time of military service inhabiting boxes of family photos, internet sites, and flea market booths across the former country still unfold as "sites of epistemological uncertainty."[38] A spectator is similarly faced with this epistemological uncertainty after watching the final scenes of Karpo Aćimović Godina's film *O ljubavnim veštinama ili film sa 14,441 kvadratom*, discussed in chapter 4. After contrasting group portraits of soldiers and female factory workers, we see soldiers running in lines in the moonlike landscape of eastern Macedonia. At the very end of this short film, the camera meets individual soldiers, one after another, all in the same uniform, all the same but also clearly unique in this sameness, escaping the categories by which people are usually judged—those of class, ethnicity, education, social capital, and taste.

As we look at these photographs today, our gaze is inevitably refracted through the prism of the catastrophe that tore Yugoslavia apart. There is almost nothing we can say with certainty about the people in them, except that they were JNA soldiers. We cannot determine their education, social background, ethnicity, or whether they come from a city or a village. We cannot guess what their destiny would be in the disastrous years in which Yugoslavia dissolved and in the aftermath of that catastrophe—which greatly depended on their ethnicity, which is indecipherable in these ritualized, uniformed photographs. This inability not only gives the photos the capacity to counter the ethnicized gaze that became the only way to see and to be seen in the time of the catastrophe and its aftermath, but also reconnects the men in the photographs with the futures that could belong to them, the futures forever lost in the killing, suffering, and violence of the 1990s.

The utopian moment is frozen in these ubiquitous, highly formal photographs in which men in neat uniforms all look young and the same. That moment is seeded in the possibility enabled by uniformity and sameness—of seeing and recognizing others and being recognized by one's moral qualities, irrespective of one's ethnic, linguistic, or social background. That possibility disappeared in the dawn of the Yugoslav catastrophe, when the forms and infrastructures for uniformity and sameness that generated possibilities of transcending frames set by identity categories started dissolving, and moral qualities were replaced by ethnic belonging as a basis for recognition and solidarity, but also as a criterion for life and death.

6

Dissolution of Form

Vladan Jovanović, a historian born in a central Serbian town, still keeps the note his parents received from the base in Kovin when he went to serve in the JNA in 1987 in a unit that trained drivers. With a card decorated with a stylized portrait of a uniformed soldier drawn in gold, the JNA invited them to come to the oath-taking ceremony and informed them about their son's first days of military service:

> Dear parents, we are glad to let you know that your son arrived in our unit safely and in good health. Our officers will assume care for him and will help him adapt fast to new life and work circumstances. On our base, your son will have all he needs, and the army will offer him new skills and make everything possible for him to become an even more respectable member of our socialist homeland, its guardian and builder. You can visit your son on Saturdays in the afternoon and on Sundays the whole day. Please write your son about your intention to visit him, so that we

Figure 6.1 The oath-taking ceremony on a Yugoslav army base.

can prepare a pass so he can go out to the city. Use your first visit to talk
with his officers.

In the prevalent understanding of public and private spheres in socialism,
whereby "the public/private distinction was aligned with a discursive opposition between the victimized 'us' and a newly powerful 'them' who ruled the
state," while "private activities, spaces, and times were understood by people
throughout the region as 'ours' and not the state's," this note to a soldier's
parents easily reads as yet another symptom of the socialist state's intrusion
into the private sphere and its ambition to thoroughly control all aspects of its
citizens' lives.[1] However, the ritualized character of JNA service and the fact
that many of its elements were shared by various social domains—the family
and the state, the private and the ideological—point to the relationship between citizens and the state as one of coordination and sharing rather than
of hegemony and hierarchy. Parents and the state (with the military as one
of its pillars) shared the parental role and care for young men, with mutual
trust and confidence. In turn, many rituals that made up military service in the
Yugoslav People's Army (JNA) were also incorporated in familial registers;
the language patterns were shared, and the values overlapped.

In the late 1980s and early 1990s, with the end of Yugoslavia approaching and the contours of the coming catastrophe becoming clearer, the JNA was in the process of swiftly losing its syncretic character and was transformed from an army of peace into an army of war. Much of the Yugoslav military leadership aligned with the Serbian side in the conflict. The political elites did not leave much space for universalist, citizenship-related, and moral values, but imposed the organicist notion of society and ethnic identity as defining social and political reality. In Slovenia and Croatia, which were the first of the Yugoslav republics to proclaim independence, the JNA became "the biggest enemy."[2] At the same time, public demands for the option of conscientious objection increased during the 1980s, particularly in Slovenia, where it was one of the important issues raised by civil society.[3] Military service—which used to be an honor, a citizen's duty, a rite of passage that made boys into men, and an important socializing process, as well as a citizenship-related project and a way to provide support and aid to citizens in case of crises and natural disasters—became for many a violation of rights and freedom, a work of the totalitarian apparatus that needed to be evaded. The idiom of "human rights" that emerged as a new conceptual language on the eve of Yugoslavia's disintegration was one of the salient global symptoms of the Cold War's end. As David Scott argues, this idiom was used to legitimate liberal democracy as a universal political project and as the only alternative in transition from what was labeled an illiberal regime.[4]

In such circumstances, in which ethnic belonging became the only available means of (self-)identification, the socialist past could be seen only as illiberal or totalitarian, and when there was only a single way to imagine the political future—in ethnically homogeneous nation-states—the institutional infrastructures that generated meanings and values shared by different actors of Yugoslav socialism dissolved, rendering certain forms and possibilities for collectivity politically problematic, illegitimate, and meaningless. Consequently, the trust and "coordination" of parental duties between soldiers' parents and the military institution that characterized decades of JNA military service disappeared. When the wheel of armed conflict and ethnic violence was set in motion, many parents headed to bases where their sons served in the JNA, concerned about their destinies, and started making plans for how to protect and save them. Tomo Buzov, a former JNA officer, boarded a train from Belgrade on a February morning in 1993, when the Yugoslav wars were well underway, to visit his son at the JNA base in Podgorica and make sure

Figure 6.2 Goran Jevremović, a soldier from Serbia, on the JNA base in Ljubljana, Slovenia, with his mother, who came for a visit, concerned for his safety. The photo is reproduced from the newspaper *Borba*, July 13–14, 1991.

he was well and safe. Two years earlier, in 1991, when Slovenia and Croatia proclaimed independence, many parents, in an attempt to get their children back from bases in other parts of the disintegrating country, got organized, reclaiming their parental authority and demanding that the civil authorities intervene.[5] The Parents' Committee for the Protection and Return of Slovenian Soldiers was established in Slovenia in spring 1991. In early July of the same year, several hundred parents from Serbia, mainly mothers, entered the parliament building in Belgrade and interrupted its work, demanding that their children who served in the JNA be brought back to Serbia. Some days later, these parents boarded buses and came to Ljubljana, concerned about their sons in newly independent Slovenia, from which the JNA was refusing to withdraw. Slovenian parents met them and offered accommodation during their stay in Slovenia.[6]

This disentanglement of state and family was a direct consequence of the radical shrinking of Yugoslav citizens' possibilities for being, recognizing each other, and belonging; this shrinkage came hand in hand with shrinking horizons of political alternatives. With the coming catastrophe of the Yugoslav wars in the 1990s, who you were in ethnic terms not only became the only possible way of identification, but also determined one's fate. Mila Dragojević provides an account of this process of shrinking possibilities, zooming in on the formation of ethnically based communities of Croats and Serbs in wartime Croatia between 1991 and 1995. She defines these newly fixed frames of belonging as "amoral communities," singling out as their important characteristic the fact that "the connection between ethnicity and political identity extends into everyday facets of life."[7] In such communities, "instead of perceiving each other in terms of personal traits or community roles, people first consider ethnicities."[8] In workplaces, public spaces, schools, and playgrounds, they started to group along ethnic lines.[9] This logic of recognition and organization significantly closed political horizons for individuals. As Dragojević points out, amoral communities are "places where individuals don't feel free to express their personal views if those views don't align with . . . dominant views or narratives [of their perceived ethnic group]." In such places, "a person of a certain cultural identity automatically has certain political views and one doesn't give them any space to think otherwise."[10]

UN-UNIFORMED

The ethnicizing logic of structuring life that accompanied the destruction of socialist Yugoslavia was poignantly exposed in a series of photographs by Jane Štravs, a Slovenian art and fashion photographer, and lucid visual chronicler of the alternative and cultural avant-garde of 1980s Slovenia, who served in the JNA in Belgrade in 1986. Jane took a number of portraits of JNA soldiers with whom he shared time and space in the barracks.[11] Three of these portraits became iconic of his photographic work from the 1980s and are part of the permanent exhibition of the Museum of Modern Arts in Ljubljana. Featuring soldiers in front of a military tent, dressed in shabby grey uniforms, looking directly into the camera, Jane's portraits sharply diverge from the generic conventions of JNA studio portraits, coming close to the war photography genre and disturbingly anticipating the conflict that would take place only a couple of years later (see figures 6.3, 6.4, and 6.5).

In these three portraits, the setting, posture, look of the uniform, and the strong emphasis on the facial expressions of the photographed soldiers all suggest that these photographs are placed outside and in opposition to the performative and ritualized norms prevalent over the decades of the existence of military service in the JNA. The deviation from these norms seems to suggest the photographs' spontaneity; they were supposed to be "real," devoid of the

Figures 6.3, 6.4, and 6.5 Jane
Štravs, *Yugoslav People's Army
Soldier I–III* (1986).

romanticism and staginess that strongly marked studio portraits discussed in the previous chapter. They also seem to individualize the persons photographed, to open a space for them to be who they really are, a space otherwise sealed off by the uniform they wore and by the ritualized character of military service. Here, in Jane's photographs, are soldiers in their barracks, in front of an army tent, and in JNA uniforms, but they look distinguishably individual, their faces remarkable, memorable, and unique.

If the tight uniform and formal posture of the studio portraits resulted in epistemological uncertainty as to how to interpret and classify the photographed men, thus providing certain autonomy and protection for them, what did Jane's series of photos, which deviated from the uniform and formalized, mean to the men depicted in them?

The photographic realism of these images is misleading, stresses Marina Gržinić, who writes that Jane's photographs make us "refuse the early and 'innocent' belief that the camera merely presents us with visual facts that were simply 'out there' and which are now objectively observed and recorded."[12] As Jane explained to me in an interview, he took the three portraits using a wide-angle lens that slightly distorted the photographed subjects. This photographic technique made the faces in these photographs remarkable and memorable, but it simultaneously moved the images much further away from the people photographed than the uniforms, disciplining, haircuts, and ritualization of everyday routines inside the barracks did. In the studio photographs discussed earlier, the difference between reality and portrayal was made explicit by the absence of eye contact and by strict photographic conventions. On the other hand, in the ritualized setting of military service, this explicit difference did not automatically make the photos less "real" for the soldiers depicted in them, the same way that the experience of military service was very real, even though it was simultaneously far removed from the everyday, normal, and ordinary and was liminal and often surreal. Similarly, the overt staginess of normality in Franci Virant's series of photographs of men in civilian clothes in the barracks discussed in chapter 4 did not distance soldiers from their photographed selves.

Jane's portraits, however, lack sincerity about the difference between the real and the photographically staged. They conceal the staginess, the wide-angle lens's distortion of the faces, not only from spectators but also from the very men photographed. These men have neither autonomy nor control over the context of photographing and its result. After being photographed, these three men, Jane's army buddies, never saw the photographs, and according to the photographer, it is quite certain that they would not like them. For them, these photographs are not "the ones that are wanted," unlike Franci's photographs from Polygon C, snapshots made by soldiers in which they enact fighting or playing instruments standing on a table, or standardized, staged studio photos that are still carefully kept in family albums and photo boxes and widely shared on social media.[13]

Jane's portraits of JNA soldiers who served together with him in Belgrade in the 1980s share two important features with the identity-card photographs made immediately after soldiers were dressed in their uniforms, such as the photo of Antonije Pušić, aka Rambo Amadeus (figure 4.1): the position of the person photographed, who is facing and looks straight at the camera, and an estrangement between the person photographed and the person in the photograph. Known as frontal portraits, these photographs, as John Tagg suggested, have often been associated with a "code of social inferiority" and documentation of human beings for diverse scientific, legal, and medical purposes.[14] Both social hierarchization and "othering" may be read into Jane's three portraits of JNA soldiers.

Concealing the staginess of these portraits may be the price for the expression of uniqueness and individuality of the men portrayed. But the claim to individuality, however, is untruthful as well. Jane explained to me that the intention behind the series of portraits was that each of the men portrayed stands for one of the three "typical" former Yugoslav ethnic groups; they supposedly represent a Serb, a Gypsy, and an Albanian—although the persons in the photographs were not necessarily actual members of the purported ethnic group. The persons in the photographs thus come to be "typified"— "identified indexically and often iconically with socially recognized characters and moral positions."[15] This artistic technique brings Jane close to nineteenth-century attempts to systematize photographic archives according to physiognomic characteristics.[16] It requires "that distinctive individual features be read in conformity to type."[17] But the type is far from an "objective category"; as the Victorian Francis Galton argued, "The usual way is to select individuals who are judged to be representative of the prevalent type, and to photograph them; but this method is not trustworthy, because the judgment itself is fallacious. It is swayed by exceptional and grotesque features more than by ordinary ones, and the portraits supposed to be typical are likely to be caricatures."[18] Here, too, the facial distortion produced by a wide-angle lens was made to produce a type, whereby the unique and individual cannot be separated from the grotesque, caricatured, and derogatory.

The use of such a technique to make the persons in these photographs representatives of a national/ethnic type does not reflect the photographer's own perception of these groups. Here, Jane was more interested in the spectator's gaze at the moment of the already ongoing ethnicization of Yugoslav society. As Gržinić stresses, this is a crucial feature of Jane's work, which is "directed towards analyzing and reflecting the act of looking at photographs."[19] Nevertheless, whatever the photographer's intention was, the typology he made inevitably entails a generalized look and objectifying of photographed individuals. Furthermore, the typology enabled generalization through labeling: each of the three portraits in the series is labeled *Yugoslav People's Army Soldier*.

Figure 6.6 JNA soldiers at the entrance of a barracks in Ljubljana. Photo by Tone Stojko. Courtesy of the Slovenian Museum of Contemporary History.

In this way, the classified, distorted, and (nationally/ethnically) typified portraits become a representation of the JNA as a whole and "came to establish and delimit the terrain of the other, to define both the generalized look—the typology—and the contingent instance of deviance and social pathology."[20] These photographs by Jane became a commentary on his continuous artistic critique of social and political tensions and exclusions. In the 1980s, Jane was a member of the Slovenian alternative scene, connected with the intellectual and civil society movement that articulated sharp criticism of Yugoslav socialism. According to Marina Gržinić, "Štravs' work in the eighties is the rearticulation of life on the margins of a totalitarian structure."[21] The critique in Slovenia was intensely directed at the JNA as the most rigid and totalitarian element within that "totalitarian structure." The portraits of three Yugoslav army soldiers were no doubt part of the critique. During protests in Slovenia in 1988 against the military trial of four Slovenians that was supposed to be conducted in Serbo-Croatian, the JNA was clearly established as the enemy and a "terrain of the other." This othering was iconically visualized in Tone Stojko's reportage photographs, shot in front of the JNA barracks in Ljubljana. In one of these photos, JNA soldiers stand at the entrance to the barracks, while civilians toss flowers at them (figure 6.6). The young men wearing uniforms of the Yugoslav army became an embodiment of the military in which they served. From "our children" they became solely soldiers of a hostile military, or at best someone else's children.

Placed next to each other, the studio photographs of JNA soldiers discussed in the previous chapter and Jane Štravs's photographs seem to offer visual expression of this transformation of the Yugoslav army, which unfolds with the loosening of fixed forms and ritualized conventions in the photographic practice. The dissolution of forms also had its equivalents on JNA bases, in a secluded, liminal microworld where young men from all over the dissolving country were still gathered. The ethnic differences that used to be a source of jokes and cheerful teasing became a reason for hatred or fear. The soldiers' ethnicity became crucial for their position and often their well-being and security. As the only Albanian on his base, Elmaz had to endure a lot of torment from a Serb officer during his military service on the eve of Yugoslavia's disintegration. Neither the fact that he spoke very good Serbo-Croatian nor the uniform he wore was of much help. That uniform, which for decades played an important role in providing a context for the moral recognition of men who wore it, in 1990 and 1991 put young men still gathered from all parts of the dissolving country in danger. Many were trapped in their barracks, left without food and supplies. Many were sent to the front, and many were killed in that uniform, trying to protect the country and its foundational principle of brotherhood and unity on which too many of those in "the real world," outside the barracks, had already given up.[22]

Interlude

The Catastrophe

On May 6, 1991, Saško Gešovski, a young soldier from Kavadarci in Macedonia, was killed by Croatian nationalists in the town of Split. He was among the soldiers guarding naval headquarters, in front of which fifty thousand protesters were demanding that the Yugoslav People's Army (JNA) take a clear position on self-proclaimed Serb autonomy in the Knin area in Croatia. Someone shot at the soldiers, killing Saško and wounding another soldier from Macedonia, Toni Stojčev of Makedonska Kamenica.[1] Saško is known as the first JNA soldier to become a victim of the Yugoslav wars.

∞

At the same time, Jure Gombač, a JNA soldier from Ljubljana, Slovenia, was serving in Split in Battalion 490 of the military police. The atmosphere was tense, and his unit had often been sent to Knin and other ethnically mixed areas where there was a possibility of conflict between Serbs and Croats. He realized that the Yugoslav military would not be able to handle a serious conflict and that many young men performing their military service would be victims of this inability, just like his friend Saško Gešovski, with whom he served in the same unit. He managed to leave the base and meet his parents, who carefully organized his escape and took him back to Slovenia.

∞

That May, I was in my third year of high school. The news of the tragic death of Saško, who was just a little bit older than my schoolmates and me, did not reach us then at the college-prep high school "Svetozar Marković" in Sveto-zarevo, Serbia. The war seemed to be somewhere else and unrelated to us. But one day in the following school year, we stood next to an open grave, saying goodbye to David Jakovljević. David, a tall, quiet, kind young man with curly dark hair, used to be our schoolmate. He loved music and played guitar. A year older than the rest of us, David was a dropout from another school before he joined us, becoming one of only two boys in our language-oriented high school class. When he failed to complete the first year, he gave up, supported by our teacher who told him that college-prep high school was too demanding for him. As he had just turned eighteen, he was called up for military service. He was killed in Croatia, in the area of Karlovac, in the uniform of a JNA soldier.

∞

Bahrudin Kaletović was from Tuzla, Bosnia and Herzegovina, and he was serving in the JNA in Slovenia in 1991. On June 27, in the midst of a short conflict that led to Slovenian independence, Bahrudin was recorded by YUTEL, the only all-Yugoslav television station in Yugoslavia, which broadcast between 1990 and 1992. Lying down somewhere in a Slovenian wood next to his machine gun in a green camouflage uniform that was supposed to conceal his position, and looking lost and desperate, Bahrudin told the journalist that, as he understood it, the war between the JNA and Slovenian Territorial Defense units was being waged because "they, like, want to secede, and we, like, will not let them, but in fact, we just want to go back to the barracks, nothing else."

∞

On the evening of the same day, Slovenian Territorial Defense forces downed a light JNA helicopter, shooting from a tall building on Republic Square in Ljubljana. The helicopter exploded and fell into Ljubljana's Rožna dolina neighborhood. Two JNA soldiers died—a Slovenian, Toni Mrlak, and a Macedonian, Bojanče Sibinovski. The helicopter was unarmed and was transporting bread from the military bakery in Ljubljana to Vrhnika for the JNA soldiers trapped on the base there. The two Territorial Defense soldiers who shot down the helicopter were later decorated for this action.

∞

That same summer of 1991, the JNA base 4 July on Metelkova Street in Ljubljana, Slovenia, where Goran Jevremović from Svetozarevo in Serbia was performing his service, was surrounded daily by civil society activists and citizens protesting against the Yugoslav military. A state of emergency had been declared weeks earlier. The soldiers could not leave the base. To prevent desertions, the Slovenian soldiers were confined to barracks. Goran and other soldiers had to guard them, but they were actually all trapped. To make the days shorter and release tension, they told jokes and played table football together.

∞

In autumn 1991, Saša Ilić, a future literature student I was in love with, had to postpone the beginning of his studies at the University of Belgrade for a year to serve in the JNA on the Montenegrin coast. I liked his photos in the navy uniform he sent me, accompanied by long letters that contained much more than the longing and despair of a young man uprooted from his world. Unlike many before them, Saša and his generation could not separate their military service in the JNA from the war in which Yugoslavia disintegrated. In his letters, Saša wrote about military ships that left the harbor every night, sailing toward the border with Croatia and coming back in the morning with emptied ammunition containers that he and other "rookies" had to unload. Later, he wrote about recurrent journeys on the navy ship to Pula and back, transporting weaponry as the JNA withdrew from Croatia; about Albanian soldiers who used every opportunity to escape from the army; about officers whom from one day to another the soldiers had to address as "Sir" instead of "Comrade." Despite all I read in these letters, and despite how much they meant to me, I could not really grasp what was going on with Saša and with the country in which we both grew up. He was all alone. In the summer of 1992, I went to visit him, taking the night train from Belgrade to Bar with my two girlfriends. This journey was fun and an adventure for us, and we were not fully aware of the tensions and violence happening all around. Saša was happy to see me, but also very afraid for my safety.

∞

On February 27, 1993, just half a year after I boarded the Belgrade-Bar train to visit my boyfriend, who was serving in the disintegrating military of an already dead country, twenty men were taken off that same train. As soon as it started from Belgrade, the conductor, accompanied by an armed man, checked the passengers' tickets, but also asked for and recorded their names. Hours later, the train was stopped at Štrpci, near Priboj, where a small stretch of the railway crossed the territory of Bosnia and Herzegovina. Using the conductor's list, members of the "Revengers" special unit of the Republika Srpska (the Serb-controlled part of Bosnia), led by Milan Lukić, ordered the Muslim passengers from the train, robbed and killed them, and threw their bodies in the Drina river. Two of these passengers were not Muslim, and one of them was Tomo Buzov, a Croat born in Kaštel Novi, a retired first-class captain of the JNA who lived in Belgrade. Concerned for his son's safety in these tumultuous times, Tomo had embarked on the train in Belgrade that morning to visit him, while he was performing his military service in Montenegro's capital, Podgorica (formerly Titograd). Tomo was taken from the train and killed, together with Muslim passengers—because he tried to protect them and refused to sit in silence.

∞

In summer 1992, when I took the Belgrade-Bar train, Hariz Halilovich was in Prijedor in Bosnia and Herzegovina. He had come to this town in northwestern Bosnia from Sarajevo, where he studied, for a reason similar to the one that made me travel to Bar: to visit his girlfriend. But the tension and threat that I could feel in Bar that summer were much more real for Hariz in Prijedor, which was under the control of the Serb paramilitaries. He became stuck in the town, but managed to escape the destiny of thousands of local Muslims who were killed. Hariz was imprisoned in Trnopolje concentration camp, where he took on the role of a "doctor," using knowledge he had acquired in the medical high school he graduated from in Zvornik and during his army service in Novi Sad and Senta in 1988 and 1989, where he had served in the infirmary.[2] Trnopolje was one of more than six hundred camps and other sites of torture and suffering established on the territory of the former Yugoslavia for members of various ethnic groups. Buildings, facilities, and institutions established in the course of the Yugoslav modernization project—factories, mines, cultural centers, schools, museums, cinema halls—were turned into concentration camps and sites of torture.[3] Lora military harbor in Split, where Jure was based during the escalation of the conflicts, was turned into a torture camp for incarcerated Serbs not long after he clandestinely left the military.

∞

On January 27, 1993, in the main square of the small town of Trebinje in Bosnia and Herzegovina, a 26-year-old Bosnian Serb, Srđan Aleksić, tried to stop a group of Serb soldiers from assaulting his Muslim friend, Alen Glavović. The soldiers turned to him and beat him so heavily that he fell into coma and died six days later.[4] Alen managed to escape and eventually left for Sweden. He lives there with his family; every summer he returns to Trebinje and visits Srđan's grave. Srđan Aleksić became a symbol of humanity in the post-Yugoslav area. The most recognizable image of him circulating in public space is his photograph in the JNA uniform, taken while he was doing his military service when he was 18 years old.[5]

∞

In July 1995, Bosnian Serb military units killed more than eight thousand men and boys near Srebrenica in Bosnia and Herzegovina. In the worst war crime in Europe since the end of World War II, Hariz Halilovich lost most of his male relatives. Two and a half decades later, thousands of victims have still not been identified and properly buried. Srebrenica is the most painful node in a dense web of war crime sites in the former Yugoslav lands. Many mass graves are still to be discovered.

∞

On April 27, 1999, a month after the NATO bombing of Yugoslavia (then comprising Serbia and Montenegro) started, Elmaz Jonuzi decided to go to downtown Pristina, the capital of Kosovo, to try to get some groceries. The city was empty because of airstrikes and the violence of Serb paramilitary forces. Only a couple of stores, with a very limited selection of wares, were open in the city center. At the time, Elmaz lived with his wife, a baby daughter, and his parents. He left for the city together with two of his neighbors. The three of them were caught by a group of Serb soldiers and taken separately behind buildings. The soldier who took Elmaz shot six times in the air and shouted, "Run away!" Elmaz ran. His two neighbors never came home.

7

The Aftermath

In the late 1990s, after the wars in Croatia and Bosnia had ended and before NATO's intervention in Serbia and the violence in Kosovo, Mitko Panov, a former JNA soldier who had completed his military service in Titov Veles in 1982 and left for the United States to pursue a career as an artist, came back to his homeland with a particular goal: to find out "what became of [his] army buddies. Did they find themselves carrying weapons again? Did they have to use them against each other? Who prospered and who was caught in the tangles of the war?"[1] Looking for the men with whom he shared a year in the JNA uniform, Panov traveled through landscapes laid to waste, and across newly established borders controlled by the international forces trying to prevent new outbreaks of conflict. This was a devastatingly painful journey, and it is painful to watch the documentary he made of it.[2] Reaching addresses where his army buddies were supposed to live, he finds burned houses, ethnically cleansed towns and villages, and his friends missing, dead, displaced, or economically struggling, with ruined health and ruined lives.

This is what a decade of violent conflicts left of disintegrated Yugoslavia: burned villages and towns; thousands killed, missing, displaced, or emigrated; and economic deprivation and humiliation for those who survived and stayed. Observed more broadly, for the citizens of the former Yugoslavia, this terrible decade was a kind of temporal corridor through which Yugoslavs walked from a time when the future was "not merely possible but imminent; not only imminent, but possible," to a time "in which the present seems stricken with immobility and pain and ruin."[3] That present, as David Scott puts it, is a time when "a certain experience of temporal afterness prevails in which the trace of futures past hangs like the remnant of a voile curtain over what feels uncannily like an endlessly extending present."[4]

In the aftermath of the Yugoslav catastrophe, people were left amid the ruins, not only of their houses and neighborhoods, but also amid the ruins of hopes for the future. In the "desert of post-socialism" in which they found themselves, two intertwined, mutually exacerbating processes further foreclosed any possibility for such hopes: "the capitalist 'transition' leading toward the establishment of the neoliberal paradigm, and ethnocentric restoration leading toward the renewal of an organicist national state."[5] In this new reality, the world Yugoslav citizens used to live in and everything they dreamed of and hoped for in socialism became a problem, a deviation, and their attachment to that world became a sign of a malady, something to be overcome. From the onset of Yugoslavia's disintegration, former Yugoslavs' biographies were reduced to a single trait: their ethnic identity and adjacent religious ones. They became Croats, Serbs, Albanians, Slovenians; Muslims, Catholics, Orthodox Christians. They were killed, beaten, expelled, displaced, threatened, erased from official records, or put in concentration camps because of what they were. And they were killing, beating, expelling, threatening, or burning houses because of what they were.

UNBECOMING

Decades after the end of the Yugoslav wars, those wars still shape the social and political reality of people inhabiting post-Yugoslav space—in some cases as a source of national pride and piety, in others as a source of pain, trauma, or humiliation, but always as a handy political instrument to maintain the status quo. Ethnic belonging has become normalized as the only available—

and imaginable—mode of identification, eliminating all the alternatives and eradicating reminders of the possible futures anchored in those alternatives. Former Yugoslavs are tightly caught in the event-aftermath straightjacket.[6] As a result, the socialist past is not seen in any other way than as a prelude to the conflicts of the 1990s, while the present is seen exclusively as their aftermath. This narrow, reductionist gaze defines how the past can be viewed and regulates what is possible and acceptable in the present. It also shapes the relationship between former Yugoslav men and their experience of military service in the Yugoslav People's Army (JNA) and its place in their biographies.

Many former Yugoslavs have felt the effects of this narrowing and reduction quite literally on their own skin. Vladimir Nešković, a Macedonian who presently lives in Slovenia and works there as a software engineer, served in the JNA in the late 1980s, first in Zagreb and then in Surdulica, a town in southern Serbia. Like many men who performed military service in the JNA, he has a visible souvenir from his army days: a tattooed (Cyrillic) inscription "JNA" on his arm (see figure 7.1). In the early 2000s, he frequently went with friends and colleagues from Ljubljana to the nearby Croatian coast. Each time he would go to the beach, he would cover the JNA tattoo with a bandage, afraid that someone might react negatively to the symbol of the once common army, as its meaning and history had been reduced to the fact that in the 1990s it became an instrument of the Serbian side in the wars.

If the ritualized everyday life of military service allowed engaging in practices such as tattooing without profound consideration of their meaning, former JNA soldiers cannot afford any insouciance toward their tattooed bodies in the aftermath of the Yugoslav catastrophe. In that aftermath, these bodies have become unfitting, inappropriate, something to be ashamed of, to hide, and to rewrite. "Everything was great in the JNA . . . Only this tattoo fucks me up. Especially when I am on the coast," wrote a commentator on an internet forum where JNA experience was discussed.[7] Many also reached for solutions that made their tattoos from the army invisible more permanently than an adhesive bandage would, by removing or overwriting them. An owner of a tattoo studio wrote in his blog that most of his customers who want to cover old tattoos are those "who have tattoos from the past, so-called JNA tattoos. These were made using a technique that used to be typical for the military and prison: a needle and a thread—and you have a tattoo and you are a cool guy." He added, "I always laugh a lot when I see these tattoos, but then I get to work and cover them so that my customers and I are both satisfied."[8]

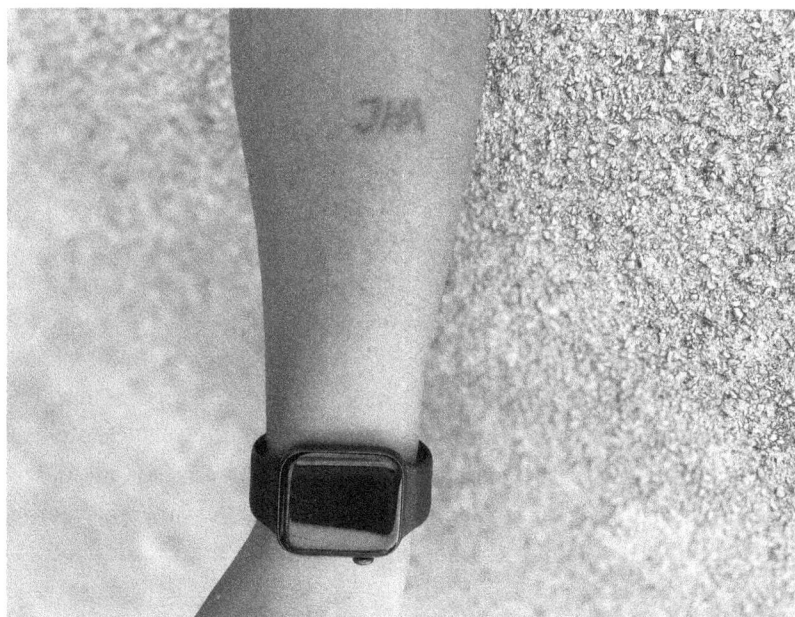

Figure 7.1 Vladimir Nešković's tattoo from his time in the JNA.

How profoundly the aftermath shapes stories, histories, and biographies, often flattening, erasing, or rewriting them, becomes particularly visible when the forms and narrative threads central to military service in the JNA are revealed to the public eye, for example, in films made since the end of Yugoslavia.

In late 1996, the Croatian film *Kako je počeo rat na mom otoku* was released.[9] Written by Ivo and Vinko Brešan, the film was shot on an abandoned JNA base near Šibenik. The plot is set in 1991, at a point when Croatia had already declared independence from Yugoslavia, but the JNA still held bases across the country and refused to withdraw from them. The film starts with the arrival of a father determined to rescue his son, who is trapped in the barracks under the command of the fanatical Serb officer, Aleksa. The inhabitants of the island, led by local members of the newly formed Croatian defense forces, try to persuade the officer to give up and release the soldiers, a request he refuses. Posing as a high-ranking officer, the father manages to get into the barracks and rescue his son and some other soldiers. Enraged by the deception, Aleksa orders soldiers to start shooting at the people gathered in front of the barracks. As a result, the film, abundant with jokes and recognizable humorous references to army life, ends in tragedy.

Made in the immediate aftermath of the war in Croatia, the film brings together two interrelated narratives about the JNA that became dominant in the early 1990s. The first is the story of parents rescuing their sons from bases and bringing them home; the second is the narrative about JNA officers that depicts them as tragic men, detached from "real life" and pathologically faithful to the crumbling ideology of Yugoslav socialism and its army, and ready to sacrifice the young and innocent lives of the soldiers under their supervision for this ideology. The Slovenian film *Outsider* was released a year later, in 1997.[10] The film, which many regard as the first Yugoslav film after Yugoslavia, also paints a portrait of a JNA officer in such ideological colors. *Outsider* is set in an earlier period, in Ljubljana at the end of the 1970s. Living in an alien setting, in a mixed marriage, the rigid JNA officer comes into severe conflict with his adolescent son, who grows up under the influence of the Ljubljana punk culture of the time. The conflict ends in the most tragic way, with the boy's suicide.

These cinematic portraits of JNA officers reflect the dominant view of them in the aftermath of Yugoslavia, a generalized view that sees them as directly linked to the violence and war crimes that marked the dissolution of the country. When the federation broke down and national armies emerged in its successor states, former JNA officers became the most problematic elements for the "national bodies" of these new states.[11] They often did not fit into these bodies ethnically but, as Miroslav Hadžić observes, even "the right" ethnic origin could not guarantee a stable position in new national armies for former JNA officers: as soon as they were not needed for war operations, they were relieved of their posts.[12] In the former Yugoslav republics that most severely suffered from the wars of independence, a negative attitude toward the part of the officer cadre that bore actual responsibility for violence and war crimes swiftly spread to include all the individuals who served professionally in the JNA and the Yugoslav military as a whole.

Such a view normalizes a particular narrative of the end of Yugoslavia in which the JNA as an institution and its officers have a distinctly negative role. This narrative supports the organicist imagination of the national bodies prevalent in post-Yugoslav lands, silencing stories like those about JNA officers who did all they could to protect the young soldiers they were responsible for or to save the places they found themselves in as military commanders. Such is the story of Vice Admiral Dragoljub Bocinov, a Macedonian by origin, commander of the military naval base in Split, who refused to follow Belgrade's orders to bomb the city in the summer of 1991.[13] A similar story is that of Admiral Vladimir Barović, a Montenegrin, who as commander of the Pula garrison assured the citizens that there would be no destruction of their city and Istria as long as he was charge, and if any destruction were to happen, it would be because he was not there anymore. When he later took over the command of the Split military-navy domain, realizing that he would not be able to prevent destruction of Croatian cities in southern Croatia, Admiral Barović committed suicide on the island of Vis on September 29, 1991. There is the story of Tomo Buzov and his selfless act in Štrpci, mentioned in the interlude, for which he paid with his life. And finally there is the story of General Vladimir Trifunović, who surrendered the Varaždin garrison to Croatian authorities in September 1991 to save the lives of the soldiers besieged in the barracks. And these are not the only stories of this kind.

These officers' biographies do not fit any of the national narratives shaped during the 1990s. They have been forgotten, or even prosecuted as war criminals or traitors, often at the same time and by the judicial systems of different Yugoslav successor states. For example, Vladimir Trifunović was found guilty of war crimes in Croatia and sentenced to fifteen years in prison in 1991. In 1994, the Federal Yugoslav authorities in Belgrade charged him with treason and sentenced him to eleven years in prison, but he was pardoned and released in 1996. He was also tried in Slovenia for war crimes. On the other hand, the great majority of members of the paramilitary units on all sides of the conflict have never faced trial, although many of them were directly responsible for war crimes.[14] Officers of the JNA have often been deprived of the possibility of a decent life in the aftermath of the conflicts.[15] In Serbia, many of them and their families never got appropriate housing. In Slovenia, "approximately five hundred JNA officers, many of whom did not see active service and had intermarried with Slovenes" were among "the erased," the approximately twenty-five thousand permanent non-Slovenian residents who disappeared from all official records in 1992 and consequently faced very serious complications regarding their legal status and lives in independent Slovenia.[16]

The normative lens that defines the experience of serving in the JNA (for both officers and conscripted soldiers) means that the present cannot be seen in any way but as related to the violence in which Yugoslavia disintegrated. This seems to be particularly clear in another film portrait of military service in the JNA, *Karaula/The Border Post*, which appeared in cinemas across the former Yugoslavia in 2006. The novel *Ništa nas ne smije iznenaditi* (Nothing should surprise us) by the Croatian writer Ante Tomić, published in 2003, was the basis for the screenplay, coauthored by Tomić and the Croatian film director Rajko Grlić, who also directed the film.[17] The novel's title is a recognizable phrase from the lexicon of JNA and Yugoslav socialist jargon, the one that Laci playfully cited on the postcard he sent from the army to the town of Kranj in 1988 (see chapter 5). Set in 1983, the novel shows ordinary everyday life at a small border post on the Yugoslav-Albanian frontier. Yet another generation of soldiers awaits the end of their military service, tormented by Lieutenant Imre Nadj, and making their army days shorter in every possible way. Lieutenant Nadj has a medical problem and seeks help from the only doctor among the soldiers, Siniša Siriščević, a Croat from Split, who tells the lieutenant that he has syphilis. Not wanting his wife to know about it and trying to find excuses not to go home, Lieutenant Nadj declares a state of emergency, claiming that the Albanian army is preparing an attack against Yugoslavia. The only person who is allowed to leave the border post is Siniša, who goes to the nearby town to get medicine for the lieutenant and inform his wife that he will not be home for the next three weeks. Siniša has a love affair with Lieutenant Nadj's wife, while his best friend, Ljuba Paunović, an urban guy from Belgrade, announces that he wants to go on foot to Kuća cveća (the House of Flowers, the memorial center in Belgrade where Yugoslavia's president Josip Broz Tito is buried) to honor the great memory of Tito on the anniversary of the late president's birthday—although he is in fact searching for a way to escape from the army, a project in which he eventually succeeds. Siniša goes back to Split when his military service is over, and his first step back into the normal life that he left behind a year earlier ends the novel.

Devoid of dramatic turns and tragic denouements, Tomić's novel would not normally be expected to attract and hold the attention of a broad segment of the public because of the action, the complexity of its characters, and the depth of the story being told. Nevertheless, it gained a wide readership all over the former Yugoslavia and enjoyed unusual popularity—it was translated into Slovene and Macedonian (the weekly magazine *Vreme* published the novel in installments), while in Serbia it was published in Cyrillic script. The Kerempuh Theater in Zagreb also produced a play based on Tomić's novel.

What made this novel so appealing to former Yugoslavs was its authentic depiction of everyday life during military service in the JNA—every former

JNA soldier could find chunks of his own experience in its lines. The humor and recollections of the atmosphere in socialist Yugoslavia made the novel interesting also for those former Yugoslavs who did not share the army experience. Without dramatics, without heroes, and with none of the moralizing or self-censorship that usually frame narratives on the Yugoslav experience in the aftermath of Yugoslavia, the novel brings back the atmosphere, recognizable jokes, rituals, and the formulaic language used within the JNA. And this simple, but authentic picture is the main quality of the text.

The atmosphere, ritualized patterns of language, and everyday routines of service in the JNA were successfully transferred from the page to screen in the film *The Border Post*. However, the film differs from the novel in several significant ways. It seems that all the differences between the novel and the film's screenplay were introduced to concretize the story and strengthen its relation to the tragic breakdown of Yugoslavia that followed. The narrative is moved closer in time to the breakup of Yugoslavia—to 1987—and the film is supposed to be an allegory of Yugoslavia's tragedy. As the film's director, Grlić, stated:

> On the eve of any natural disaster, be it a summer storm or a total cataclysm, there is always a moment of total silence. It's that fine moment when everything stops, but also the moment when no one wants to talk about it. It happens to nature, to societies, and to entire civilizations. *Border Post* is a comedy taking place at one such moment. The film enquires about those people who were to transform in a matter of months into soldiers, refugees, victims and criminals. How did they live? What did they really want? What was the everyday life that engendered war and who were the ones who had war implanted into their minds so quickly and so easily?[18]

The main difference between the narrative of the film and the novel is in the film's tragic ending: the fight between the soldier from Belgrade and the lieutenant (in the film this character is a Bosnian and not a Hungarian), which in the novel ends with no serious consequences, turns into a massacre in the film—the Bosnian lieutenant is killed by the Serb soldier, while many other people also die, including the lieutenant's wife. The obvious reference to the violent end of the country, which the main characters in the film serve as soldiers, should automatically prevent any association with nostalgia—as one of its critics has stressed, the film has to be an allegory, because otherwise it would be nostalgic, which is by no means good.[19] Public discussions of the film in post-Yugoslav societies also focused on its allegorical aspects. What was said in these discussions resembles the dominant official narratives that circulate in the wake of Yugoslavia's disintegration and fails to see the film in any other way than through the national/ethnic lens. In Slovenia, there were complaints that Slovenes were underrepresented in the film. In Serbia, criticism was directed toward the way "representatives" of various nations were presented, and the film was perceived as anti-Serb, because the Serb soldier is depicted as a cheater, provocateur, and troublemaker, the Bosnian officer as a victim, while the Croat soldier is presented in a positive light as an intellectual and seducer waiting for a bright future once his military service is over. In Croatia, on the other hand, some saw the film as anti-Croatian, having a tendency "to bring Croatia back to its own past."[20]

In spite of such negative responses, the film was met with great enthusiasm among former Yugoslavs and enjoyed exceptional popularity: during the first two weeks of its showing, it topped the box office in all the former Yugoslav republics simultaneously (another record set by this film in the post-Yugoslav era), while the first showing in Sarajevo was screened at the Zetra Hall and drew an audience of 7,500.

What attracted such immense interest in *The Border Post* among people all over the former Yugoslavia? It seems that, as in the case of Tomić's novel *Ništa nas ne smije iznenaditi*, people expected to see on screen everyday life in the JNA, to hear its language, to laugh at the humor typical of it, and all that makes the telling of army stories so important and necessary. It also seems that the film's authors and producers were well aware of this. Although they insisted that the film was an allegory of the violent destruction of the country, this allegory is present only in the film's last fifteen minutes.[21] The rest of the film is, in fact, a humorous story about everyday life in the JNA, in which most former Yugoslavs will recognize bits and pieces of their own past. This is exactly the opposite of *Good Bye Lenin!*, a film about East German socialism, which portrays everyday socialist objects and practices recognizable and understandable to former East Germans, thereby excluding West Germans, emphasizing the East/West divide—although the film was hailed for "uniting easterners and westerners in laughter."[22] However, *The Border Post* produces a feeling of solidarity among former Yugoslavs by showing recognizable details of and references to their common past, much more than dividing them by insisting on the tragic end of their common history. The allegorical and

tragic denouement of the film seems a somewhat inappropriate and unnatu-
ral end to this cheerful and unburdening story: the Slovene journalist Andrej
Gustinčič wrote that "the film's end with the spilling of blood, which is meant
to be a symbol of the bloody destruction of Yugoslavia, is in discrepancy with
the rest of it—it is like a prolonged joke to which a tragic end is attached."[23]

The film's authors, who received financial support from state institutions
of the Yugoslav successor states, and who at the same time made the film
for an audience, many of whose members experienced socialist Yugoslavia,
faced a difficult task in considering both "officially" acceptable narratives of
the Yugoslav past and the knowledge, experience, and feelings of the people
to whom that past belongs. Setting the violent conflict as a necessary frame
for the cinematic story of the JNA made this film project more the "product
of the memory industry" than an attempt to grant legitimacy to experiences
and memories of military service in the JNA by making them publicly visible.[24]
Such framing made these memories and experiences inevitably archaicized,
in Raymond Williams's terms, put in the service of the dominant ideologies
of the present, and thus unable to question or complicate the logic of the aftermath that limits horizons of individual people and reduces them to their
ethnic identification.[25] In the post-Yugoslav present, for the history of the
JNA to be told publicly through the experience of individuals, these individuals had to be made representatives of (ethnic) types—a process disturbingly
anticipated by Jane Štravs's photographs of men with whom he served in the
JNA, which I discussed in chapter 6.

Public commemorations of victims of the 1990s wars and condemnation of
perpetrators in public discourse and collective imagery also place men's ethnic
identity, their destinies in the catastrophe, and their roles in the wars in only
one, well-defined, and unquestionable relation to the JNA uniform. In Slovenia and Croatia, the JNA has been interpreted solely as an aggressor, although
Slovenes and Croats served in it during the decades preceding the 1990s. The
ten-day war between the JNA and the Slovenian Territorial Defense force became a central reference in discourses of national sovereignty. The Slovenian
Anton (Toni) Mrlak, a JNA pilot who intended to cross to the Slovenian side
but was shot down and killed while flying in a helicopter over Ljubljana carrying bread for soldiers trapped in the JNA barracks, has an important place in
these discourses as a Slovenian victim. The name of the Macedonian Bojanče
Sibinovski, the other JNA soldier killed in the helicopter, is almost never mentioned alongside Mrlak.

Captain Tomo Buzov, a Croat, a JNA officer whose army disintegrated, and who was taken from the train and killed in Štrpci because he tried to protect Muslims, has been "no one's victim" as he did not fit any national framework: a JNA officer living in Belgrade, a Croat among Muslims killed by Serbs, he could not be part of any collective "we." As Boris Dežulović has written, "Tomo Buzov is no one's concern: he was not statistically a Bosniak to be commemorated with other Muslims; in Croatia, he was seen as a traitor and an officer of an aggressor army."[26]

Public recognition and respect for Tomo Buzov's brave act came late, almost two decades after the war crime in Štrpci. A memorial plaque was placed in his birthplace Kaštel Novi in Croatia in autumn 2015, with the inscription "In memory of a man who could not remain silent [as one of the passengers from the same train described Buzov in the court trial]. One among a thousand of them [passengers on the Belgrade-Bar train]." In April 2016, a similar plaque, with the inscription "In memory of the humanity and braveness of the men who lived at this address," was placed at the entrance of the apartment block where he lived with his family in New Belgrade.

The municipal government of the Croatian city of Split remains deaf to numerous initiatives to place a plaque that would commemorate the death of Saško Gešovski, a JNA soldier and the first victim of the Yugoslav wars, who was murdered by a mob protesting against the JNA in front of its headquarters. This protest was, on the other hand, fixed in the official memory in Croatia as "an important date in Split history, but also in the history of the homeland war."[27] On the day that Saško was killed, Eugen Jakovčić from Split was on the Goce Delčev JNA base in Skopje, Macedonia, doing his military service. He remembers every second of that day:

> My mother called me in a panic from Split. I talked to her from a telephone booth in the post office on the base. Crying, she told me, 'They killed a little Macedonian' (*Ubili malog Makedonca*). My commander, colonel Ivan Terzić, who was in charge of the base, lined us up and loudly said: "There are comrades from Split among us. No one should even look at them in a bad way, or you will be heavily sanctioned." Later he called me to his office and we drank whiskey and cried together. That May day on the base in Skopje I realized for the first time that something terrible is coming.

In the aftermath of Yugoslavia's destruction, a time defined by the logic of ethnic belonging as the single structuring principle of social and political life, there can be no place for the recognition and memory of JNA officers who cried in fear for the lives of young men they were in charge of and who did everything they could to protect them. These officers, together with many young men who died in the JNA uniform during the conflicts in the 1990s, became "the forgotten soldiers of a dead country."[28]

BIOGRAPHIES UNMADE

In 2015, to mark the twentieth anniversary of the genocide in Srebrenica, where Serb forces killed more than eight thousand Bosnian men and boys, journalist Dženana Halimović started collecting photographs of victims. Her aim was to give faces to numbers, since in dealing with the mass killings in the aftermath of the Yugoslav wars, names have turned into numbers and DNA samples. "As humanity seemed to disappear, so did any semblance of personhood," wrote Halimović in her explanation of the collection of Srebrenica victims' portraits.[29] Making an online gallery of Srebrenica's victims, she wanted to restore the lost personhood and biographies of men reduced to numbers and remind us that "in each of the thousands of pictures is a human being with a history. And a future cut short."

A visitor, while scrolling down this seemingly endless, but still incomplete, gallery, with thousands of photos of men of different ages, will recognize many JNA soldiers among them. There are identity card photographs, studio photos of young men in JNA uniform in which they have the recognizable posture seen in chapter 5, with their gaze away from camera, as well as photographs taken more informally. The photographs in the JNA uniform are often the only visual reminders of the men killed in Srebrenica. Painfully frozen in another time, they stand out in the multitude of other, quite diverse photographs of men of various ages. A promise of the future inscribed in these uniform photographs was brutally eradicated in horrifying violence done by other men, many of whom also had photos of themselves in the JNA uniform in family albums in their homes.

The Bosnian cultural theorist Damir Arsenijević sees the fact that JNA photos are the only ones left of victims of genocide in Bosnia as a result of the impossible constellations that make a social reality of its aftermath: "All the while," he writes, "life after genocide continues like this: in this photo, a woman is holding a framed picture. In the framed picture, there are three figures: the woman, a young man in uniform and a young girl. The young man in uniform is her missing husband. The image of him that she holds—the most beloved image of him—is one of him wearing the uniform of the Yugoslav People's Army, the same army that took him away, killed him and buried him in a clandestine mass grave."[30]

Here, Arsenijević exposes the impossibility of recuperating "normal" life after genocide and trauma. As he also shows elsewhere, this impossibility is eagerly perpetuated by local political elites imposing ethnic hegemony as the only logic of political life.[31] But what Arsenijević also does is to enforce the event-aftermath perspective and equate the military that millions of men served in during the era of Yugoslav socialism with the forces that killed them in the 1990s. Most of these men, if they could have a voice, probably would not make this equation themselves. It deprives them of their own biographies, in which both the experience of serving in the JNA and photos in JNA uniforms as material memories of that experience may have occupied an important place. They spent a year of their life in that uniform, visited places far away from their homes, and made friends who mattered to them long after their military service was over. They, not least, participated in the political project that stands in sharp opposition to its aftermath. The fact that those who killed them probably had the same studio photos, wore the same uniform, and had similar memories from their time in the JNA does not make their biographies, abruptly cut by genocide, meaningless or absurd. It does not make the only photos of these men less precious for those who outlived them. This is not how life pulsates under the debris left by unthinkable violence.

Amid this debris, DNA technology has been extensively used to identify human remains exhumed from mass graves. Many dead and missing victims of the Yugoslav wars have been identified, thanks to DNA matching with their loved ones, who continue to live, often scattered around the globe, re-settled in distant places and foreign countries. Hariz Halilovich writes about Fatima, now living in St. Louis, Missouri, who lost her two sons and husband in the Srebrenica genocide in 1995. Their remains were identified thanks to DNA matching, and Fatima traveled twice, in 2004 and 2006, from St. Louis to Bosnia to attend a collective burial at Srebrenica Memorial Cemetery.[32] Fatima hoped to get some material belongings that might have been found at the sites where her family members were exhumed, thinking of "her husband's pocket watch, wedding ring, and cigarette holder, as well as a silver necklace her younger son was wearing," but also of "personal ID cards they had in their pockets as well as the clothing they had on, the very jackets and trousers she had patched and stitched during the war."[33] However, she had to accept the official explanation that these material artifacts are pieces of evidence to be used by the International Criminal Tribunal for the former Yugoslavia (ICTY) and that "one day all the artifacts would be returned to Bosnia and then relatives would be asked to identify each item which thereafter might form a part of a genocide museum collection or be appropriated by the surviving relatives."[34] But in 2009, Fatima learned "that the ICTY officials had destroyed material recovered from the mass graves of the Srebrenica genocide," justifying this action with a sanitized, cold, bureaucratic explanation that it "is standard procedure if the material is no longer being used as evidence during UN court proceedings and if it poses a risk to public health."[35]

In her living room in faraway St. Louis, Fatima keeps a framed photograph of her husband "dressed in an olive-green shirt and a Titovka cap with a red star on his head, a Yugoslav People's Army uniform."[36] It stands next to the photo of the two sons she lost in Srebrenica. For Fatima, these two photographs are the only material mementos of her lost sons and husband. In her words, "these pictures bring a bit of the old home here . . . without them I would feel like a complete stranger in this foreign world."[37] In the social world torn apart by the war and genocide of the 1990s, the photograph of her husband in the JNA uniform is not a symptom of the impossibility of normality, but rather the opposite—the only reminder that normality once used to be possible and real.

Portraits of young men in JNA uniforms, marking visually important points in the biographies of men in the former Yugoslavia, may actually work as visual staples that stitch together the past and the present cut apart by the catastrophe of the 1990s, recovering normality in places torn by and frozen in conflict. The same year in which Dženana Halimović established the online gallery of photographs of men killed in Srebrenica, a small exhibition on Srebrenica was on display at Sarajevo's Historical Museum of Bosnia and Herzegovina. The exhibition's emphasis was on ties, maintained or restored, that connect people in Srebrenica and serve as a foundation for restoring "a normal life" in the town. On display were mostly photographs from family albums, and many of them were familiar individual or group portraits of men in uniforms of the JNA. In one of the frames, there was a photo of a father and a son and

Figure 7.2 Photographs displayed at the Historical Museum of Bosnia and Herzegovina, Sarajevo, August 2015.

two smaller photos of young children—the family's third generation. This combination of photos clearly emphasizes continuity and sheds an optimistic light on Srebrenica, emphasizing the resilience of life in this place that was so gravely marked by mass killing in 1995, when all the male members of so many Bosnian Muslim families lost their lives. A "connecting chain" in this displayed frame, a son of the older man and the father of two children, is in the JNA uniform (see figure 7.2).

The photographic portraits of men in the uniform of the army that is no more circulate in the post-Yugoslav space within families, among relatives, friends, colleagues, across generations, following their own logic of love, remembrance, and attachment. Neither the limits of the uniform and the standardized posture, nor the normative dictate of the aftermath that makes these portraits unbefitting, affect the gaze of those who, taking them in hands, see their fathers, grandfathers, sons, friends, colleagues, brothers, cousins, husbands, and lovers.

In February 2016, my father passed away. After forty days, in accordance with tradition, the family, relatives, and friends gathered around the still fresh

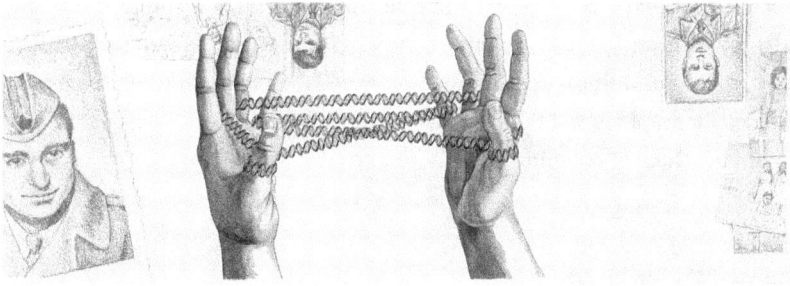

Figure 7.3 An illustration from Samira Kentrić's *Balkanalije*.

grave in a small cemetery in a village in central Serbia. An elderly man whom I vaguely knew from the village that I left at the beginning of the 1990s to study in Belgrade approached me and stretched both hands toward me, holding carefully in them a studio photograph of my father in the Yugoslav army uniform. The photo was not new to me: I had the same one in one of the boxes that held old family photographs. My aunts and uncles also nodded in recognition: they, too, owned the same photo. The black-and-white photo was taken in a photo studio in the Croatian town of Karlovac, where my father spent the first part of his military service in the JNA in 1966. He probably sent it to his parents, uncles and aunts, cousins, neighbors, and friends. This is one of the recognizable images of my father, one that will remain in the memory of many people, now that he is gone. It is he, young and gentle, in uniform, looking away from the camera, in a black-and-white photograph with serrated margins.

The photo I received from the elderly villager at the cemetery on that gray March day in 2016 was one of the photographs of JNA soldiers taken in local studios, just like the photos left of men who were killed in Srebrenica. These photographs remain important for the men portrayed, as well as for people to whom these men matter: their family, friends, and relatives. A couple of years after my father died, I received several black-and-white photographs of my father from my uncle. He decided that these photographs should belong to me rather than be stored among old photographs in a box in his basement. The only photo of his brother he decided to keep was the one from his time in the JNA.

In her autobiographical graphic novel titled *Balkanalije*, the Slovenian artist Samira Kentrić writes that her mother saw her father for the first time in a photograph of the same kind. She fell in love with a man in the JNA uniform, a fact that gives this recognizable army photo not only importance, but also a fateful and destiny-defining capacity. With such a place in family histories, these uniform photos and the uniformed men in them resist forces that flatten biographies and reduce full, rich, and complex lives to single threads, stripping them of meaning and emotions.

LEARNING WHO YOU ARE

These images of young men in the JNA uniform, firmly placed among other images their loved ones keep and cherish, are quite often all that remains of people lost in the darkness of war, the only proof that these people ever were. When Mitko Panov started out on his quest to find his army buddies, he sent several letters to addresses he got from them before they departed from Titov Veles once their military service was over. Many of the letters he sent to Bosnia and Herzegovina returned, undelivered; when he visited those addresses, no one had heard of these men. Their photographs from the JNA seem to be the only proof that they really existed. These photographs are also a reminder of a possibility of living a different reality, albeit one confined by the fences of a military base, and of imagining a future from that confined space that was different from the future that came.

On a Facebook group page used by former JNA soldiers, who post on it photos and information on when and where they performed their military service and who try to learn the whereabouts of their army mates, there was a photograph of two cheerful young men. They stand among beds in an army barracks. They are in civilian clothes, and a bag with packed belongings is on the bed on the left, suggesting that the photo was taken on the last day of their military service. The owner of the photograph, one of the two men pictured in it, wrote the following when he posted it in the summer of 2019: "I am a Serb, he is a Muslim . . . We were like brothers!!! Last minutes in the barracks in Kranj, June 1990."

Among several friendly comments and congratulations about the friendship, there are also those pointing to the contentious nature of this ethnic (and religious) identification in the post accompanying the photograph.[38] "Good for you, I did not know who was who back then. I was not interested in that either. I did not even know who I was," one of the group members wrote. Another pointed out that the ethnicity of former soldiers should not be specified in such posts, as these issues caused too much hatred and suffering. "It does not matter who you are, but what kind of person you are," wrote another. "We were all humans (*ljudi*) and loved and respected each other, and sang together," added a group member from southern Serbia.[39]

This thread (and many similar ones on this Facebook group's page) points to the possibility of (self-)identification based on premises of morality, virtue, rightness, and honor—the possibility citizens were offered in socialist Yugoslavia and its military and largely lost when ethnicized logic prevailed. The possibility of alternative interpretations and identifications has caused significant social anxiety since the 1990s. The purpose of the uniform by definition—to make all the men the same—was problematic in times when these men, both those dead and those still alive, *had* to be seen as different— as Croats, Muslims, Serbs, Albanians, Macedonians, Montenegrins, Slovenes, Hungarians—because the reality and the logic governing social, economic, and political life were based on that difference.

Mitko Panov left Yugoslavia too early to be gradually exposed to this differentiation process. As he traveled through the devastated lands of the former Yugoslavia to produce his documentary, tracking down his army buddies whom the JNA uniform had once made all the same, he had to learn who they had become since they had left their barracks. Mitko knew them by their names and nicknames and remembered them because of their skills, sense of humor, sporting achievements, talents, and diligence. But in the meantime, they had become defined by their ethnicity. This ethnicizing logic not only defined their destinies, sending some of them to their deaths and others into exile, it also crucially affected Mitko's prospects of finding his friends, particularly in ethnically cleansed Bosnia. In the city of Zenica, he looked for Boris, but Boris had left the city like most of the local Serbs, never to return there. In Drvar, he hoped to find Marinko. The policemen whom he asked for directions to Marinko's village kept him for hours in the police station because he was suspicious about Mitko asking after a Serb in an area that has been dominated by Croats since the war. In the city of Doboj, he tried to find Dino, but no one remembered him. Mitko did not know which ethnicity Dino belonged to, which seems to be crucial for whether he could still be there or not. As a woman he met in the apartment building where Dino used to live explained to him, if Dino was either a Muslim or a Croat, then he was certainly not in Doboj anymore.

Who you are ethnically has become so overwhelmingly and inescapably defining of the reality and the possibilities of everyone in the former Yugoslavia that I had no choice but to obey this logic of ethnicization in this book, systematically attaching national/ethnic qualifiers to the former Yugoslav soldiers I am writing about. Depending on who they were, these soldiers could be dead or alive; remembered or forgotten; they may have had to flee their homes or remained in them; they could have been mobilized and found themselves in trenches attacking towns and villages or defending them; or they could have hidden in basements and shelters trying to survive the shells. As these possible destinies were not a matter of choice, thinking and writing about the men these destinies were assigned to cannot escape the logic of who they were ethnically. That moment in Kranj in 1990, when two friends took a photo just before they departed for their homes in different parts of Yugoslavia, was the last moment in which who they are could be thought of outside the logic of ethnicity and when who they are ethnically was not the only identification that mattered. The absence of alternatives in thinking about who we are is just another symptom of life in the aftermath of the catastrophe, in the present among the ruins of possible futures.

8

Form and Life

The aftermath is singular, motionless and constricted. It freezes the present, flattens biographies, narrows perspectives on the past, and reduces horizons of the future. In the aftermath, modalities of being for the former Yugoslavs are limited to what they are ethnically, and their reality is defined by the tight causality between the event and its aftermath, again reducing who they are to seemingly clear categories of victims and perpetrators under the long shadow of the wars of the 1990s. But the forms that constituted the experience of military service in the Yugoslav People's Army (JNA)—all those routines, rituals, objects, photographs, best friends' names, geographical places, jokes, chunks of formulaic language, and their afterlives in post-Yugoslav space and beyond it—possess the capacity to unsettle the present and point to lost alternatives.

The capacity of these forms to defy the aftermath in its solidity, singularity, and surface smoothness, and to question the neatness of the categories in which the aftermath is organized is closely connected to the affective ties of solidarity, friendship, and care among the soldiers gathered from all corners of Yugoslavia, very different but made the same by the uniform they wore and the rituals and routines of army life. For these ties to emerge, and for their subsequent capacity to unsettle, question, and destabilize the stillness of the aftermath, the forms that made up life on JNA bases—performative, ritualized, lacking variation, and distanced from was what was perceived as a "normal" and meaningful life and often resulting in surrealness and absurdity—had to be taken *as life* and embraced as such by men in uniforms performing their military service. To be capable of producing affective forces that unsettle the ruins in Yugoslavia's aftermath, these performative, semantically limited forms themselves had to be filled with affect; they had to become *forms of life*.

Theorizing affect, a fashionable academic enterprise of our time, tends to keep form outside its scope.[1] Life, like ethics, politics, and aesthetics, necessarily appears in some form and "must be enacted in the definite particular."[2] But forms are often seen as irreconcilable with affect's universality, pre-culturality, intensity, and ability to escape articulation. As Margaret Wetherell points out, what makes affect special for many is its "dramatic and turbulent qualities, along with the random, the chaotic and the spontaneous"—and these features stand as the opposite of well-defined and repetitive forms emerging as patterns, habits, and rituals, which are thought to have disciplining and emotion-numbing effects.[3] Many scholars, however, point to the fact that such forms also enable "the body's potential for engaging in the new, change and creativity," and recognize the capacity of patterns, habits, routines, and rituals to lead to social transformation "through accumulation and reverberation of 'minor' affective responses, interactions, gestures and habits."[4] Nevertheless, firmly structured, repetitive, ritualized collective forms and routines, with limited variety and emerging in a context provided by a robust state institution like those that concern me in this book, remain decoupled from affect, solidarity, and other politically meaningful engagements that are seen through the lens offered by the ontological turn as fluid, fleeting, networked, and movable. These collective forms and routines are, on the other hand, firmly linked to notions of governance, control, and domination, with hegemonic power relations, totalitarian societies, and oppressive contexts.[5]

In studies of twentieth-century state socialisms, extensive attention has been given to repetitive and ritualized forms of politics, language, culture, and ideology. The increasing gap between forms of ideological representation and their literal (semantic) meanings has been understood as a symptom of socialism's inevitable implosion and as an explanation of how it was possible, in the first place, that socialism's end brought little surprise to those who lived it, although it seemed eternal to them while it lasted.[6] These forms of socialist life have been largely associated with the negative pole of the binary oppositions between truth and lies/dissimulation, repression and freedom, oppression and resistance, official culture and counterculture, totalitarian language and people's language, and the public self and private self.[7] In his study of ideological forms of late socialism, Alexei Yurchak persuasively dismantles these binary categories, which permit only two mutually exclusive possibilities for a socialist subject in his or her positioning toward hegemonic ideology and the state: a "real" support or "simulation" of support.[8] These binary models, Yurchak further argues, imply that meaning is fully defined in the speaker's mind before the act of speaking. However, the slippage between the form and the meaning also involved an element of unpredictability.[9]

In Yurchak's analysis, the subject's relationship to the forms of hegemonic discourse of communist ideology and meanings inscribed in ideological performance and representation, and his or her engagement with these forms, were largely situated in the domain of knowledge and interpretation. Asking "how Soviet people in fact interpreted the lived ideology and reality of socialism," Yurchak directs us toward "knowledge that is always-already partial, situated, and actively produced" and dialogical, a knowledge that "accounts not only for 'semantic' (literal) meanings for which ideological discourse supposedly stands, but also for 'pragmatic' meanings that emerge in discourse as a situated activity."[10]

This knowledge and the interpretative tools that it enabled provided socialist subjects with an ability to navigate both the ideology and the reality of late socialism, in circumstances of the widening gap between the form and meaning, where "copying forms of ideological representation into other domains became more meaningfully constitutive of everyday life than the adherence to literal (semantic) meanings inscribed in those representations."[11] This copying practice, which became known as "overidentification," required mastering the hegemonic discourse and the ritualized protocols of its use. It was employed by socialist subjects in concrete pragmatic contexts in the way that best responded to their needs and interests. We saw some instances of such strategic use in chapter 5.

On the bases of the Yugoslav army, where millions of young men spent a year or more performing their military service, many practices that constituted life were overtly decoupled from their literal meaning. In many spheres, this decoupling was necessary for the very functioning of the military. Life on the base was made of performative, scarce bits of language, and ritualized, repetitive routines. Yurchak looks at socialist subjects' engagements with the hegemonic discourses of communist ideology for an answer to the question of the conditions that made the collapse of the socialist system possible and simultaneously rendered that collapse unexpected until the very end, while I ask how the limited and hegemonic forms of discourse and other practices that constituted life on JNA bases acquired the capacity to unsettle the present and recall lost alternatives in the aftermath of the Yugoslav catastrophe. To answer this question, I propose to look at hegemonic, standardized, and ritualized forms beyond the knowledge-interpretation framework that implies the subject's positioning vis-à-vis these forms and the extent of his or her distance from and control over them. Instead, I ask about the affective work of these forms, about the emotional fabric they were productive of in the context in which the subject's position was not one of distance and control necessary for interpretation and strategic use, but one of embracing ritualized, performative experience of military service that lasted for a year or longer *as life as such.*

To highlight the difference in outcomes of ritualized, hegemonic, and monotonous workings of forms that depended on how the uniformed subject stood vis-à-vis these forms, in this chapter I discuss the life of forms that made up military service in the JNA—forms prescribed, predictable, limiting, and limited—as that life unfolds in the JNA archives created by two artists during their military service, Dušan Mandić and Franci Virant. I then discuss male friendships made in the JNA as the most important affective fabric that shaped life on military bases, and which was shaped by its formalized, standardized, repetitive forms.

ON SOLDIERS AND ARTISTS

Uprooted from Ljubljana and the city's intense alternative life "on the social, cultural and artistic margins of Socialism," which he was observing and interpreting through the lens of his camera, and caught within the fences of a Belgrade JNA base in 1986, Jane Štravs did not embrace the reality of his army service as life.[12] He saw the forms that constituted that reality as the opposite of life, as imposed upon him, limiting, and a deprivation of freedom. Jane experienced the reality of life in the JNA uniform as the totalitarian work of

Yugoslav socialism in condensed form, the same work that he was artistically exposing and critiquing with his photographs. As a JNA soldier, he turned to making art as a survival strategy and saw it as a way to remain who he really was despite the oppressive mechanisms he was involuntarily exposed to. What he did as an artist-photographer on the army base sought to connect him with the world he had left when he entered through its gates. Because of that, Jane's photographs of JNA soldiers that I discussed in chapter 6 easily fit into his broader artistic opus of portraits made in the 1980s, which aimed to offer an insight into life at "the margins of totalitarian structure."[13] These margins encompass Ljubljana's underground spaces, shabby clubs, galleries, concert stages, and JNA barracks as well.

Like Jane in Belgrade, Dušan in Niš, despite his role as "garrison painter," pursued his own distinctively outward-oriented artistic project, firmly placed within the alternative art politics of the ŠKUC Gallery in Ljubljana and not within the military base in southern Serbia. Dušan sent the artistic material he created during the year of his service to his girlfriend in Ljubljana. These artworks make up the exhibition *Die Welt ist schön: Private D. M.*, which was shown for the first time at the ŠKUC Gallery in October 1982, immediately after Dušan returned from military service, and in Belgrade a couple of months later. More than three decades later, in 2014, the exhibition was on display again, this time in City Art Gallery Ljubljana, and three years later it was shown in Belgrade for the second time.

The first thing a spectator encounters in the exhibition is the juxtaposition of a portrait a young JNA soldier and the image of a Latin cross. The portrait is a drawing, the cross is of metal with layers of oil paint applied to it, but both are transformed by being photographed and projected onto the gallery's wall (see figure 8.1). The installation is accompanied by a text explaining that both images, the cross and the soldier, are symbols of the mighty ideological state apparatus—a symbol of thousand-year-old Catholicism and a symbol of the young, but strong, ideology of the Yugoslav socialist system. According to the text,

> the exhibition deals with a social situation from the position of the subject (the exhibition's author) toward the (Yugoslav) People's Army, a fundamentally repressive apparatus of the state stemming from the tradition of the National Liberation Movement. Simultaneously, the exhibition points to the relocation of the subject: from the position where he seemingly has

Figure 8.1 Dušan Mandić in front of his installation *Private and Cross*, City Art Gallery Ljubljana, 2014.

control over the situation in which he lives and acts to a position in which he finds himself dressed in the JNA uniform and is from that moment on only a small wheel in the totalitarian mechanism.[14]

It is clear from this framing, as well as from the very title of the exhibition, that it has a distinctively self-reflexive character. Although the text states that "every male citizen shared such a destiny during the previous socialist regime," it is the author's particular situation, shaped to a great extent by his biography up to the point when he left to serve in the JNA, where he was forced to exchange "personal freedom for non-freedom, civilian clothes for a uniform, time and labor committed to art in the ŠKUC Gallery in Ljubljana for time 'in jail,'" that is at the heart of this exhibition.[15]

Although the exhibition is largely self-reflexive, the soldier portrayed next to the projection of the metal Latin cross is not Dušan Mandić. The soldier is anonymous and serves as a symbol, a generalized signifier of the situation the exhibition reflects upon.

The distance between the author and the JNA soldier who is the subject of the author's artistic reflection and the lack of equivalence between them, even though the exhibition speaks of the author's own experience in the JNA, are the result of a need to regain control over the self and the place in the world that Dušan felt he lost once he dressed in the JNA uniform. He was eager to remain an artist, unchanged by any of the effects of the military and its world, as close as he could get to the world of alternative culture and art in Ljubljana that he belonged to and had to leave for the period of his military service. He wanted to retain his voice unchanged by the effects of the military institution. The same was true of Jane Štravs and his photographic opus from his time in the JNA.

These artists strove to stand above the situation in which they involuntarily found themselves. Such an artistic position forced them to detach themselves from other soldiers with whom they shared everyday life on military bases. In their works of art, the soldiers they portray are not present as who they are, but are rather types, symbols, and/or a means of transmitting specific artistic and political messages. They are instruments in the artistic process and were often put in an interpretational context with which they probably would not identify.

To convey an artistic message highlighting the oppressive effects of the JNA, Jane and Dušan needed to ignore, conceal, and compromise other effects of that institution, those resulting from the space and time shared with other men who wore the same uniform. The relationship between Jane and the three men he photographed, or between Dušan and the young man whose portrait is displayed next to the Latin cross, is limited to that between the artist and his artistic subject. It conceals that both the artists and their subjects were made the same by the uniforms in the confined space of the barracks they lived in and through the rituals that constituted army life; and it does not make visible any affective ties that might be woven between them during their military service.

At approximately the same time that Dušan served in the JNA in Niš, another Slovenian artist, the photographer Franci Virant, came to the barracks in Sombor in northern Serbia. After brief training, he was transferred to Osijek and spent most of his military service at the training ground Polygon C. As an "official" unit photographer, Franci was allowed to photograph, so he took photos, mostly at the request of his army buddies. In 2011, in a small gallery in Ljubljana, he had an exhibition titled *Polygon C 1980/81*. The twenty-five photographs he selected for the exhibition depict daily life at the training ground—soldiers on watch, in their leisure time, or during routine activities. Since the training ground was detached from the main barracks and soldiers were on their own in the afternoons after the officers went home, in many photographs the soldiers are not dressed according to regulations: they pose half-naked, or dressed in an undershirt, or with slippers on their feet. Nevertheless, we see recognizable patterns and forms in these photographs: in some, young men in uniform pose with machine guns and other weapons. In contrast to these, there are also very formal portraits, strongly resembling the army identity-card photos discussed in chapter 4 or the studio photos discussed in chapter 5. These photos, in all their diversity, were taken at the request of the soldiers themselves. Unlike Jane Štravs's photo series, the soldiers photographed by Franci undoubtedly identified with their photographic selves, and this identification was not conditioned either by the formality and staginess of the photographic act or by the absence of these characteristics. Like Ante Tomić's novel *Ništa nas ne smije iznenaditi*, these photos have no ambition to serve as signifiers of some larger truth. The men in them are not symbols of types that would corroborate this larger truth. All have names, places they come from, and unique stories. Their names, places, and stories are inseparable from them. When I spoke to him in the gallery in Ljubljana, Franci remembered them all and was very fond of the memories they still shared, or might have still shared, because he neither knew nor dared to explore what the wars of the 1990s and the deterioration that followed them have done to the young men smiling while posing for his camera on the isolated training ground near Osijek in 1981.

Unlike Dušan Mandić and Jane Štravs, Franci Virant has waited a long time to display the photographs he took during his time in the JNA. In his own words, by taking these photographs, he did not make art but "captured life." And more than "artistic quality," it is life caught in these rather standardized photographs that catches the observer's attention. That form of life—lived by young men whose uniform prevents us from knowing whether they were Serbs, Croats, Muslims, Albanians, or Hungarians; or whether they came from big cities or remote villages—unfolds in the exhibited photographs as remote, irreversible, and irreparable. The very site where these forms existed and were captured by Franci's lens, Polygon C, was heavily damaged in the war. The military unit of people featured in the photographs and the life they depict were assemblages, possible only within the fenced-in limits of Polygon C.

One of the photographs shows part of Franci's unit, a group portrait of young men probably taken on a summer afternoon (see figure 8.2). Some of the soldiers are not in uniform and are dressed lightly; they might have just

Figure 8.2 Part of Franci Virant's unit at Polygon C near Osijek, 1981. Franci is in the front row, third from the left. From the archive of Franci Virant.

finished a soccer match. Some have parts of their uniform on, while others are fully dressed, probably because they were on duty at that moment. The remoteness and isolation of the place where they served enabled such variation in their dress; it would not have been possible in the barracks, where the presence of officers was constant. Despite differences in the way they were dressed, these young men all went through the same routine day after day, counting the days, longing for the homes, girlfriends, and lives they had left behind, and dreaming of the moment when life would resume. But still, life on Polygon C was also life, a meaningful life in which the young men made friends, joked, cared for each other, exchanged secrets, played soccer, and laughed.

This is how Franci described the group of his army buddies, pointing them out in the photograph:

The first in the upper row from the left is Branko Dujmović. He received the Exemplary Soldier badge, and was indeed an exemplary man. The second from the right is Duje, from a place near Omišalj. He was a great colleague and is one of those I would like to visit. Then, here is Dino from Prijedor. He never took a shower. The first from the left in the lower row is Franjo

Pečnik, from Maribor. He was an electrotechnical engineer and was in charge of the radar. And there is a soldier, Mijatović, a Roma *Gastarbeiter* who came to serve in the army from Vienna. I had to take ten portraits of him, for all his relatives. Once his relatives came to Osijek to visit him and brought a bear that danced for us in the yard of the military base. They did not want any money for the performance, of course. Mitrović was extremely well behaved, a skilled accordion player, and a great friend. They were all in my unit, the intermediate class of August of 1980.

Mitko Panov's years-long quest to find his army buddies that we follow in his documentary film *Comrades* started with a similar photograph, shot at roughly same time. Panov's film begins with this photograph. It captures his unit, assembled on the base in the Macedonian town of Titov Veles on the eve of the year 1982, a playful crowd of young men in uniforms, smiling cheerfully, with bottles of beer in their hands, looking in different directions, some directly at the camera, some away from it. The camera travels over the faces of these young men, one by one. It starts with the author, a smiling, dark-haired boy in the middle of the photograph, with the delicate moustache of someone who had hardly started shaving. His voice guides us as the camera stops for a moment on each cheerful face:

> Standing above me, I recognized Zoran, whom we called Zuba because he was missing his front tooth. Next to him is Srđan, who was the fastest runner in the unit. Above Srđan is Kadri, from a tiny village in the hills on the Serbian-Kosovo border. At the picture's top stand Džigi, the class clown, Miško, the rock star, and Nehad, the junior ping-pong champion. On their right stands Slavko, who was the quietest guy in the unit. Then come my Bosnian comrades: Dragan, whose first shave was in the army, Mustafa, who was the most diligent among us, and Pejo, whom I remember as the loudest.[16]

Looking at men in Franci's group portrait and in the photograph at the beginning of Mitko's documentary, it is hard to imagine that they experienced the continuity in their lives that was taken for granted at the moment these photographs were taken. The rupture of the 1990s opened too many possibilities, some of them quite dark and frightening. But at the moment these photographs were made, there was life with its countless promises waiting for them once their service was over; and back then in the early 1980s, the future seemed possible, placed within familiar coordinates, and easy to imagine and look forward to. These young men were there together, sharing routines of military service and knowing and befriending each other despite the tremendous differences among them. Their friendships were based on their moral qualities, because in this shared, confined space filled with ritualized, repetitive practices, these qualities mattered much more than who one was in ethnic terms or from what kind of place one came to serve in the JNA. Despite generic and genealogical differences, it is possible to recognize in these photographs the same utopian spark of alternative identifications and possible futures that lurks in the highly formalized studio portraits of young men in JNA uniforms. It is there, directing our gaze toward many possibilities, some lived, some imagined and hoped for, that were destroyed during the Yugoslav catastrophe and have been eradicated during the decades of its aftermath.

IMPOSSIBLE FRIENDSHIPS

Embracing the experience of army service as life, lived through ritualized and repetitive forms that often held a tinge of surrealness, JNA soldiers made friends in the army. Friendship is central to the ideological build-up of most all-male groups and institutions, such as the military. Usually observed as "thin and pragmatic," "dependent on shared values and similarity between friends," male friendship is the basis of familiar notions of the "brotherhood of man" and political solidarity.[17] It is nurtured, together with other manly characteristics such as physical fitness and strength, discipline, and self-regulation in institutions strongly characterized by the ritualization of everyday life and subsequent hyper-aesthetics, such as boarding schools, religious orders, and the military.[18] Describing the life of male students at the Doon boarding school in India, David MacDougall argues that male friendship, built within defined social aesthetics and by sets of everyday rituals and performances, aims to keep a new generation of Indian leaders connected.[19] He suggests that the boarding school can be seen as a "training ground" where boys are modeled into political subjects who should share not only knowledge, but also interests, aspirations, and views.

We can similarly think of the Yugoslav military as a training ground for making Yugoslav men. However, the universal character of military service made this experience more radically detached from young men's usual or desired biographical paths than a boarding school would: the latter was carefully chosen with the aim of giving these paths direction and increasing the boys' prospects for a bright future. Obligatory service in the JNA was, in a way, more of a distraction, an unchosen, albeit expected and mandatory one-year pause on the way to the future and its promises. Moreover, and even more importantly, the young men gathered in JNA barracks and exposed to the routines and rituals of the military were far more diverse than carefully selected boarding school students, whose uniforms came with a certain status and signaled a certain social background. In contrast, the JNA uniform and military mechanisms made all Yugoslav men radically equal in their diversity. These facts significantly affect and complicate the connections made among men in the JNA and the ways these connections relate to the future.

In the barbed-wired space of Yugoslav military bases, bonding among young soldiers was certainly based more on shared cultural preferences than on any shared geographic origin or ethnic background. Similar age, education, and interests, the same taste in music, similar family situations—they all provided the foundation for friendships. That was true for Branislav Ković and Ivica Krajina, whose friendship was forged during military service in Pirot in southern Serbia in 1984 and whose reunion after thirty-four years made it into the news on Serbian media in 2019. Branislav recalls that in 1984 they had just graduated from high school and were still kids: "We were not thrilled by the fact that as soon as we left school, our freedom was taken from us, our hair was cut, and we found ourselves in the barracks surrounded by fences. What brought us together was the same worldview and similar energy—we listened to the same music and were attracted by the same books. We were inseparable for a year, and shared the good and the bad."[20]

Božidar, a transport engineer from Zagreb, befriended Đura from Belgrade's peripheral neighborhood, also because of the many similarities between them: both came to serve in 1977 after they graduated and were older than the majority of conscripts in their garrison in Postojna. As Božidar remembers, of eight hundred newly arrived conscripts, only five were university graduates. Unlike others who served at that time for a year and a half, they served only one year because of their college education. Both Božidar and Đura were already married when they came to serve in the army. Their family situations, desires, plans for the future, thoughts, and worries were much different from those of eighteen-year-old conscripts and provided a common ground for friendship between them. Božidar fondly remembers

Đura and the days they spent together in the Postojna garrison: "My unit officer was responsible for food and supplies. His name is Đura and he is from Serbia. He became my best friend. He was two meters tall and everyone was a bit overwhelmed by him. He was also married, came to serve in the army late, and already had a small child."

Two artists, Nebojša Šerić Šoba and Dejan Dimitrijević, were both born in 1968—Šoba in Sarajevo, Bosnia and Herzegovina, and Dejan in Pančevo, Serbia. They met at the bus station in Pula, on their way to the base in Mali Lošinj, where they were heading for military service. They became friends even before the bus reached Mali Lošinj: as soon as they exchanged a couple of words, their shared affinities and interest in art made them "click." Their friendship solidified during basic training; then they were sent to different places for the rest of their military service—Nebojša to Sinj and Dejan to Split. After the JNA, they both graduated from art academies and maintained contact, occasionally exchanging letters. The breakup of Yugoslavia cut the ties between them. They both survived wars and mobilization and experienced multiple uprootings over the years to come. They met again in New York in 2015, almost thirty years after their army service in Mali Lošinj.

Many men, like Božidar and Đura, Nebojša and Dejan, or Dušan Mandić and the nuclear physicist from Belgrade whom he befriended during his military service in Niš, became friends because of commonalities and affinities they brought with them to the barracks. But service in the Yugoslav military, bringing drastically different men together and molding their experience with repetitive, ritualized routines, made possible another kind of friendship, the "impossible" friendship that would not be probable outside the base: one based on affection stemming from mutual care, protection, and help. The educated soldiers would write letters for the illiterate ones. The physically able protected weaker ones from hazing by older soldiers or in fights with local young men that sometimes broke out when soldiers went into the city. Božidar taught Serbo-Croatian to an Albanian from his unit and helped him persuade their commander to give him permission to leave for home for two weeks. Dušan taught a fellow soldier how to use a typewriter. The philosopher Boris Buden remembers his friendship with Jeton from Kosovo. The two soldiers did not even share the same language, but found a way to enjoy spending time together in free afternoons when they were allowed to leave the barracks and go to downtown Belgrade.[21] In Radosav's unit, there was a young man whom they called the Intellectual (Intelektualac) because of his education and the very thick glasses he wore. He knew everything about weapons and the physics of shooting, but could never hit the target during target practice. Each of his unit buddies would shoot one bullet into his target, so that he, too, could reach a satisfactory score. For Elmaz, this protection was critically important and tightly connected to friendship during his military service in the JNA in the Serbian town of Kragujevac in 1988–89. Being surrounded by his four closest army buddies made Elmaz, an Albanian in JNA uniform, feel safe and protected both within the barracks and outside, in the city. "When I was with these four, I felt safe and knew that nothing bad could happen to me," Elmaz told me as we gazed over Pristina's net of streets and buildings from the window of the café on the top floor of one of Kosovo's newly built shopping malls. When his military service in Kragujevac came close to its end in 1989, demonstrations against oppression by the Serbian government started in Kosovo. Serbian authorities imposed a curfew on the province, and Elmaz's military service was prolonged by thirty-five days. He remembers those thirty-five days as extremely difficult to get through: "I barely survived. All my friends were gone, new soldiers came, and I felt unprotected and constantly in danger."

"In my unit in Maribor," remembers Radosav, "there was Kamenko, a boy from Kakanj. In the dormitory, he slept above me. Every night, his blanket would fall down while he slept and he would start shivering. I kept covering him [throughout his] whole military service." "We took care of each other (*pazili smo se*)," was one of the first things Hariz Halilovich told me about his friendship with Đurica. When we met for the first time, Hariz was in his early forties. He is now a social scientist in Australia and we improvised an interview about his experience in the JNA during a conference dinner in Edmonton in 2010. Over a beer, we laughed together about his stories from the army. He recalled anecdotes and tried to remember the expressions and specific vocabulary of the last decade of socialist Yugoslavia's military institution. At the end, with a bit of hesitation, Hariz told me a story of his army buddy Đurica, a peasant and a talented accordion player from central Serbia, not far from the place where I was born. Hariz, who was assigned to serve in the garrison infirmary because he had graduated from medical high school, would put Đurica in quarantine giving him a diagnosis of "suspected scabies," a condition that required strict isolation from other soldiers and thus saved him from being assigned night watch duties, which he was terribly afraid of. "My Đurica!" said Hariz softly. "His parents brought him the accordion. He could not do night watch because he was scared, and I would put him into isolation. We would deliver him food until 4 p.m., and when the officers left, he would go out."

The friendships between men that were made in the JNA were greatly constrained by the confinement and liminality of the place where they emerged and were informed by the norms of the military institution. As such, they do not fall into the category of "ideal friendship" or "friendship in its purest form" made between "unconstrained people who come to feel spontaneous affection for, and so befriend, each other."[22] These soldiers did not have the freedom to decide whether they would be there or to choose with whom they would spend time in an enclosed, fenced-in space. Forged at the heart of a totally masculine institution in an institutionalized, ritualized, and normative setting, the bonds established between men in JNA barracks appear, on the other hand, to be almost exemplary of "typical" male friendship, understood as superficial, devoid of intimacy and emotions, strongly dependent on social norms, and resulting in formal and rigid relationships incapable of transgressing and questioning the existing order.[23] These male friendships exhibit limitations both in their reach and their linguistic and emotional expressive means. Numerous photos from time in the JNA that are visual reminders of these friendships seem to reflect these limitations. They replicate ritualized forms of everyday life on military bases. In both studio photos and those taken on bases, performativity prevails over other characteristics: men pose, standing facing each other, or looking away from the camera in the studio photos; in other photographs, they hug each other looking into the camera in the familiar way that schoolboys or athletic-team members have their photos taken with their buddies; or they just stand next to each other. Ritualization and the performative character of studio photos and snapshots alike confirm what John Ibson argues in his book on the American tradition of all-male photographs, that the difference between studio photos and snapshots is not as defining as it seems and as their very definitions seem to suggest: "Although by definition a snapshot would not be taken in an actual studio, it would nonetheless be taken in a particular cultural context—a 'cultural studio'—a site with its own expectations and constraints."[24]

Standardization, predictability, performativity, and processes of routinization and ritualization that characterized reality on JNA bases across socialist Yugoslavia also shaped the friendships made during military service in the JNA. It is reflected in both visual material and the language that accompanies that visual material. On the reverse side of army photographs, as well

Figures 8.3, 8.4, 8.5, and 8.6 Studio photos and snapshots of army buddies.

as in some books and other objects from the period of military service, one can find dedications to an army friend. Highly formulaic and made with very limited lexical resources—a usual combination of words and expressions such as "sincerely," "from the heart," "as a memory," "for long remembrance of army days"—they inevitably recall Bernstein's notion of the restricted code, "where the lexicon and hence the organizing structure, irrespective of its degree of complexity, are wholly predictable."[25] Before it ended up at the New Belgrade flea market where I found it, a large, richly illustrated monograph on the Yugoslav armed forces used to belong to a JNA soldier, Ivan.[26] He received it as a present from an army buddy. We learn about that on the book's first page, where a man whose signature is unintelligible wrote this dedication: "To Ivan, sincerely and from the heart, from his friend from army days in Maribor in 1983" (*Iskreno i od srca Ivanu, od prijatelja iz armijskih dana u Mariboru 1983*). This book about the JNA given as a sign of friendship from one soldier to another, with a formulaic and depersonalized dedication written in a recognizable, precise, "technical" style of handwriting that many men adopted when young, illustrates the limitations and paucity of the experience of socialist military service and of the expressive means those exposed to it had at their disposal. Does it also signal the shallowness, rigidity, and emotional thinness of friendships made in the JNA?

"Real," "creative" friendship between men, argues Kingston, emerges only in marginal spaces that are open to men's intimacy, sentiments, and fondness.[27] In the context of the military, deep and meaningful friendship is believed to be possible in extreme conditions of war, violence, and suffering. Michel Foucault insisted that emotional ties woven among men in the trenches of World War I were crucial for them to fight, survive, and keep living in the aftermath of extreme events:

> During World War I, men lived together completely, one on top of another, and for them it was nothing at all, insofar as death was present and finally the devotion to one another and the services rendered were sanctioned by the play of life and death. And apart from several remarks on camaraderie, the brotherhood of spirit, and some very partial observations, what do we know about these emotional uproars and storms of feeling that took place in those times? One can wonder how, in these absurd and grotesque wars and infernal massacres, the men managed to hold on in spite of everything. Through some emotional fabric, no doubt. I don't mean that

it was because they were each other's lovers that they continued to fight; but honor, courage, not losing face, sacrifice, leaving the trench with the captain—all that implied a very intense emotional tie.[28]

Peacetime military service, as Tom Smith notes, has usually been overlooked as a possible site of men's friendship, intimacy, or even desire.[29] The friendships made during JNA service, a central masculine institution in socialist Yugoslavia, seems to fit this common view. Made by the same ritualized, repetitive, semantically limited patterns as the reality of military service, these friendships seem unable to create meaningful ties or destabilize firmly set hegemonic relations. But, as Foucault warned us, the military, in all its ideological and social rigidity, is a contradictory institution with regard to the feelings it generates among men, gathering them within fenced-in space: relations based on affection, solidarity, and friendship "at the same time keep [the military institution] going and shake it up."[30] "These relations," writes Foucault, "short-circuit it and introduce love where there is supposed to be only law, rule, or habit."[31] What emerged in the limited and liminal space of JNA military bases, away from the ordinary, was not only a seemingly solid category of male comradeship that militaries around the globe strongly propagate, superficial and firmly set within the constraints of "real manliness." An emotional fabric much softer and subtle could emerge precisely because of the liminality of the army world. This fine emotional fabric could be caught by a photographer's eye in periods free of drill, exercises, and ideological education. The very normative masculine space of the all-male institution of the JNA was simultaneously a rare realm in which the kind of expressions of fondness and friendship among men we see in the photographs from Franci Virant's archive from the JNA were possible and socially acceptable (see figures 8.7, 8.8, 8.9, and 8.10).

Writing about the history of male relationships in American culture and overt expressions of emotion between men in photographs, John Ibson outlines a clear temporality in which such expressions were common in the early days of photography, "from daguerreotypes, ambrotypes, cartes de visite, and tintypes, through cabinet cards, simple paper prints, and the enormously popular photographic postcards"—it was customary for two or more American men to pose for a photo together and show intimacy and mutual fondness in it.[32] This cultural practice of expressing emotional attachment among men "appear[s] to have either vanished or became sadly attenuated or redirected"

Figures 8.7, 8.8, 8.9, and 8.10 Army buddies at Polygon C near Osijek, 1980–81.
Photos by Franci Virant.

with modernization, and was replaced with emotional restraint caused by "the fear of being thought gay."[33] Yugoslav socialist society and its military were no exception in setting barriers to overt expressions of feelings among men. But the liminal space of army service, and the even more liminal space of the remote training ground near Osijek, allowed for photographic practices very similar to the visualization of the emotionality of American maleness from the earlier period that Ibson discusses. The playful affection we see in these photographs is not outside of or in opposition to the ritualized reality of JNA barracks, in which young men lived through ritualized and monotonous forms, but in a rather complex relationship with it. This affection was a result of care, mutual help, and friendship woven in the long days of military service, in which young men were far from the extremes of war and violence, but still in a setting in which ritual forms and protocols governed power relations and shaped everyday life. It was also a result of the possibility of mutual recognition based on moral and universalist terms, possibilities also enabled by these standardized forms and protocols that shaped army experience.

Asynchronous with other photographic practices of the time, Franci's affectionate photographic images of young men would hardly have emerged outside the limited and liminal space of military service in the JNA. Similarly, it has not been possible to transfer into "ordinary life" the feelings of affection, solidarity, and care that inhabited the forms of life and wove ties among young Yugoslav men on JNA bases. These feelings were conditioned by proximity and intimacy, which were replaced by physical distance between army friends once they went home after military service was over—and by the different rhythms of everyday life once they resumed their non-uniformed lives. Many of the friendships between very different men would be impossible to form, but also to maintain, outside the JNA, where the uniform and ritualized practices and protocols, working as an equalizer, opened a space for them. These friendships and feelings, although bound to a temporary discrete experience, liminal and placed outside the "normal" and the ordinary, and untransferable to these spheres, keep living their afterlife in the aftermath of Yugoslavia and the catastrophe through which it fell apart. What is more, they exhibit an unexpected agency and a capacity to question the seemingly fixed relationship between the past, present, and future that marks the aftermath. The next chapter focuses on this capacity and on the forms in which it manifests itself.

9

Afterlives

The prevalence of dystopian visions of the future that marks our present makes us increasingly attentive to and interested in past utopian visions and imaginations of a future yet to come that were present in a time when "horizons of utopian possibility" were still open.[1] It hardly comes as a surprise that concepts such as afterlife, remains, traces, debris, ruins, ruination, and archive became keywords in academic works trying to grasp social worlds around the globe. While many scholars use these concepts to explore enduring effects of violence and catastrophe, others follow the ways in which past utopian visions of the future linger in the present. The driving force of this growing body of research comes from the acknowledgment that the relationship between the past, the present, and the future is not fixed and given, as well as from the necessity to think of, imagine, and articulate nonlinear histories that defy the theological notion of universal historical flow.

Among these concepts, *afterlife* has become particularly prevalent, with its usage moving "away from longstanding meanings in religious, archaeological, and art studies," building instead upon Walter Benjamin's reflection on *Nachleben* connected to the idea that "works, lives, languages, and media possess a historicity that cannot be reduced to the continuum of temporal unfolding preferred by the nineteenth-century German historicism associated with such proper names as Leopold von Ranke."[2]

The focus of the new academic interest in afterlives remains on the affective, sensory, bodily, and embodied workings of unresolved traces of the past, but has become increasingly linked to political affects. An important body of this research has been dedicated to the afterlives of socialist projects across the globe and the ability of their material, cultural, and political remains to transmit collective affects across time and space.[3] Unlike aftermath, ruins, residues, remains, relics, or memories, afterlife suggests an agency, not a mere repetition, but "a living on and after that both remains attached to what came before and . . . departs from it in ever-new directions."[4] This is not a mere presence, but one that does something in the present in not always predictable ways. Exploring the afterlife of military service in the Yugoslav People's Army (JNA) in the aftermath of the Yugoslav catastrophe therefore invites us to ask what memories of it *do*, but also what are the *forms* in which their faculty unfolds.

With time inexorably passing, both material and emotional residues of the Yugoslav military become subordinated to the logic of the aftermath. Remnants of military infrastructure were remade to serve other purposes, left to nature to reclaim, or are still objects of contention over property rights.[5] Former JNA soldiers keep living their lives, some even manage to maintain friendships with their army buddies, some reconnect with them after many years. The passage of time allows for recuperation, reconciliation, and healing, but rarely outside the frames in which the possibilities of existence were fixed in the 1990s by ethnic violence.

Spring 2019 marked the twentieth anniversary of the NATO bombardment of Serbia and the conflict in Kosovo, the last stage of the long and painful dissolution of Yugoslavia. It was also twenty years since Mitko Panov ended his quest for his army buddies and boarded a US-bound plane back to his new home. In the former Yugoslav lands, exacerbating ethnic tensions is still a reliable card that politicians eagerly play to remain in power, and too many people still struggle to make ends meet. Still, some kind of normality has returned. Some destroyed houses have been rebuilt, others remain in ruins, left to disintegrate and be overtaken by nature. Borders between the newly independent nation-states that emerged from the wars became fixed and it seems as if they have been there forever. Today, some of these borders are external borders of the European Union. They continue to be sites of violence for many of those fleeing from the Middle East, but local people cross them without the fear and formal complications that were commonplace in the 1990s.[6]

Reunions of former JNA buddies are part of this restored normality. On September 29, 2018, a Serbian internet news portal published an article about two friends from the JNA: a Serb, Branislav Ković from Bogatić, and a Croat, Ivica Krajina from Đakovo, who met again for the first time since their military service in 1984. The article reports that Ivica and Branislav have often thought of each other over the years, especially after the war started and the old country fell apart.[7] Numerous stories of this kind circulate in the post-Yugoslav space in social and digital media. On the page of the Facebook group Pronađi drugove iz bivše JNA (Find friends from the former JNA) that has more than 318,000 members as of summer 2023, there are daily posts that inform readers about encounters between men who were best friends in the army after many years of having no contact or clue about each other's destiny.[8]

Often, these army friends' reunions in the decades after Yugoslavia's disintegration confirm the order of the aftermath, structuring the logic of existence along firmly set lines of ethnic belonging. Almost always marked by hesitation and fear of discovering the tragic destiny of army friends or opening scars that the war has left on their souls, many of the reunions became possible only after enough time had passed since the rupture of the 1990s, when the smoke of burned houses dissipated and when once-imaginable alternatives were irrevocably dismissed. In the reality of the aftermath, these reunions are readable only within the set framework defined by the ethnicity of their actors. The encounter of Branislav and Ivica would not have become media news if they had not been a Serb and a Croat. This is also how they were defined in the article's headline: "A Serb and a Croat, friends from the JNA, met after 34 years: They used to share the good and the bad, were inseparable, and now destiny brought them together again." "Of course, we also talked about divisions, war, and the dissolution of Yugoslavia," reported Branislav and Ivica on their reunion. "As mature and serious persons, we respect that each of us loves his country and nation. Such a degree of nationalism does not harm our friendship."[9] This piece of news about the reunion of former JNA soldiers who befriended each other cannot disrupt or challenge the new, ethnically defined order. It unproblematically fits that order, confirming the completion of the process in which people's biographies were reduced to a single trait: their ethnicity.

The friendships made during military service in Yugoslavia, on the other hand, are also capable of doing important work against this order. This work is related to former Yugoslav men's biographies, and it resists flattening and reducing. Sometimes it complicates the relationship between former JNA soldiers and their past, revealing their biographies as discontinuous and unsettled. Božidar's friendship with Đura did not survive the catastrophe of the 1990s and the new ethnicized reality, with which it was starkly incompatible.

> Now, this is what happened with Đura. After one year of service, I went home, and naturally, at the first opportunity, I headed to Belgrade to find him. So Đura and I met. There were so many tears, we both cried. We revived our memories . . . you know, in the army we had shared everything. But then, in 1990, when the war started and Yugoslavia disintegrated, I called Đura. His wife answered the phone. She told me that Đura did not want to talk to me, that all of us Croats were . . . well . . . Ustaše, and that he would go to Knin to defend his (Serb) brothers.[10] I tried to talk to him, to persuade him that I was also against many things happening in politics at that moment . . . To ask him whether he really believed that I could change after everything we had been through in the army . . . Look, I could not believe what he was saying. We had shared everything. I had met his wife and little kids, and I knew everything about his family. There was no politics there. His name was Đura, my name was Božidar . . . he was like a brother to me. But then the 1990s came . . . I was so disappointed. I do not know what happened to him later, whether he went to Knin or not. We have never been in contact again.

For Božidar, the break-up of his friendship with Đura not only makes the past painfully unrelatable to the present, it also makes it difficult to perceive his own biography as a continuous trajectory, revealing life in the aftermath of the Yugoslav catastrophe as all but based on a fixed and unproblematic relationship between the past, the present, and the future. For many soldiers, on the other hand, friendships resulting from confined and ritualized life on army bases have become an anchor that helps keep together a life that is scattered by the catastrophe of war and violence. Whether maintained over the many years or only carried along life paths as a reminder of social, political, and affective horizons alternative to those that prevail, for many former Yugoslav men, these friendships work as a stitch that binds the past with the present, assuring them that they managed to endure and save what matters most: their moral, virtuous selves and universal human qualities, and the ability to recognize these same qualities in other humans.

When violent conflicts in Yugoslavia started accelerating, Hariz received a phone call from his army friend Đurica, who offered him shelter in his family's home in a remote Serbian village near Rekovac. The offer went unaccepted because Hariz managed to go far away to Australia, escaping the horrifying destiny of most of his male relatives, killed in Srebrenica in 1995. "Because of everything that happened to me and my family, I am not usually keen to hear Serbian pronunciation, but I really like that dialect of central Serbia, because it reminds me of Đurica," Hariz concluded our conversation when we met in Edmonton for the first time. That was the idiom of my own grandparents, who lived in the same area as Đurica, and I wondered if Hariz could recognize familiar linguistic traits in the way I spoke, hidden below other language layers picked up in years of living in Belgrade and then in Ljubljana, where my mother tongue lost most of its local color.

For Hariz, the memory of Đurica holds together two distant, incompatible parts of his life, the one before and the other after the catastrophe in the 1990s, separated by an ocean of loss and pain. Đurica's call, coming from an unexpected place at the moment when Yugoslavia was disintegrating along ethnic lines, remains for Hariz a precious reminder of humanity in the lands he left to escape death and unthinkable destruction. When we met several years later at another conference, this time in the Croatian coastal town of Zadar, and I mentioned Đurica, Hariz's face glowed with surprise and emotions. "You still remember my Đurica!" he said, smiling.

The artists Dejan Dimitrijević and Nebojša Šerić Šoba became friends during their military service in Mali Lošinj. After it ended, their life paths took different directions. When the war started, each coped with the new reality in his own city and in his own way. In Pančevo near Belgrade, Dejan fathered two girls and struggled with the reality of 1990s Serbia as defined by UN sanctions and the lack of such basic goods as diapers and baby food. In 1999, he moved to Canada with his family—first to Montreal and a year later to Toronto, where he still lives. Šoba survived the three-year siege of his home city, Sarajevo, and in 1999 moved to Amsterdam for an art residency and study program. He currently lives in New York City. In 2019, Šoba and Dejan participated in the Museum of Yugoslavia's exhibition *The Nineties: A Glossary of Migrations* in Belgrade, for which they jointly produced a project titled *Then and Now*.[11] Their installation's first part consisted of a map of the world on which different places were connected in a complex net of their intertwined biographical paths. Mali Lošinj, a small town on the island of Lošinj in today's Croatia, where Šoba and Dejan spent the first part of their service in the JNA on the Kovčanje military base and became friends, was the important node on this net. The second part of the installation consisted of two juxtaposed photographs. In the first photograph, taken in Mali Lošinj in 1987 by Nebojša's mother, who came for a visit, the two friends are in JNA uniforms, young, standing close to each other. The second photograph is a reenactment of the first one, shot in 2015 in New York by Dejan's wife. The two men's posture is the same and they stand in an urban space in both photographs. In both of them, portraits of two men are placed against a backdrop of cars, buildings, and flags—a Croatian socialist flag in the first one and some corporate ads in the form of flags in the other. In the second photograph, the two friends are in "civilian" clothes, older than the two uniformed men in the first one, but still recognizable (see figure 9.1).

The link made between then and now, between two moments in their biographies and two places very far away from each other, is clear, made intentionally so by replicating the posture. This link is invaluable and necessary: it points to what is continuous and constant in their fragmented and manifoldly uprooted lives. It points to something close and important, but irretrievable and also very far away. As Šoba put it, "It seems as if it was yesterday, but also three-hundred years ago. And that is why we are making this exhibition." When I met Dejan in Toronto in late summer 2019, he explained to me the intention behind their photographic assemblage: "We wanted to say here we are, it is still us, in spite of everything."

What was constant in the time of ruptures, violent changes, and multiple uprootings that marked the biographies of so many Yugoslav men was who they are, not in terms of ethnicity, but in universal terms of humanity and moral virtue, of being good men. Within the fences of army bases, in conditions defined by the simultaneity of radical sameness and dramatic difference, what mattered and was recognized were men's human characteristics and

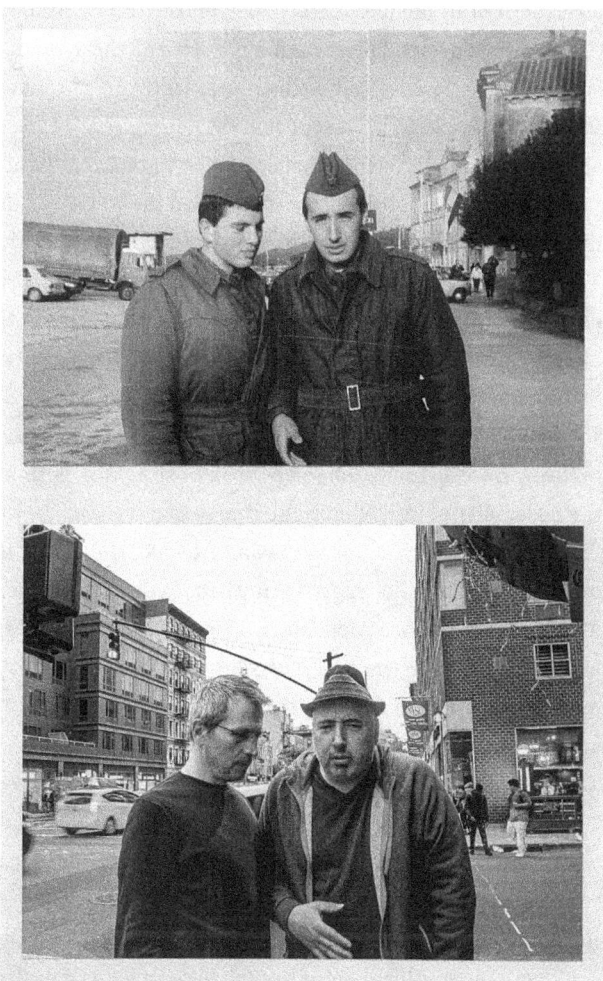

Figure 9.1 Dejan Dimitrijević and Nebojša Šerić Šoba, composite photograph from their installation at the exhibition *The Nineties: A Glossary of Migration*, Museum of Yugoslavia, Belgrade, December 2019.

qualities—what made them men, or humans. Insisting on these qualities also meant managing to preserve themselves in the tumultuous, fractured, and shifting reality of post-Yugoslavia. The desire to preserve oneself and others, to have the possibility of recognizing other men as men, as humans, and because of that as friends, is what one sees in the net of interwoven trajectories of Dejan's and Šoba's life, spanning the distance from Lošinj to North America.

Insisting on the importance of affective ties and friendships made in the confined space of military bases, former JNA soldiers are not blind to all the ambiguities that shaped life through the Yugoslav catastrophe and its aftermath. Talking about his JNA friends from Zagreb, Želimir Žilnik says, "They went through different things during all these years, some of them even supported Tuđman—but we were friends from the army and we remained friends."[12] Božidar, who still regrets deeply that his Serb friend from the army rejected their friendship because he was a Croat (and thus automatically "Ustaša"), joined the Croatian army when the war started. He considered it a moral duty and a way to do everything he could to protect his three daughters. This still did not distort his view of friendship with Đura or of the value of the experience of serving in the JNA. Dejan and Šoba were both mobilized, in two different armies, Dejan in Serbia when the NATO intervention started in 1999, Šoba in Sarajevo during the city's siege from 1992 to 1995. Šoba described what so many men experienced in the 1990s with these words: "Once we woke up in the war, we all found ourselves on opposite sides, without a choice, without the possibility of influencing the course of our lives."

A little-known fact about Srđan Aleksić, the young man whom the soldiers of the Republika Srpska army beat to death when he tried to protect his Muslim acquaintance Alen Glavović in Trebinje in 1993, and who became an anti-war symbol in the post-Yugoslav period, is that, in 1991, Srđan joined a paramilitary unit to fight on the front near Mostar, and "then created, with some friends, his own paramilitary unit, the Trebinje Guard (Trebinjska garda), with which he led a military action on the Dubrovnik front in spring 1992."[13] Alen, on the other hand, was a soldier of the Republika Srpska army—which, according to Nicolas Moll, "was not unusual, especially in Trebinje, where in 1991–92 many Muslims were drafted first into the JNA and then into the Army of Republika Srpska in order to hold the Dubrovnik front."[14]

These biographical details point to complexity, messiness, contestation, troubling coexistence, and uneasy choices—to what constitutes life lived in time of catastrophe. Insisting on their friendships with men with whom they served in the JNA while simultaneously being aware of the many shifts and complex choices each of them had to make, and embracing the ambiguity and disorder inherent to life, men of the former Yugoslavia oppose the logic of the aftermath in which their biographies are often ignored, flattened, and simplified to fit ethnic classifications and adjacent categories of heroes and traitors, victims and perpetrators. They also invite us to look at men in the post-Yugoslav space as men—as complex, insecure, affectionate, troubled, hesitant, and eluding any binary understanding in which they fit either nationalistic, hegemonic masculinity or its opposite.[15]

Recalling recognition and solidarity based on moral and personal qualities, on being virtuous humans and good men, friendships made in the Yugoslav army contradict and question the ethnicized logic of structuring reality established by the Yugoslav wars and normalized in the decades that followed. But the afterlife of friendships made in the JNA in the post-Yugoslav reality, manifesting as a force able to contradict, question, unsettle, and trouble what is given, normalized, and taken for granted, does not lie in what is explicit, preserved, present, revived, maintained, and said. Instead, it unfolds from absence, silence, suspension, hesitation, uncertainty, and impossibility.

We tend to think of the past and the futures that the past used to contain through the forms of presence, duration, and continuity; we access them as residues, legacies, material remains, and cultural reminders. However, the afterlife of friendships made in the JNA and their capacity to question the seemingly fixed relationship between the past, present, and future emerges from discontinuity, from voids and absences that are impossible to fill. In the course of his quest to find his friends from the army, Mitko Panov abandoned his original idea of finishing the film and journey by throwing a reunion party for his army buddies. For a reunion party to make sense, there should be a perception of a continuous passage of time and the possibility of imagining a future that derives naturally from the past and the present. In the post-Yugoslav lands, that natural flow was irreparably disrupted by the violence of the 1990s. For Mitko and his army buddies, Franci and his friends from Polygon C, Oto and his four friends, and other former soldiers connected by ties forged during time spent in the JNA, whatever direction their life paths took, there is no imaginable future in which they can be together beyond the time and space that brought them to JNA military bases, made them all the same, and made them friends. Individually, their lives might take very different paths—some tragic, some sad, some successful. The men in the photographs could become accomplished university professors or artists, hardworking peasants, diligent workers and loving family men . . . or they could be dead or missing. They could emigrate or stay in the places where they grew up, become successful and wealthy, or struggle to make ends meet from one month to another. But the present they live now is not any of the futures they could imagine when they were gathered in the JNA barracks. Those futures were forever lost with the failure of the political project within which they served in the army. As the author's voice tells us at the end of *Comrades*, in the "old photos that made this film come to life, the party is still on. It is still 1981 and the soldiers of the signal company unit in Veles are still celebrating New Year's Eve. We are 18 years old and life is a bright adventure eagerly awaiting us."[16] One cannot move forward, one only keeps returning to that moment, so disconnected with one's present that it is difficult to explain its meaning and importance to anyone else—like the successful Slovenian man who could not possibly explain to his French wife why the remote locality of Žabljak in Montenegro was so important for him. She could not understand the journey he took her on, not only because she was French, but also because of the profound disconnection between the present and the past that renders the meaning and meaningfulness of the man's military service inaccessible.

The friendships made in the JNA live in the present as a lingering reminder of the futures past, pointing to the impossibility of recovering what was in the past and the simultaneous need to constantly return to it.[17] This is what makes these impossible, unreconstructable friendships still alive and important. These remainders of impossibility persist in fragments of life and dispersed geographies that are difficult to put together. Sometimes these diffused geographical paths unexpectedly intersect. In the early 1990s, the Croatian writer Renato Baretić found a postcard from Samarkand in his mailbox, sent by his army buddy Željko Tešanović of Belgrade. They served together in a special mixed artillery battery of navy infantry, first in Trebinje and later in Šibenik, during 1981 and 1982. A trained geometer, Željko fled Serbia to avoid mobilization and ended up working for a construction company in Uzbekistan's capital. Some of his colleagues were traveling to Zagreb and agreed to look for Renato's address and deliver the postcard to him. They personally came to the address and left it in the mailbox. Renato held in his hands the postcard from an army friend, depicting a scene from the faraway city of Samarkand, wrapped in a Russian envelope with Cyrillic characters, with no stamp, that miraculously found him in the middle of the Yugoslav wars. He had no way to write back to Željko back then in 1992, but a year or two later, when Željko moved to Moscow, they exchanged many letters. Renato and Željko saw each other again in Belgrade in 2005, when Renato was visiting for the launch of his first novel.

Mostly, however, in the aftermath of Yugoslavia, its army, and the catastrophe in which they were destroyed, the life of friendships made in the JNA appears in modalities of absence, silence, voids, and hesitation, but also durability, quiet insistence, and perseverance. That life can be seen in Božidar's incapability to accept the fact that his friend rejected him only because they come from two different ethnic groups. "He still constantly speaks of Đura, after all these years they have not been in contact," his daughter told me after I met Božidar in Zagreb. It is also evident in Oto's insistence in keeping the studio photo of himself and his four army buddies in a special place, in spite of his wife's teasing comments. It is there too in the hesitant, but persistent questions Kadri, an Albanian from Kosovo, poses to Mitko Panov about the destiny of Dragan, a Bosnian Serb with whom they were very good friends during their military service in Veles. It can be seen in the unresolvable discrepancy between sporadic, short, almost formulaic messages on Facebook that Hariz and Đurica occasionally exchange from two remote parts of the globe—Melbourne, Australia, and Rekovac, Serbia—and in the deep meaning of connection between two men that bridges the abyss of genocide, violence, and pain. Finally, it exists in the prolonged but never materialized intention to look up and reestablish contact with a friend from the JNA. "My best friend was Zoran, from Srem. He was short and thin, just like me. Zoran was with me during training. Then we went to different places and lost contact. He was a great guy. Zoran Milivojević. I often think about trying to find him." Thus spoke Marko Jevnikar from Ivančna Gorica in Slovenia about his friend from Serbia with whom he spent the first part of his military service in the Croatian town of Karlovac in 1989–90. Radosav similarly told me that he was in phone contact with many of his army buddies, but they had never met since they left the barracks in Maribor in 1984. "Many of them called me, but we have never seen each other again," he said. Similarly, Franci Virant told me: "Each time I drive along the Croatian coast down to Dalmatia, I think of looking for my friend from the army, Duje. But I am always afraid to learn that he fell in the war. This is true also for the other men from my unit."

Marked by the impossibility of recuperating the lost future that was imaginable in the JNA uniform, and the simultaneous need to constantly return to it, friendships made during military service exhibit the capacity to destabilize what seems to be an unquestionable narrative about the past and the present that has no alternative in post-Yugoslav reality. The existence of a man who was a friend, somewhere else in another former Yugoslav republic that is now an independent state, the possibility that a postcard written by him may arrive from a strange and distant place, constantly remind one of a world gone and made impossible by the wars and violence of the 1990s, and of different, but irrevocably vanished, possible futures. Absence, hesitation, suspension—as forms in which these impossible, but durable friendships continue their life in the aftermath—unsettle the past and reveal men's biographies as complex and troubled. They point to a rather unexpected role that the generational experience of serving in the army and its affective archives have in the aftermath of the Yugoslav catastrophe. The postcard from Samarkand that found its way to a mailbox in an apartment building in wartime Zagreb, and all the postcards that were never sent or never found their addressees, a phone call never made but often thought about, a warmth and softness with which names of friends from the army are uttered, a carefully kept photograph—all these forms in which the afterlife of military service in the JNA manifests itself—should not be taken only as a symptom of generational melancholia in which the past can return only as nostalgia.[18] The afterlife of military service in the JNA—with its subtle, silent, but persistent manifestations disrupting the aftermath— also point to an intimation of a political desire, revealing another important faculty of monotonous, standardized, and repetitive forms that shaped the collective male experience of the socialist military: to keep past futures alive.

Epilogue

An Infrastructure for Feelings

The outbreak of the COVID-19 epidemic in 2020 triggered a health crisis in the Yugoslav successor states, painfully exposing yet again the inability of state institutions to take responsible, coordinated action to protect citizens, states' dependence on global power relations, and the devastating consequences of a decades-long neglect of the public health system. In those hectic and chaotic times, former Yugoslavs often recalled and were reminded by the media of how their socialist country dealt efficiently and with good coordination with the smallpox epidemic half a century ago. Yugoslavia could swiftly and efficiently react to the spread of a dangerous virus because "the state was prepared for such emergencies" and "the fight was fought with the joint forces of the experts and the state or, in the language of those times, 'all factors of our society, socio-political communities, and other social organizations at all levels.'"[1] The deadly disease, which had been eradicated decades earlier, was brought to Yugoslavia by Ibrahim Hoti of Đakovica in Kosovo, a pilgrim who returned from Mecca on February 15, 1972. The virus spread to Kosovo, the

Sandžak, Čačak, and Belgrade areas of Serbia, as well as to northern Montenegro. The authorities introduced strict measures, quarantined villages and neighborhoods, closed borders, and prohibited meetings and travel. In early April, through coordinated action in which the Yugoslav People's Army (JNA) provided logistical support, 18.2 million Yugoslavs were vaccinated, and the epidemic ended by the end of the month.[2]

At the same time as numerous texts in the media were critically juxtaposing these two responses to health crises that were fifty years apart, politicians were yet again filling the public space of post-Yugoslav societies with initiatives to reintroduce conscription-based, mandatory military service. In February 2020, marking the twelfth anniversary of Kosovo's independence, newly elected Prime Minister Albin Kurti renewed his old promise to make military service compulsory "because experience and lessons in military service are needed even to cope with the battles of peace."[3] In early 2021, the president of Serbia, Aleksandar Vučić, announced the possibility of reintroducing conscription, and in spring 2022 the possibility became a concrete proposal for a 90-day period of mandatory military service to be introduced starting in 2023.[4] In Slovenia, after two unsuccessful attempts to bring mandatory military service back, the government tried in spring 2021 to change the law on military duty to make it relatively easy to reintroduce conscription in case of "worsening security conditions."[5] Meanwhile, in May 2021, Croatia's defense minister, Mario Banožić, confirmed that the government was considering introducing mandatory military service and stressed its centrality in maintaining the values of "security, stability, serving one's country and the ideals built into foundations of the Croatian army, as well as courage and the desire for safety and unity."[6]

Significant numbers of citizens of the Yugoslav successor states seem to support these state-led initiatives to reintroduce mandatory military service, but their reasons differ from those that state authorities propagate citing vague notions of defense capacity, national security, regional tensions, and national unity. Polls indicate that this support is strongest in the age group of 45 years and older—among citizens who experienced life in socialism firsthand. Most of the supporters do not link the need for mandatory service to security threats coming from the outside. Rather, they point to its importance for teaching youth discipline and providing them with skills for independent life, and they see it as a way to maintain tradition, build a sense of community, fight corruption, and secure a more transparent and credible political system.[7] Post-Yugoslav youth, on the other hand, largely see the states in which they live as incapable, and unwilling, to organize a socially meaningful conscription-based military. Nebojša Radovanović, a twenty-three-year-old man from Belgrade, told Radio Free Europe: "I would go to serve in the army, but in the old one, as it used to be before, where one could learn many things. Today, as far as I am informed, that is not the case."[8] Jelisaveta Petrović stated that she would never fight for the Serbian state: "How could I fight for the state that does not fight for me?" she asked.[9]

The specter of the 1990s still looms from the darkness each time a universal draft is mentioned in the former Yugoslavia, recalling the time when many young men had to hide or leave the country to avoid conscription and being sent to the front line, while many who performed military service, like my schoolmate David, were sent back to their families in coffins. Nevertheless, seeing citizens' support for reinstating mandatory military service exclusively as a sign of the continuous militarization of post-Yugoslav societies, pervasive nationalism that learns nothing from the past, and the prevalence of patriarchal values would be a very partial view, confined by the event-aftermath straightjacket.[10] Current public debates on reintroducing mandatory military service may be alluring for their populist promise to "take things into our own hands," but, like recollections of the efficient handling of the smallpox epidemic in the 1970s, they also point to a desire for an imagination of the state, agency, and political subjectivity different from those that are presently available.

Universal military service and universal vaccination of the population against a contagious disease both presuppose a relationship between individuals and the state in which individual freedoms and choices are not necessarily placed above collective priorities. I remember how in my early teenage years in the mid-1980s, while attending send-offs for my older male relatives, I was perplexed that these boys simply had to go into the army for a year (an amazingly long time in the eyes of a thirteen- or fourteen-year-old girl)—regardless of what they want and plan for their lives or what they are doing at the time. I wondered how this was possible and thought I was lucky that I was not a boy.

How this was possible is still the right question to ask. In socialist Yugoslavia, military service was mandatory for all men, and the efficient containment of the deadly virus and the vaccination of almost the entire population were possible not simply because that is how things were done in illiberal states.[11] Nor do the citizens of former Yugoslav societies refer favorably to these two instances today because they are incapable or politically too "immature" to fully and responsibly embrace liberal democratic values.[12] Rather, the very possibility of these forms of social organization and action resulted from a relationship between citizens and the state based on the idea of collective acting within coordinates that allow for mutual trust, coordination, and coherence.

The political elites of post-Yugoslav societies recognize their citizens' desire for such a relationship with the state and count on it as they keep bringing the topic of mandatory military service into public debates. It is pretty clear that these recurring initiatives are hardly anything more than a populist performance: the possibility of reintroducing mandatory service in any of the post-Yugoslav states is very slim, as these states lack the financial and infrastructural capacities to maintain large numbers of recruits, care for their well-being, and provide for their daily life. Many of the facilities in which JNA soldiers spent their military service are no more. They were repurposed, left to decay or, as in case the Polygon C near Osijek, where Franci spent an important part of his service, destroyed during the conflicts in the 1990s and left in ruins.

Citizens' positive attitudes toward mandatory army service do not result from their naive belief in the feasibility of its restoration or from a shared perception that universal military service would fit well into the existing social and political order. They point rather to what is absent, missing, and impossible within that order: a political community in which they could share values and visions of the future with the state. From Slovenia to Macedonia, citizens increasingly perceive their states as hostile and jeopardizing the very conditions needed for the future by their negligence of bare life and their maltreatment of natural resources. Citizens mobilize and self-organize to prevent the eviction of families from their homes, to protect and preserve water sources, and to demand cleaner air to breathe.[13] The future, once inscribed into the socialist project through industrialization, urbanization, and extensive education, became "an excuse for neoliberal modernity and its state violence" and an object of contention in which the citizens and the state stand on opposite sides.[14]

This change in the nature of the relationship between the state and its citizens, their conflicting imaginations of the future, and the social anxieties this conflict arouses are by no means exclusively a post-socialist condition.[15] But in the case of Yugoslavia they resonate in a specific tonality because of the particular kind of individual and collective agency that was inscribed in the country's "self-management in domestic and non-alignment in international politics," as well as in Yugoslavia's "internal internationalism."[16] The *Enciklopedija samoupravljanja*, or "encyclopedia of self-management," published in Yugoslavia in the late 1970s, defines self-management, "the main principle of social organization in Yugoslavia," not only in terms of social ownership of the means of production and as "a mode of production in which the means of production and management are given back to the subjects of associated labor."[17] It also understands self-management as socially transformative and productive of qualitatively new social relations and social organization. According to the encyclopedia's authors, self-management is "a social relation and a system based on an individual's sense of belonging to the basic values of the society, to qualified and responsible participation and decision-making."[18] It enables "a new social organization in which, truth be told, not everyone can decide about everything, but that makes possible responsible decision-making under conditions of interdependency, mutual social responsibility and solidarity, and that leads to the liberation of individuals."[19] It is, furthermore, "a relation and a system that establish many new human rights," and "a system that, in the sphere of human interrelations, naturally results in the politics of non-alignment."[20] This quote points to the infrastructure for interconnectedness, coordination, and a degree of coherence and mutual trust among different social actors as an important outcome of self-management. This infrastructure made it possible for state authorities, experts, organizations, and citizens to act in coordination against the smallpox epidemic in 1972 in a way that almost seems unreal from the present-day perspective.[21] It also made it possible for parents and military authorities to share care for young men serving in the Yugoslav military.

Coordination and coherence were by no means absolute: the history of the Yugoslav socialist project abounded with internal conflicts, criticism of existing social and political relations, and a restless quest for alternatives and new forms of organization. But most of these alternatives were formed, imagined, and demanded *within* the infrastructure provided by the state and within the ideological horizons of Yugoslav socialism. For example, conceptual performance art practices (which Branislav Jakovljević explores in close relation to the concept of self-management) were developed within a network of state-supported institutions, such as Belgrade's Student Cultural Center (Studenski kulturni centar, or SKC), the Student Center (Studentski centar, SC) in Zagreb, the Student Cultural Center (Študentski kulturni center, ŠKUC) in Ljubljana, and the Youth Tribune (Tribina mladih) in Novi Sad.[22]

Forms of aesthetic practice and social organization are the focus of interest in Jakovljević's study. He claims that "for a brief moment in the aftermath of 1968, and within the confines of state-funded art institutions in Yugoslavia, the protagonists and supporters of conceptualism saw process art and self-management as inextricable, thus bringing into the closest possible proximity two poles of a broad semantic range of 'performance': on one end, an artistic practice largely seen as 'unproductive,' and on the other, industrial production."[23] Jakovljević sees conceptual performance art as an instance par excellence of self-management, while for him the JNA, together with the police and the (communist) Party, stand at the opposite pole: they are "inherently opposed to self-organization and self-management" due to their rigid organization.[24] The forms of organization and life in the JNA were also why Marko Milivojević sees it as contrary to the system of self-management: "The [JNA], in direct contradiction to the principles of self-management society, has always been organised on the basis of hierarchy, ranks, elitist decision making, iron discipline, order, political centralism and extreme conservativism in political, economic, social and ideological matters. The very institution that is the defender of self-management society is, at one and the same time, the *only* institution in which the principles of self-management society have never been applied."[25] The army itself did not deny its remoteness from these principles and the challenges it entailed. As a 1971 volume devoted to cultural life in the JNA states: "A particular problem for young people of our self-managing society is a discontinuity with practices of self-management ... The special circumstances result in almost complete reduction of self-managing activities for a soldier during his army service. A soldier follows a predefined work program, with strictly prescribed content and mode of implementation, and there is no option for him but to realize this program entirely and without objection."[26]

If we move away from the centrality of notions of personal liberties and freedoms that have meanwhile been coopted by neoliberal, individualist ideology and look carefully at the workings of the rigid, strictly prescribed forms of life and organization on JNA bases, we will see, however, that in spite of its organizational and formal rigidity and its paucity of forms—or more precisely, due to these very characteristics—the JNA *was* part of a broader Yugoslav socialist infrastructure that enabled relationships of "interdependency, mutual social responsibility, and solidarity" as well as recognizing self and others beyond frames of being predefined by class, ethnic, or religious identity.[27] This book reveals how the monotonous, repetitive, ritualized, and performative forms, rigid hierarchies, and strictly prescribed protocols that structured the reality of military service in the JNA were able to provide a framework for radically different men to live together in the "closest possible" intimate proximity, as well as the capacity of these forms to generate feelings of solidarity, care, love, and friendship among these different men.

These feelings and their effects in the aftermath of socialist Yugoslavia and its army were at the heart of my interest in this book. A large-scale project of mandatory military service aimed at national cohesion and homogenization was far from being unique to Yugoslavia. Nevertheless, the specific temporality from which we observe the afterlife of military service in the JNA offers a valuable perspective not only for our understanding of the past experience of "socialism in its real, existing form[s]," but also for grappling with our own anxious, fragmented present void of possibilities to collectively imagine the future.[28]

Close attention to the limited range of performative forms and the ways they enable and produce feelings in the controlled, rigid institutional context of the JNA and within the isolated and confined space of army bases and their silent, but powerful afterlife in the aftermath of Yugoslavia offers an insight into Yugoslav socialism and one of its central institutions that acknowledges the complexity of lives of subjects and forms of organization that we often tend to homogenize: socialism, the military, and men. It directs the gaze toward forces that work against the grain of greater historical flows and that refuse to take for granted what is fixed and presented without an alternative in the time following the tragic end of the socialist project.

Exploring the feelings that subtly, but tenaciously question the givenness of the present and the inevitability of historical flows, this book sheds light on the infrastructure that rendered these feelings possible and meaningful during socialism and which persisted through the dramatic shifts that followed. Pointing to the importance of this infrastructure for feelings, I want to widen the scope from structures of feeling (a concept with significant currency in studying social experience in conjunction with political, social, and economic changes, with which Raymond Williams described the "particular quality of social experience and relationship, historically distinct from other particular qualities, which give the sense of a generation or of a period") to the concrete sociopolitical framework that fostered these structures of feeling.[29] I see this infrastructure as a set of political, social, and material conditions that enable certain feelings, recognitions, and imaginations to emerge.[30] As Maria Todorova suggests, the importance of Williams's concept lies in emancipating "the effective component of social reality by suggesting a third layer—affective infrastructure—alongside the social and material infrastructure."[31] But it is also important, particularly for socialism as a historical period and the way we understand and make use of its legacies, to acknowledge that shared socially and politically meaningful and relevant affects could not exist outside the infrastructure connecting institutions and very diverse individuals and enabling them to share visions of society and an imagination of the future. Acknowledging this allows us to approach emotions and their workings in socialism and in its aftermath as resulting from and productive of political and social relations; such an approach to emotions can transcend the still-dominant microanalytical framework and limited focus on individual lives and subjectivities.[32] It opens up an avenue for thinking about socialist and post-socialist emotions, including those intrinsic to JNA service, as resulting from the concrete working of the emancipatory political project, outside depoliticizing interpretative frames of nostalgia, melancholia, and pastness.

The existence of the material, social, and political infrastructure that enabled a collectivity based on interdependency, mutual responsibility, and solidarity, as well as proximity, recognition, and feelings of care, love, and friendship among very different men and women across class, religious, ethnic, cultural, social, and educational boundaries was essential to Yugoslav socialism and self-management as its central organizational principle. It proves to be no less important in our own present, devoid of utopian visions of the future, in which global neoliberalism supported by states that neglect their citizens' dignity, health, and security keeps us confined in fragmented realms defined by identitarian categories. This is what Silvia Federici points to when she warns about the nature of the community we need in the present and for the future: "'Community' is not intended as a gated reality, a grouping of people joined by exclusive interests separating them from others, as with community formed on the basis of religion or ethnicity, but rather as a quality of relations, a principle of cooperation and responsibility to each other, the earth, the forests, the seas, and the animals."[33]

The compulsory, hierarchical, highly structured experience of military service in the country that dissolved into nightmarish violence may not be the most likely place to look for tools to build an alternative and to open collective spaces necessary for imagining a future based on premises different from those that shape our present. After all, every army is about learning to kill. We are being reminded of this fact all over again, and in the 1990s, former JNA soldiers tragically proved that the Yugoslav military was no exception to this pattern. But if we strive for an "education for collective governance and recognition of history as a collective project, which is perhaps the main casualty of the neoliberal era of capitalism," and simultaneously a precondition for regaining the lost capability of utopian imagination, looking back to a socialist military that insisted on bringing together radically diverse people and that created the infrastructure in which they could live, be friends, and care for each other unrestrained by confines of class, status, and ethnicity, and in which they could paint, take photographs, read books, and even write haiku poems, may help us reconsider the limits of our own horizons of the possible and the imaginable.[34]

Notes

INTRODUCTION

1   The *JNA* abbreviation I use in this book was used in Serbo-Croatian and Macedonian (standing for *Jugoslovenska/Jugoslavenska narodna armija*), while in Slovenian *JLA* stood for *Jugoslovanska narodna armada*. The Yugoslav military force was called *Armata Popullore e Jugosllavisë* in Albanian and *Jugoszláv Néphadsereg* in Hungarian.

2   Four locations of clandestine mass graves of Albanians from Kosovo killed in the 1990s by Serbian police, special units, and paramilitary forces have so far been discovered in Serbia—Batajnica, Petrovo Selo, Perućac, and Rudnica—and 941 bodies have been exhumed. In addition, bodies were burned in places like Mačkatica (an aluminum complex near Surdulica), the Feronikl factory in Glogovac, and the Bor mine and smelting basin. See "Secret Mass Graves in Serbia," https://warinserbia .rs/secret-mass-graves-in-serbia/.

3   Milićević, "Joining the War," 266.

4   See, e.g., Archer, Duda, and Stubbs, *Social Inequalities and Discontents*.

5   Patterson, *Bought and Sold*, 38; Taylor and Grandits, "Tourism," 17. Olga Shevchenko argues in her study of post-socialist Moscow that the notion of a "golden age" is not in opposition to crisis and hardship, nor are the boundaries between them clear and fixed (Shevchenko, *Crisis and the Everyday*, 70–71). The same is also true for the Yugoslav "golden years."

6   Koselleck, *Futures Past*; Scott, *Omens of Adversity*.

7   Richter, *Afterness*, 2.

8   Lasch, *True and Only Heaven*; Lowenthal, *Past Is a Foreign Country*; Sontag, *On Photography*. For discussions of the meanings and potentials of nostalgia in the

aftermath of socialism and Yugoslavia, see Velikonja, *Titostalgia*; Petrović, "Nostalgia for the JNA"; Petrović, "When We Were Europe"; Petrović, "Mourning the Lost Modernity"; Petrović, "Toward an Affective History"; Slavković and Đorgović, *Nostalgia on the Move*.

9 Quotation from Gordon, *Ghostly Matters*, 139.

10 Schwenkel, *Building Socialism*, 8.

11 Quotation from Jameson, "American Utopia," 1. See also Scott, *Omens of Adversity*.

12 Hunt, "Afterlives."

13 Scott, *Omens of Adversity*, 13.

14 Derrida, "Archive Fever."

15 Kurtović, "Archive." See also Petrović, *Yuropa*; Dzenovska, "Emptiness."

16 See, e.g., Galjer and Lončar, "Socially Engaged Architecture"; Hofman, "Disobedient"; Kirn, *Partisan Counter-Archive*; Stubbs, "Emancipatory Afterlives"; Štiks, "Activist Aesthetics."

17 Stoler, "Introduction," 9.

18 Richter, *Afterness*, 187.

19 On "rogue archivists," see De Kosnik, *Rogue Archives*.

20 Mbembe, "Power of the Archive," 20.

21 Scarboro, "Living after the Fall," 281.

22 The quoted passages are taken, respectively, from Georgiescu, "Between Trauma and Nostalgia," 285, and Scarboro, "Living after the Fall," 281. The Archives of the Peace Movement, stored in and managed by the Peace Institute in Ljubljana, contain testimonies from men who evaded the draft for the JNA, as well as from conscientious objectors who refused to use weapons during their military service.

23 Cvetkovich, *Archive of Feelings*.

24 Cvetkovich, *Archive of Feelings*, 241.

25 Cvetkovich, *Archive of Feelings*, 7.

26 Quotation from Cvetkovich, *Archive of Feelings*, 9.

27 See Mbembe, "Provisional Notes on the Postcolony," 3.

28 Boyer and Yurchak, "American Stiob"; Mbembe, "Provisional Notes on the Postcolony"; Wedeen, *Ambiguities of Domination*.

29 Kruglova, "Social Theory and Everyday Marxists," 761.

30 Dimitrijević, "In-Between Utopia and Nostalgia," 31.

31 See *Jugoslavija: kako je ideologija pokretala naše kolektivno telo/Yugoslavia: How Ideology Moved our Collective Body*, dir. Marta Popivoda (Serbia/France/Germany, 2013).

32 On subversive affirmation, see Arns and Sasse, "Subversive Affirmation." On *stiob*, see Boyer and Yurchak, "American Stiob," and Yurchak, *Everything Was Forever*. The word *stiob* is the slang term used by Yurchak to refer to "the ironic aesthetic"

and "a peculiar form of irony that differed from sarcasm, cynicism, derision, or any of the more familiar genres of absurd humor. It required such a degree of overidentification with the object, person, or idea at which this stiob was directed that it was often impossible to tell whether it was a form of sincere support, subtle ridicule, or a peculiar mixture of the two. The practitioners of stiob themselves refused to draw a line between these sentiments, producing an incredible combination of seriousness and irony, with no suggestive signs of whether it should be interpreted as the former or the latter, refusing the very dichotomy between the two." (Yurchak, *Everything Was Forever*, 249–50). On Eigensinn, see Lindenberger, "Eigen-Sinn."

33 Yurchak, *Everything Was Forever*, 25, emphasis in original.

34 Kruglova, "Social Theory and Everyday Marxists," 762; Luerhman, *Secularism Soviet Style*.

35 Kruglova, "Social Theory and Everyday Marxists," 766, emphasis added.

36 Yurchak, *Everything Was Forever*, 115.

37 Yurchak, *Everything Was Forever*, 117.

38 Yurchak, *Everything Was Forever*, 121. "The term *svoi*," writes Yurchak, "can mean 'us,' 'ours,' or 'those who belong to our circle.'" It designates a particular form of sociality among young Soviet people "that differed from those represented in authoritative discourse as the 'Soviet people,' 'Soviet toilers,' and so forth" (Yurchak, *Everything Was Forever*, 103).

39 Yurchak, *Everything Was Forever*, 121.

40 Yurchak, *Everything Was Forever*, 121.

41 Benjamin, *Arcades Project*.

42 Hunt, "Afterlives."

43 On the event-aftermath straightjacket in the context of post-colonial Congo, see Hunt, *Nervous State*, 5.

44 Hunt, "Afterlives."

45 Bebler, "Political Pluralism"; Bieber, "Role of the Yugoslav People's Army"; Hadžić, *Sudbina partijske vojske*; Hadžić, "Army's Use of Trauma"; Niebuhr, "Death of the Yugoslav People's Army."

46 Feldman, "Memory Theaters," 165. On the institutional history and technical characteristics of the Yugoslav military, see Marković, *Jugoslovanska narodna armada*; Dimitrijević, *Jugoslavenska narodna armija*; Mikulan and Smutni, *Partizanska vojska*.

47 This is part and parcel of a broader process whose workings are well illustrated by the European Union–funded project significantly named COURAGE (Cultural Opposition—Understanding the Cultural Heritage of Dissent in the Former Socialist Countries). Aimed at connecting collections, this project seemingly unproblematically brings together and into coexistence very different, ideologically sharply opposed people and cultural practices during the socialist period. For example, we

find next to each other Želimir Žilnik (discussed later in this book as a JNA soldier), a prominent filmmaker and part of New Yugoslav Cinema, who was born in a Nazi concentration camp in Niš where his mother was murdered soon after giving birth and his father was killed by Serbian Nazi collaborators; and Zagreb's archbishop Alojzije Stepinac, who supported the Croatian fascist puppet regime during World War II. Dubravka Ugrešić has written poignantly about these revisionist practices; see Ugrešić, "Archaeology of Resistance" (a title she borrowed from the Zagreb exhibition organized in the framework of the COURAGE project).

48 Feldman, "Memory Theaters," 165; see also Petrović, "Mourning the Lost Modernity." On narratives of "larger entities," see Ginzburg, "Microhistory," 31. On naturalization of ruins of modernist utopia as an unexceptional consequence of the end of history, see Blackmar, "Modernist Ruins."

49 Milojević, "Transforming Violent Masculinities." For a broader post-socialist context, see Eichler, *Militarizing Men*; Hallama, "Men and Masculinities."

50 Pankhurst, "Post-War Backlash Violence," 313. See also Fraser, *Military Masculinity*; Cahn and Ni Aolain, "Gender, Masculinities, and Transition"; Hamber, "Masculinity and Transitional Justice"; Moran, "Gender, Militarism, and Peace-Building"; Theidon, "Reconstructing Masculinities."

51 The prevalent normative view of socialism in Europe is strongly informed by the narrative of Europe's two totalitarianisms; see Ghodsee, "Tale of 'Two Totalitarianisms.'" This paradigm significantly influences memory politics in the former Yugoslav societies as well. For an insightful discussion of the consequences of applying the signifier "totalitarian" in the field of Yugoslav art, see Komelj, "Function of the Signifier 'Totalitarianism.'"

52 Cf. Bilić, *LGBT Activism*; Milojević, "Transforming Violent Masculinities"; Niarchos, "Women, War, and Rape"; Schroer-Hippel, *Gewaltfreie Männlichkeitsideale*; Sivakumaran, "Sexual Violence against Men"; Wilmer, *Social Construction*; Žarkov, *Body of War*.

53 Baer, *Spectral Evidence*, 107.

CHAPTER 1. HISTORY, STORIES, AND SELVES

1 Rusinow, "Yugoslav Idea."

2 Rusinow, "Yugoslav Idea," 26.

3 Bertsch, "Ethnicity and Politics," 89. On the abandonment of Yugoslav identity as an alternative to ethnic identities in the 1960s, see Grandits, "Dynamics of Socialist Nation-Building."

4 See Spaskovska, "'Heteroglossia' of Loss," 35.

5 Kirn, *Partisan Ruptures*, 15.

6 Kirn, *Partisan Ruptures*, 15.

7 Bieber, "Role of the Yugoslav People's Army," 302.

8   Milivojević, "Yugoslav People's Army," 2.

9   Milivojević, "Yugoslav People's Army," 5.

10 Milivojević, "Yugoslav People's Army," 14. There was no provision for conscientious objection in socialist Yugoslavia until the mid-1980s, and draft evaders were subject to legal prosecution. Even when conscientious objection was allowed, the status of conscientious objectors was given to religious believers only, and they had to serve in the military but without arms (Garb and Jelušič, "Cultural Gap," 171).

11 Milivojević, "Yugoslav People's Army," 14. Milivojević's stark dichotomy between partisan forces in World War II and the JNA overtly diminishes the Yugoslav character of the partisan liberation forces. While the partisan units were indeed predominantly organized territorially, the broader, Yugoslav framework was inseparable from their operations; separating the Yugoslav idea from what partisans fought for and so many died for is a revisionist take on the history of World War II in Yugoslavia. The legendary First Proletarian Division, for example, had a distinctively multiethnic character. In one of most important battles on the Sutjeska River in eastern Bosnia and Herzegovina, partisans lost more than a third of their number, men and women who were from Croatia, Bosnia and Herzegovina, Serbia, and Montenegro. From the coastal region of Dalmatia in Croatia alone, more than 3,000 partisan fighters lost their lives in the battle.

12 On intertextuality in the context of Rhodesian army conscription, see White, "Civic Virtue," 108.

13 *Vojnikova ljubav*, dir. Svetislav Pavlović (Yugoslavia, 1976).

14 *Nacionalna klasa*, dir. Goran Marković (Yugoslavia, 1979).

15 *Kad sam bio vojnik*, dir. Stjepan Zaninović (TV series), TV Belgrade/Zastava Film, 1969–70; *Vojnici*, dir. Stjepan Zaninović (TV series), Union Film/Zastava Film, 1981.

16 Andersson, "Constructing Young Masculinity," 145, quoting Søndergaard, "Poststructuralist Approaches."

17 On all-male conversations, see Coates, *Men Talk*. On memories of all-male institutions other than the army, see Mouzelis, "On Total Institutions"; MacDougall, *Corporeal Image*.

18 See, e.g., Das, "'Kiss Me, Hardy'"; Herzog, *Brutality and Desire*; Martin, *Napoleonic Friendship*; Smith, *Comrades in Arms*.

19 Mouzelis, "On Total Institutions," 117.

20 Mouzelis, "On Total Institutions," 117.

21 Smith, *Comrades in Arms*, 3.

22 Smith, *Comrades in Arms*, 243.

23 Smith, *Comrades in Arms*, 243.

24 Scott, *Omens of Adversity*, 163.

25 Mazzarella, "Totalitarian Tears," 92, 94.

26 See Kalinin, "'Ugnetennye dolzhny govorit,'" and Kruglova, "Social Theory and Everyday Marxists."

27 Hanka Paldum was a folk-music singer popular in Yugoslavia in the 1980s.

28 Tanja Radež, "Tudi dekleta imamo svoje spomine na vojsko" [Girls also have their army memories], *Ambient* 18, no. 92 (2010): 82.

29 Goran Vojnović, "Ko se združijo celo skini in čefurji" [When skinheads and čefurs join forces], *Dnevnik*, August 14, 2010, https://www.dnevnik.si/1042380470.

30 Coates, *Men Talk*, 45.

31 Coates, *Men Talk*, 45.

32 Jackson, *Unmasking Masculinity*, 221.

33 Palčok, "Uloga aktivne kulturne djelatnosti," 112.

34 Smith, *Comrades in Arms*, 237.

35 Miljenko Jergović, "O romanu" [On the novel *Ništa nas ne smije iznenaditi* by Ante Tomić, 2003], *Karaula*, http://www.karaulafilm.com/novel.php.

36 The term *bilocation* was coined in 1990 by Marina Gržinić and Aina Šmid. See "Bilokacija (Bilocation) (1990)," video, *Grzinic-Smid*, February 12, 2013, http://grzinic-smid.si/?p=271.

37 Žabljak lies in the Durmitor massif in northwest Montenegro. With a population of around 2,000 people, it is located at the highest altitude of any town in the Balkans.

38 Goffman, *Asylums*, 67.

39 Ahlbäck, *Manhood*, 1.

40 Ahlbäck, *Manhood*, 1.

CHAPTER 2. A BARBED-WIRE UTOPIA

1 On the demise of the statist model of revolution, see Federici, "Feminism," 284.

2 See, e.g., for the Habsburg Empire, Deák, *Beyond Nationalism*; Cole, *Military Culture*; Stergar and Scheer, "Ethnic Boxes."

3 Krebs, *Fighting for Rights*; Ingesson, "Conscription, Citizenship, and Democracy."

4 Stover, "Armed Forces and Nation Building," 323, 324.

5 On the JNA in the 1980s and 1990s, see Bieber, "Role of the Yugoslav People's Army," 301.

6 MacLeish, *Making War*, 18.

7 On the Soviet/Russian military, see Eichler, *Militarizing Men*.

8 Quotation from Al-Qazzaz, "Army and Society," 144.

9 A sad reflection of this fact can be found in a 1993 newspaper article on the integration of refugees from Bosnia and Herzegovina in Slovenia. The article suggests that most of the refugees would probably never go back to ethnically cleansed territories. "This is particularly true for intellectuals who do not behave like classical refugees in Slovenia, but attempt to integrate into society. Many businessmen, actors

and other artists, journalists, and former politicians came to Slovenia with their families, and their children go to Slovenian schools. It is very improbable they will ever go back home. These people used to declare as Yugoslavs and as such they will hardly find peace in nationally strictly segregated environments" (Petra Vovk, "Da južnjaci ne postanu Slovenci" [Southerners should not become Slovenians], *Borba*, September 30, 1993).

10 Vukićević, "Koherentnost nacionalnih kultura."

11 Bjelajac, *Jugoslovensko iskustvo*, 13.

12 Zimmermann, *Origins of a Catastrophe*, 64.

13 *Gastarbeiter* (*gastarbajteri*, as they were colloquially called) were Yugoslav labor migrants who left to work in Western European countries in the 1960s and 1970s (see Le Normand, *Citizens without Borders*).

14 Jones, *Red Army and Society*, 35–36, quoted by Eichler, *Militarizing Men*, 19.

15 Eichler, *Militarizing Men*, 24.

16 On military service and Yugoslav citizenship, see Oliwia Berdak, "You're in the Army, Now," *Citizenship in Southeast Europe*, October 29, 2012, http://www.citsee.eu/node/104.

17 On female combatants during World War II, see Batinić, *Women and Yugoslav Partisans*; Pantelić, "Yugoslav Female Partisans." As Erica L. Fraser writes, in the Soviet Union, women were similarly "quickly demobilized at the end of 1945 and were not permitted to re-enlist," despite their "exemplary service in all fields, including combat" (Fraser, *Military Masculinity*, 6). See also Krylova, *Soviet Women*.

18 Vratuša et al., *Enciklopedija samoupravljanja*, 829.

19 Miletić, "Predvojnička obuka u Jugoslaviji."

20 See Milivojević, "Yugoslav People's Army," 22.

21 "Naša Lidija je pri vojakih, je Radgončanka" [Our Lidija is in the army and she is from Radgona], *Pomurec*, January 25, 2017, https://www.pomurec.com/vsebina/41434/Nasa_Lidija_je_pri_vojakih__je_Radgoncanka_.

22 The abbreviation SMB stands for *sivomaslinasta boja* (grey-olive color), used in the JNA for infantry uniforms.

23 Despite the extensive participation of women, anxiety over their presence and negative attitudes toward them were not alien to the partisan units during World War II either. In the biography of Josip Broz Tito's last wife, Jovanka Broz (née Budisavljević), who had also been a partisan, Đuro Zagorac writes about the first female fighting unit from Lika (*Prva ženska lička četa*), composed exclusively of young, unmarried women, that Jovanka joined in August 1942. Seventy-five young female partisans fought shoulder to shoulder with their male comrades and exhibited extraordinary braveness and efficiency. Zagorac quotes the words of Đoko Jovandić, "a legendary partisan commander from Lika," who stressed, "It is exactly their braveness that led to risks and danger." He also mentions jokes circulating among partisans about the "hollow unit," which made him even surer that this unit

should be dismantled and the young female fighters sent to other units and assigned the more traditional tasks of nurses and orderlies (Zagorac, *Jovanka*, 14–15).

24 Janjatović, *Ilustrovana YU rock enciklopedija*, 103.

25 "Ženske—vojaki že julija" [Women—soldiers already in July], *Dogovori* 11, no. 5 (1983), http://www.dlib.si/?URN=URN:NBN:SI:doc-J92DGM3H.

26 *Naša vojska*, March 9, 1984. The newspaper was published by the 5th military district (covering Slovenia and part of Croatia).

27 Dota, *Javna i politička povijest muške homoseksualnosti*, 305.

28 As Dota points out, Yugoslavia was not only more liberal in this respect than other socialist countries, but also many European ones. Over the period between 1951 and 1977, around 520 men were convicted of homosexuality in Yugoslavia, while in less-populated Austria, 12,000 persons were convicted during the same period (Franko Dota, "Homoseksualnost u socijalističkoj Jugoslaviji: Za 'muški protuprirodni blud' išlo se u zatvor" [Homosexuality in socialist Yugoslavia: For male sodomy one would go to jail], *Klix.ba*, February 12, 2016, https://www.klix.ba/lifestyle/homoseksualnost-u-socijalistickoj-jugoslaviji-za-muski-protuprirodni-blud-islo-se-u-zatvor/160212073).

29 "Kad partija raspravlja o seksualnom moralu" [When the party discusses sexual morals], an interview with Franko Dota by Helena Puljiz, *XXZ*, December 20, 2017, https://www.xxzmagazin.com/kad-partija-raspravlja-o-seksualnom-moralu.

30 Požgaj-Hadži, "Language Policy," 62; see also Radovanović, *Planiranje jezika*, 47; Naylor, "Sociolinguistic Situation," 80.

31 See, e.g., Avšič, "Za enakopravnost slovenskega jezika"; Avšič, "O poveljevalnem jeziku NOB Slovenije."

32 See Jan, "O problemima kulturnog života"; Vukićević, "Koherentnost nacionalnih kultura."

33 Korošec et al., *Vojaški slovar*.

34 Vukićević, "Koherentnost nacionalnih kultura," 97; Jan, "O problemima kulturnog života," 101.

35 Ali Žerdin gives a detailed account of reactions in Slovenia to the military trial. See Žerdin, *Generali brez kape*; see also Bugarski, *Jezik u društvenoj krizi*, 31.

36 Avšič, "Pismo zvezni ustavni komisiji." This was the first time the letter was published. This issue of *Časopis za kritiko znanosti* was dedicated to the topic of the "equality of languages in the military forces."

37 Avšič, "Pismo zvezni ustavni komisiji," 33.

38 Koleva, *Biografija i normalnost*, 40.

39 For a similar framing of military service, albeit in very different political circumstances, see White, "Civic Virtue."

40 Koleva, *Biografija i normalnost*, 51–52.

41 See Abram, "Na koži pisana Jugoslavija," 70.

42 Verdery, "Socialist Societies," 849.

43 Tikhomirov, "Grammar of Trust and Distrust," 327. The quotation is from Pine, "Inside and Outside," 100.

44 The British historian E. P. Thompson participated in one of the Youth Labor Actions, spending a month on the building of the Šamac-Sarajevo railway in 1947 as leader of the British brigade. The next year, together with other brigadiers, he published a booklet of impressions of Yugoslavia. The texts offer a valuable insight into the qualitatively new relations built through joint labor on the railway. See Thompson, *Railway*.

45 Observers have often questioned the voluntary character of the Youth Labor Actions, claiming either that there was a significant degree of coercion or that volunteers sought direct personal benefit from participation—getting a better workplace, an opportunity to enroll at university, and so on. E. P. Thompson also addressed this issue, writing: "The part which these strong national organisations, assisted by the schools, played in the recruitment campaign may seem to have put a measure of compulsion on the volunteers. This is quite true. But the compulsion was the moral pressure of a society whose total effort was directed to reconstruction. It may be fairly compared with the social pressure on a young man in a nation engaged in a fight for its independence, when no conscription exists and volunteers are wanted at the front. And this is only a fair comparison when it is understood that the pressure came not only from society, but from the conscience and inclinations of the individual as well" (Thompson, *Railway*, 12–13).

46 Quoted from the documentary film *Comrades/Jarani*, dir. Mitko Panov (Macedonia, United States, 2000).

47 *Rani radovi/Early Works*, dir. Želimir Žilnik (Yugoslavia, 1969).

48 See, e.g., Galjer and Lončar, "Socially Engaged Architecture."

49 Žilnik and Buden, *Uvod u prošlost*, 133.

50 Quotation from Dzenovska, "Emptiness," 11. See also Miljački, "Once Upon a Time"; Kulić, "Orientalizing Socialism."

51 Plato, *Republic*; Jameson, "American Utopia."

52 Jameson, "American Utopia," 19.

53 Jameson, "American Utopia," 30.

54 Jameson, "American Utopia," 28.

55 See Jameson, "American Utopia," 58. In *Comrades/Jarani* (dir. Mitko Panov), the JNA is described as "the army of peace."

56 Jameson, "American Utopia," 61.

57 On the army as a vehicle for the fraternization of classes, see Jameson, "American Utopia," 62. Yugoslav socialism strove, not always successfully, to come close to the ideal of social equality and classlessness, but what characterizes its four-and-a-half-decade history is its intense and overt dealing with and attempts to overcome social

inequalities, ethnic tensions, and conflicts. See, e.g., Archer, Duda, and Stubbs, *Social Inequalities and Discontents*; Jelača, Kolanović, and Lugarić, *Cultural Life of Capitalism*.

CHAPTER 3. THE ROUTINE

1   Milivojević, "Yugoslav People's Army," 13–14.

2   Quotation from Deakin, *Embattled Mountain*, 103. William Deakin was a British historian and the leader of the British military mission to Tito's headquarters.

3   "Intervention impérative," December 27, 1944, "Notes by Koča Popović 1922–1953," file no. 3, Legacy of Konstantin-Koča Popović and Leposava-Lepa Perović, Historical Archives of Belgrade.

4   "Operations," March 1945, "Notes by Koča Popović 1922–1953," file no. 3, Legacy of Konstantin-Koča Popović and Leposava-Lepa Perović, Historical Archives of Belgrade.

5   See "Za učvršćenje vojske" [To solidify the army], November 11, 1945; notebook dated May 11, 1947; notes for the lecture on discipline in the army, 1953, all in "Notes by Koča Popović 1922–1953," file no. 3, Legacy of Konstantin-Koča Popović and Leposava-Lepa Perović, Historical Archives of Belgrade.

6   Nenadović, *Razgovori s Kočom*, 13. Although his decision was made in France, Popović was not alone among Yugoslav Surrealists in making it. As Dubravka Đurić writes, "Most Surrealists quit the avant-garde experiments after 1933 and turned to socially engaged and critical writing affiliated with the revolutionary politics of the Communist Party of Yugoslavia" (Đurić, "Radical Poetic Practices," 76).

7   In the early 1980s, Slovenian critics of the JNA, led by Janez Janša, then president of the Alliance of Socialist Youth of Slovenia, argued that the army's insistence on unquestioned discipline and mechanical memorization had resulted in the underrepresentation of Slovenian officers among JNA staff. Critics also complained that Slovenian recruits were forced to abandon the principles of self-management, although it was supposed to be at the core of Yugoslav socialist ideology. See Miroslav Lazanski, "Anatomija jednog pacifizma" [Anatomy of pacifism], *Danas* 160, March 12, 1985, quoted in Dumančić, "He Who Does Not Serve," 103.

8   The acronym PAP M59 stands for *poluautomatska puška M59*. With regard to meals, SDO stands for *suvi dnevni obrok* (lit. "dry daily meal," a ready-made field ration) and GG9 derives from *goveđi gulaš*, or beef ragu. Meanwhile, SMB stands for *sivomaslinasta boja* (lit. "olive-grey color"); RAP is an abbreviation of *rezervni alat i pribor* ("spare tools and accessories"); and DRNČ is an abbreviation of *deterdžentni rastvor za naslage čađi/za nerđajući čelik* ("detergent solution for deposits of soot/non-rusting metal"). *Požarni* is a "person on duty," and *četni evidentičar* is a "unit record keeper," or company clerk.

9   For understandings of habituation that diverge from the behaviorist model of stimulus-response chains, see, e.g., Bourdieu, *Social Structures*; Akrivou and

Todorow Di San Giorgio, "Dialogical Conception." I further discuss the relationship between habits and affect in chapter 8.

10 MacLeish, *Making War*, 12.

CHAPTER 4. THE UNIFORM

1   On "mortification," see Goffman, *Asylums*, 14.

2   Hajiyski, "Psichologiya na voennata disciplina," 222, 226.

3   Smith, *Comrades in Arms*, 107.

4   *O ljubavnim veštima ili film sa 14,441 kvadratom* [On love skills or a film with 14,441 frames], dir. Karpo Aćimović Godina (Yugoslavia, 1972).

5   Zastava Film was established in Belgrade in 1948 as a film production unit in the JNA (Odeljenje za proizvodnju filmova Jugoslovenske armije u Beogradu). Its output encompassed but was not limited to short educational films and pieces of reportage on life in the Yugoslav army. Zastava Film was the largest and most important producer of both short documentary and feature films in socialist Yugoslavia. After Yugoslavia disintegrated, it became a documentation and film center of the Serbian military.

6   Quoted from "Godina i 18 minuta: KORNET intervju sa Karpom Godinom," *Kornet*, February 16, 2015, https://www.kornet.rs/2015/02/16/godina-i-18-minuta-kornet -intervju-sa-karpom-godinom/.

7   *Zdravi ljudi za razonodu* [Healthy people for fun], dir. Karpo Aćimović Godina (Yugoslavia, 1971).

8   Despite the order by JNA officials to destroy the film, it was preserved and is available at https://www.youtube.com/watch?v=cZlm4UIpOPU.

9   The song was written and performed by the alternative, provocative duo Laboratorija zvuka braće Vranešević (Vranešević Brothers' Sound Laboratory).

10 Dukovski, *Povijest Pule*, 249.

11 For most of these towns, the massive presence of the military in urban space was easily noted on city maps. For Bitola and Skopje, see Stilinović, Cattoor, and De Meulder, "Mapping the Realms."

12 Stilinović, Cattoor, and De Meulder, "Mapping the Realms."

13 Bonfiglioli, *Women and Industry*, 48.

14 *Variola Vera*, dir. Goran Marković (Yugoslavia, 1982).

15 Ljubiša Samardžić was a famous Yugoslav actor.

16 According to one of my interviewees, "All over Yugoslavia, JNA soldiers were exempt from paying for tickets for public transport, but not in Pula, because there were more soldiers than civilians in this city."

17 *Kad sam bio vojnik* [When I was a soldier], dir. Stjepan Zaninović, TV Belgrade/ Zastava Film, 1969–70. Quotation from episode 1, "*Dobro nam došli*" [Welcome].

18 GDJNA, *Vojnici—likovni umetnici 1972*. See also Radišić, *Vojaki*.

19 GDJNA, *Vojnici—likovni umetnici 1966*. On soldiers' participation in the exhibition *Vojnici—likovni umetnici*, see MCO, *Umetnička zbirka Doma vojske Srbije*, 24. Before the mid-1960s, soldiers could use their free time to work as artists, but then it became an integral part of their duties.

20 Quotations respectively from GDJNA, *Vojnici—likovni umetnici 1974*; GDJNA, *Vojnici—likovni umetnici 1966*. The 1968 exhibition catalog stressed that the repertoire could be widened to also address war and struggles for liberation (MCO, *Umetnička zbirka Doma vojske Srbije*, 24).

21 GDJNA, *Vojnici—likovni umetnici 1966*.

22 GDJNA, *Vojnici—likovni umetnici 1968*.

23 GDJNA, *Vojnici—likovni umetnici 1972*.

24 Quoted from Urša Matos, "Biografija (kdo je kdaj): Slavoj Žižek," *Mladina*, October 24, 2004, https://www.mladina.si/96679/nar-kdo_je_kdaj--ursa_matos/.

25 Zoran Predin, "Dvojni vid in sveža voda v prahu" [Double vision and fresh powdered water], *Dnevnik*, September 10, 2016, https://www.dnevnik.si/1042750778.

26 Both *burek* and *sirnica* are traditional pastries, filled with minced meat and cheese.

27 Bell, *Ritual Theory*, 217; Butler, *Gender Trouble*; Yurchak, *Everything Was Forever*.

28 Wedeen, *Ambiguities of Domination*; Yurchak, *Everything Was Forever*, 17.

29 Jullien, *On the Universal*, 10–11.

30 Although feelings of humiliation and self-degradation are usually associated with mortification and uniforming in the context of mandatory military service, these were not constitutive of estrangement in accounts of former JNA soldiers. In another context, drawing on his own experience of military service in Greece, the sociologist Nicos Mouzelis questions the universal character of mortification, emphasizing that in the context of the Greek military, "mortification processes are neither perceived nor experienced as self-degrading" (Mouzelis, "On Total Institutions," 116).

CHAPTER 5. THE RITUAL

Parts of this chapter were previously published as "Portraits of Yugoslav Army Soldiers: Between Partisan and Pop-Culture Imagery," in *Partisans in Yugoslavia: Literature, Film and Visual Culture*, ed. Miranda Jakiša and Nikica Gilić, 137–56 (Bielefeld: Transcript, 2015).

1 Quotation from Bell, *Ritual Theory*, 209.

2 Bourdieu, *Logic of Practice*, 18, quoted by MacDougall, *Corporeal Image*, 106.

3 Quotation from Bell, *Ritual Theory*, 197.

4 Foucault, "The Subject and Power," 219.

5 Feuchtwang, "Ritual and Memory."

6 Bloch, "Symbols, Song, Dance," 63.

7 Bloch, "Symbols, Song, Dance," 63.

8   Bell, *Ritual Theory*, 206.

9   Here, the term *restricted code* does not figure in a strictly Bernsteinian sense, as it is related more to the highly ordered, formalized, and repetitive reality of military service than to the limitations of forms of speech conditioned by speakers' social background. Nevertheless, in the restricted reality of JNA bases, huge social differences among soldiers exposed the limitations of expressive means available to those from lower social strata (Dušan Mandić's reuse of another soldier's letter to his girlfriend discussed below being an interesting example of such exposure). On restricted code, see Bernstein, *Class, Codes and Control*.

10 Regarding micro-politics, see Foucault, "Body/Power."

11 Mandić, "A Short Discourse on Painting," 141.

12 Podlesnik, "Die verkehrte Welt," 20.

13 Podlesnik, "Die verkehrte Welt," 20.

14 This view was also one of the central narratives of the Slovenian critique of socialist Yugoslavia in the 1980s, as I outlined in chapter 1.

15 The Slovenian groups IRWIN and NSK to which Mandić belonged were both known for extensive use of overidentification.

16 Yurchak, *Everything Was Forever*, 250. On subversive affirmation, see Arns and Sasse, "Subversive Affirmation"; on *stiob*, see Boyer and Yurchak, "American Stiob"; Yurchak, *Everything Was Forever*.

17 See also Rasa Baločkaitė, "Post-Soviet Mimicry: Grotesque but Empowering," *New Eastern Europe*, July 26, 2016, http://neweasterneurope.eu/2016/07/26/post-soviet -mimicry-grotesque-but-empowering/; Bhabha, "Of Mimicry and Man"; Onyeoziri, *Shaken Wisdom*.

18 Bell, *Ritual Theory*, 197.

19 Bell, *Ritual Theory*, 207.

20 Abram, "Na koži pisana Jugoslavija."

21 *Karaula/The Border Post*, dir. Rajko Grlić (UK/Serbia/Croatia/Slovenia/Macedonia/ Bosnia and Herzegovina/Hungary/Austria, 2006). Although an artistic "reenactment" of life in the JNA, this film had the ambition of "authentically" depicting that life, including the language that was used in the army. I write about this film and its reception in detail in chapter 7.

22 Vesna Zmijanac was a popular folk music diva in Yugoslavia in the 1980s.

23 Bloch, "Symbols, Song, Dance," 64, emphasis in original.

24 See Bell, *Ritual Theory*, 211.

25 Bloch, "Symbols, Songs, Dance," 64. See also, Bell, *Ritual Theory*, 212.

26 On the website Skarabej (www.skarabej.com), an online museum of old family photographs, along with numerous photographs of JNA soldiers there are also portraits of soldiers from all around the world (the United States, Great Britain,

Germany, Japan, etc.), as well as portraits taken in the former Yugoslav lands, but in earlier periods.

27 On soldier portrait photographs generally, see Willis, "Search for Self," 118–19. In her study of World War I postcards, Christine Brocks also discusses those in the form of soldiers' portraits (Brocks, *Die bunte Welt des Krieges*).

28 Spiegelman, *Maus*, 134. See also Hirsch, *Family Frames*, 38.

29 Posted April 15, 2011, http://www.kolekcionari.com/showthread.php?t=10564. The URL is no longer active.

30 *Svečana obaveza* [The solemn oath], dir. Božidar Nikolić (Yugoslavia, 1986).

31 Samuel, *Theatres of Memory*, 369.

32 Appadurai, "Colonial Backdrop," 4.

33 Appadurai, "Colonial Backdrop," 4.

34 Sandžak is a predominantly Muslim-populated border region between Serbia and Montenegro.

35 Gatalo, *Slika sa uspomenom*, 72. The English translations from Gatalo's novel are mine.

36 Gatalo, *Slika sa uspomenom*, 72.

37 As Corinne Kratz points out, realism is not necessarily an inherent feature of portrait photography. On the contrary, "as photographic practice developed in the United States in the late 1830s, the extreme lifelike quality of daguerreotypes was seen as a *hindrance* to portraiture. Photographic conventions that distinguished between portrait and a mere likeness developed in the 1840s, drawing on portrait conventions in other media" (Kratz, *Ones That Are Wanted*, 118). See also Trachtenberg, *Reading American Photographs*, 24–26.

38 Appadurai, "Colonial Backdrop," 4.

CHAPTER 6. DISSOLUTION OF FORM

1 Quotations from Gal, "Semiotics," 87.

2 Garb and Jelušič, "Cultural Gap," 171.

3 Milošević, "Prilog proučavanju vojnog pitanja," 99–100; Bebler, "Socialist Countries."

4 Scott, *Omens of Adversity*, 129.

5 Boris M. Gombač, himself the father of a JNA soldier who served in Split when the war started, described the chronology of the activities of the Slovenian parents committee and published the testimonies of several Slovenian soldiers who served in the JNA in Gombač, *Na drugi strani*.

6 Gombač, *Na drugi strani*, 80.

7 Dragojević, *Amoral Communities*, 33.

8 Dragojević, *Amoral Communities*, 33.

9   Dragojević, *Amoral Communities*, 33.

10 Sven Milekić, "Amoral Communities: How Ethnic Identity Prevailed in Croatia's War," interview with Mila Dragojević, *BALKAN TRANSNATIONAL JUSTICE*, November 1, 2019, https://balkaninsight.com/2019/11/01/amoral-communities-how-ethnic-identity-prevailed-in-croatias-war/.

11 These photographs are reproduced in Štravs, *Photographic Incarnations*.

12 Gržinić, "Štravs' Photographic Incarnations," 8.

13 The quoted phrase is from Kratz, *Ones That Are Wanted*, 1.

14 Tagg, *Burden of Representation*, 36–37.

15 Weidman, "Anthropology and Voice," 43.

16 Sekula, "Body and the Archive."

17 Sekula, "Body and the Archive," 11.

18 Galton, *Inquiries into Human Faculty*, quoted in Sekula, "Body and the Archive," 7.

19 Gržinić, "Štravs' Photographic Incarnations," 8.

20 Sekula, "Body and the Archive," 7.

21 Gržinić, "Štravs' Photographic Incarnations," 7.

22 Goran Duplančić's autobiographical graphic novel tells a poignant story of fear and being lost, but also of solidarity, care, and friendship in the life of JNA soldiers trapped on the JNA military base in Šentvid in Slovenia in the spring of 1991. See Duplančić, *Vojna*.

INTERLUDE. THE CATASTROPHE

1   "Med napadi na JLA v Splitu ubili makedonskega vojaka" [Amid attacks on the JNA in Split, a Macedonian soldier was killed], *Večerno Delo*, May 7, 1991.

2   Hariz describes his "war paths" in Halilovich, *Kako opisati Srebrenicu*.

3   Ivančić, Polan, and Stjepanović, *Killing Culture*.

4   Moll, "Positive Hero," 3.

5   Moll, "Positive Hero," 20.

CHAPTER 7. THE AFTERMATH

Parts of this chapter were previously published as "Nostalgia for the JNA? Remembering the Army in the Former Yugoslavia," in *Post-Communist Nostalgia*, ed. Maria N. Todorova and Zsuzsa Gille, 61–81 (Oxford: Berghahn Books, 2010).

1   *Comrades/Jarani*, dir. Mitko Panov (USA/Macedonia, 2000).

2   *Comrades/Jarani*, dir. Mitko Panov (USA/Macedonia, 2000).

3   Scott, *Omens of Adversity*, 4, 6.

4   Scott, *Omens of Adversity*, 6.

5   Dedić, "Yugoslavia," 170. See also Horvat and Štiks, *Welcome to the Desert*.

6 Hunt, *Nervous State*, 5.

7 The comment was posted on a forum on Index.hr, December 4, 2004, http://www
.index.hr/forum/default.aspx?q=t&idf=21&idt=21986&p=3. The URL is no longer
active.

8 "Prekrivanje starih tetovaža (Cover tattoo)" [Concealing old tattoos], Tattoo Studio "Zile," January 29, 2011, http://ziletattoostudio.blogspot.com/2011
/01/prekrivanje-starih-tetovaza-cover.html. See also Abram, "Na koži pisana
Jugoslavija."

9 *Kako je počeo rat na mom otoku* [How the war started on my island], dir. Vinko
Brešan (Croatia, 1996).

10 *Outsider*, dir. Andrej Košak (Slovenia, 1997).

11 Petrović, "Officers without an Army."

12 Hadžić, *Sudbina partijske vojske*, 179.

13 Ljubica Spaskovska, "The Forgotten Soldiers of the Dead Country," *Balkanist*, February 8, 2017, https://balkanist.net/the-forgotten-soldiers-of-a-dead-country/.

14 Vukušić, *Serbian Paramilitaries*.

15 Sztandara, "Expired Places."

16 Blitz, "Statelessness," 462.

17 "Synopsis," *The Border Post*, http://www.borderpostmovie.com/synopsis.php. The
film's scenario has been published as a book together with Tomić's novel: see Tomić,
Ništa nas ne smije iznenaditi; Grlić and Tomić, *Karaula*.

18 Rajko Grlić, "Director's Statement," *The Border Post*, http://www.borderpostmovie
.com/directors_statement.php.

19 Željko Luketić, "Rajko Grlić: Karaula" [Rajko Grlić: *The Border Post*], http://www
.mikrokino.net/osvrt_arh.asp?counter=15#100. The URL is no longer active.

20 Vesna Milek, "Kodak je prefin trak za politiko" [Kodak is too subtle for politics],
interview with Rajko Grlić, *Delo, Sobotna priloga*, April 15, 2006, 24.

21 Luketić, "Rajko Grlić."

22 *Good Bye, Lenin!*, dir. Wolfgang Becker (Germany, 2003). Quotation from Berdahl,
"Goodbye, Lenin," 183.

23 Andrej Gustinčič, "Brez nostalgije in ljubezni" [Without nostalgia and love], *Delo,
Sobotna priloga*, April 23, 2006, 28.

24 Quotation from Van Dijck, *Mediated Memories*, 13.

25 Williams, *Marxism and Literature*, 122.

26 Boris Dežulović, "Jedan od tisuću" [One in a thousand], *Slobodna Dalmacija*, December 9, 2014.

27 This is how Split's mayor Andro Krstulović Opara described the protest in
May 2021, announcing a roundtable discussion to commemorate the event on the
occasion of its thirtieth anniversary.

28 Spaskovska, "Forgotten Soldiers."

29 Dženana Halimović, "Here are the Faces of Thousands Who Died in Srebrenica: About Project," *Radio Free Europe/Radio Liberty*, July 2015, https://www.rferl.org /a/27114531.html#.

30 Arsenijević, "Politics of Memory," 217.

31 See, e.g., Arsenijević, *Forgotten Future*.

32 Halilovich, "Reclaiming Erased Lives," 241.

33 Halilovich, "Reclaiming Erased Lives," 241–42.

34 Halilovich, "Reclaiming Erased Lives," 242.

35 Both quotations from Halilovich, "Reclaiming Erased Lives," 242. See also Kristin Deasy and Dzenana Halimovic, "After Hague Destroys Srebrenica Evidence, Survivors Feel Pain of Lost Memories," *Radio Free Europe/Radio Liberty*, September 3, 2009, https://www.rferl.org/a/1814205.html.

36 Halilovich, "Reclaiming Erased Lives," 237.

37 Halilovich, "Reclaiming Erased Lives," 242.

38 In 1971, Muslims were proclaimed a constitutive nation of socialist Yugoslavia. See Knežević, "Inhabitants," 140.

39 See the Facebook group Pronađi drugove iz bivše JNA [Find comrades from the former JNA], https://www.facebook.com/groups/1426107641004634/permalink /2440166496265405/.

CHAPTER 8. FORM AND LIFE

1 Brinkema, *Forms of the Affects*, xv; Wetherell, *Affect and Emotion*, 13.

2 Brinkema, *Forms of the Affects*, xv.

3 Wetherell, *Affect and Emotion*, 13.

4 The first quotation comes from Blackman, "Habit and Affect," 186; the second is from Pedwell, *Revolutionary Routines*, 116. On the relationship between patterns, habits, routines, and rituals, on the one hand, and social transformation on the other, see also, e.g., Pedwell, *Revolutionary Routines*; Candiotto and Dreon, "Affective Scaffoldings"; Akrivou and Todorow Di San Giorgio, "Dialogical Conception."

5 Wedeen, *Ambiguities of Domination*.

6 Yurchak, *Everything Was Forever*, 3.

7 Yurchak, *Everything Was Forever*, 5.

8 Yurchak, *Everything Was Forever*, 25.

9 Yurchak, *Everything Was Forever*, 21. See also Yurchak, "Soviet Hegemony," 482.

10 Yurchak, "Soviet Hegemony," 485.

11 Yurchak, "Soviet Hegemony," 481.

12 Quotation from Gržinić, "Štravs' Photographic Incarnations," 7.

13 Gržinić, "Štravs' Photographic Incarnations," 7.

14 Quoted from the gallery display text next to the *Private and Cross* installation.

15 Quoted from the gallery display text next to the *Private and Cross* installation.

16 *Comrades/Jarani*, dir. Mitko Panov (USA/Macedonia, 2000).

17 Kingston, "Subversive Friendships," 7. The opening quotation is from Ibson, *Picturing Men*, 4.

18 MacDougall, *Corporeal Image*, 97–98.

19 MacDougall, *Corporeal Image*, 100.

20 "Srbin i Hrvat, ratni drugovi iz JNA, sreli se posle 34 godine: Nekada su delili dobro i zlo, bili nerazdvojni, a sada ih je život opet spojio" [A Serb and a Croat, friends from the JNA, met after 34 years: They used to share the good and the bad, were inseparable, and now destiny brought them together again], *Telegraf*, September 29, 2018, https://www.telegraf.rs/vesti/srbija/2995369-srbin-i-hrvat-ratni-drugovi-iz -jna-sreli-se-posle-34-godine-nekada-su-delili-dobro-i-zlo-bili-nerazdvojni-a-sada -ih-je-zivot-opet-spojio-foto.

21 Boris Buden, "Jeton i ja u JNA" [Jeton and I in the JNA], Leksikon YU Mitologije, http://www.leksikon-yu-mitologije.net/jeton-ja-u-jna/.

22 Carrier, "People," 21.

23 Kingston, "Subversive Friendships."

24 Ibson, *Picturing Men*, 119.

25 Bernstein, *Class, Codes, and Control*, 59.

26 *Oružane snage Socijalističke federativne republike Jugoslavije.*

27 Kingston, "Subversive Friendships."

28 Michel Foucault, "Friendship as a Way of Life," trans. John Johnston, *Caring Labor*, November 18, 2010, https://caringlabor.wordpress.com/2010/11/18/michel-foucault -friendship-as-a-way-of-life/.

29 Smith, *Comrades in Arms*, 200.

30 Foucault, "Friendship as a Way of Life."

31 Foucault, "Friendship as a Way of Life."

32 Ibson, *Picturing Men*, 1.

33 Ibson, *Picturing Men*, 7, 5.

CHAPTER 9. AFTERLIVES

1 Bloch, *Principle of Hope*, 202. See also Schwenkel, *Building Socialism*, 4.

2 Richter, *Afterness*, 2–3. The first quote is taken from Hunt, "Afterlives." Hayes and Gilburt speak of the afterlife of the image or "other lives of the image," which are "plural, distinct, discrete, and happening in 'liquid time'" (Hayes and Gilburt, "Other Lives of the Image," 13).

3 Schwenkel, *Building Socialism*; Paul Stubbs, "The Emancipatory Afterlives of Non-Aligned Internationalism," *Rosa Luxemburg Stiftung*, January 2020, https://www

.rosalux.de/en/publication/id/41631/the-emancipatory-afterlives-of-non-aligned -internationalism.

4   Richter, *Afterness*, 4.

5   Falski, "Who Has the Right to Decide?"; Kardov, Knežević, and Rogoznica, *Kome pripadaju bivše vojne nekretnine.*

6   Isakjee et al., "Liberal Violence"; El-Shaarawi and Razsa, "Movements upon Movements"; Rexepi, "Arab Others."

7   "Srbin i Hrvat, ratni drugovi iz JNA, sreli se posle 34 godine," *Telegraf,* September 29, 2018.

8   See the Facebook group Pronađi drugove iz bivše JNA (Find friends from the former JNA), https://www.facebook.com/profile.php?id=1426107641004634&ref=br_rs.

9   "Srbin i Hrvat, ratni drugovi iz JNA, sreli se posle 34 godine."

10 The Ustaše was a Croatian fascist and nationalist organization that collaborated with the Nazis during World War II and ruled the fascist puppet-state Independent State of Croatia (NDH). The name was also used as a derogatory term for Croatian nationalists during the 1990s.

11 For the Museum of Yugoslavia's exhibition, see https://www.muzej-jugoslavije.org /en/exhibition/devedesete-recnik-migracija/.

12 Franjo Tuđman (1922–99) was a Croatian nationalist politician, the first president of Croatia after independence and the founder of the Croatian nationalist party, the Croatian Democratic Union (HDZ).

13 Moll, "Positive Hero," 13.

14 Moll, "Positive Hero," 13.

15 The anthropologist Stef Jansen similarly highlights this mutual recognition of men *as men* as an important aspect of postwar reality in Bosnia and Herzegovina. See Jansen, "Of Wolves and Men."

16 *Comrades/Jarani*, dir. Mitko Panov (USA/Macedonia, 2000).

17 On futures past, see Koselleck, *Futures Past.*

18 Scott, *Omens of Adversity*, 126.

EPILOGUE

1   Vučetić, *Nevidljivi neprijatelj*, 78, 82. As Vučetić points out, the medical institutions and doctors were also well prepared because Yugoslav doctors were able to gain expertise in fighting infectious and tropical diseases through cooperation in the framework of the Non-Aligned Movement (Vučetić, *Nevidljivi neprijatelj*, 125).

2   Vučetić, *Nevidljivi neprijatelj*, 42. See also Sabina Ferhadbegović, "Past and Present Health Crises: How Yugoslavia Managed the Smallpox Epidemic of 1972," *Cultures of History*, July 22, 2020, https://www.cultures-of-history.uni-jena.de/focus /kleio-in-pandemia/past-and-present-health-crises-how-yugoslavia-managed-the -smallpox-epidemic-of-1972/.

3   Xhorxhina Bami, "Kurti Vows to Make Military Service Compulsory in Kosovo," *Balkan Insight*, February 17, 2020, https://balkaninsight.com/2020/02/17/kurti-vows-to-make-military-service-compulsory-in-kosovo/.

4   See "Vučić: Razgovarali smo o vraćanju obaveznog vojnog roka" [Vučić: We spoke about bringing mandatory military service back], *Danas*, January 28, 2021, https://www.danas.rs/drustvo/vucic-razgovarali-smo-o-vracanju-obaveznog-vojnog-roka/; Gordana Ćosić, "Obavezni vojni rok u Srbiji: Za i protiv" [Mandatory military service in Serbia: pros and cons], *Radio Slobodna Evropa*, May 10, 2022, https://www.slobodnaevropa.org/a/srbija-vojni-rok/31843110.html.

5   "Bo vojaški rok spet obvezen? Za uveljavitev dovolj že navadna večina poslancev" [Will military service be mandatory? A simple majority of parliament members would suffice to reinstate it], *24UR*, April 13, 2021, https://www.24ur.com/novice/slovenija/obvezni-vojaski-rok.html.

6   "Ministar obrane potrvdio: Razmišlja se o vraćanju obaveznog vojnog roka" [Defense minister confirmed: Reinstating mandatory military service is being considered], *Poslovni dnevnik*, May 26, 2021, https://www.poslovni.hr/hrvatska/ministar-obrane-potvrdio-razmislja-se-o-vracanju-obaveznog-vojnog-roka-4289390.

7   Ignjatijević, Elek, and Pavlović, *Naoružavanjem protiv bele kuge, kriminala i korupcije*, 7; "Obvezni vojni rok: Svi u dobi od 16 do 45 godina trebaju iskusiti vojsku" [Mandatory military service: everyone between 16 and 45 years should experience the military], *Dnevnik*, April 26, 2016, https://dnevnik.hr/vijesti/hrvatska/obvezni-vojni-rok-uvesti-ga-ili-ne---434898.html.

8   Ćosić, "Obavezni vojni rok u Srbiji."

9   Ćosić, "Obavezni vojni rok u Srbiji."

10 Hunt, *Nervous State*, 5.

11 David Scott's insights into memory politics and transitional justice mechanisms in the aftermath of the violent end of Grenada's socialist project strongly resonate with the aftermath of the post-Yugoslav situation and post–Cold War normativity, in which liberal democracy is perceived as the only viable political option, the one exempt from crime, while the transition from illiberal to liberal rule is "understood as the single direction of an acceptable political future" (Scott, *Omens of Adversity*, 128). For an enlightening analysis of (post-)Yugoslav, post-socialist transition, see Buden, *Zone des Übergangs*.

12 Writing about the consequences of the transitional ideology in Eastern Europe, Boris Buden emphasizes that this region "after 1989 resembles a landscape of historical ruins that is inhabited only by children, immature people unable to organize their lives democratically without guidance from another," and warns that "the notion 'children of communism' is . . . not a metaphor. Rather it denotes the figure of submission to the new form of 'historical necessity' that initiates and controls the process of the post-communist transition. On these premises, the transition to democracy starts as a radical reconstruction out of nothing" (Buden, "Children of Post-Communism," 133).

13 See Ivan Rajković, "Rivers to the People: Ecopopulist Universality in the Balkan Mountains," *Fieldsights*, March 24, 2020, https://culanth.org/fieldsights/rivers-to-the-people-ecopopulist-universality-in-the-balkan-mountains."; Larisa Kurtović, "Riverine Struggles against Plunder and Dispossession: Water Defenders in Postwar Bosnia-Herzegovina," *Europe Now*, May 18, 2022, https://www.europenowjournal.org/2022/05/17/riverine-struggles-against-plunder-and-dispossession-water-defenders-in-postwar-bosnia-herzegovina/.

14 Rajković, "Future Snatchers."

15 Pierre Bourdieu famously spoke about the right and the left hand of the modern state. The left hand is a caring one offering health protection, education, and welfare provisions, while the right hand is a repressive one, which is "obsessed by the question of financial equilibrium, knows nothing of the problems of the left hand, confronted with the often very costly social consequences of 'budgetary restrictions.'" According to Bourdieu, "One of the main reasons for all these people's despair is that the state has withdrawn, or is withdrawing, from a number of sectors of social life for which it was previously responsible: social housing, public service broadcasting, schools, hospitals, etc." (Droit and Ferenczi, "Left Hand"). The pandemic globally exposed disastrous consequences of this withdrawal and the abyss standing between the real social, political, and economic conditions that the neoliberal state creates and what citizens need, desire, and hope for.

16 Jakovljević, *Alienation Effects*, 8, 178.

17 Vratuša et al., *Enciklopedija samoupravljanja*, 876.

18 Vratuša et al., *Enciklopedija samoupravljanja*, 876.

19 Vratuša et al., *Enciklopedija samoupravljanja*, 876.

20 Vratuša et al., *Enciklopedija samoupravljanja*, 876. See also Jakovljević, *Alienation Effects*, 6.

21 Vučetić, *Nevidljivi neprijatelj*, 180.

22 Jakovljević, *Alienation Effects*, 28.

23 Jakovljević, *Alienation Effects*, 5.

24 Jakovljević, *Alienation Effects*, 288.

25 Milivojević, "Yugoslav People's Army," 15.

26 Palčok, "Uloga aktivne kukturne djelatnosti," 111.

27 Vratuša et al., *Enciklopedija samoupravljanja*, 876. Amateurism was another important element of this infrastructure: amateur practices in which various segments of the Yugoslav citizenry engaged in factories, amateur clubs, worker and popular universities, and cultural centers brought two modes of production (artistic and industrial) into the closest possible proximity and also, and this is particularly important, relativized and challenged class-based divisions. The Western understanding of amateurism is bound to categories of private space and free time; Yugoslav amateurism, in contrast, as philosopher and sociologist Rudi Supek points out, reconciled two usually opposed social tendencies: individual creative

expression on the one hand, and belonging to the collective on the other (Supek, "Sociološki značaj amaterizma").

28 Quote from Jakovljević, *Alienation Effects*, 2.

29 Williams, *Marxism and Literature*, 131, 133. For examples of analyses centered on structures of feeling, see Bonfiglioli, *Women and Industry*; Bonfiglioli, "Post-Socialist Deindustrialisation"; Strangleman, "Deindustrialisation."

30 Ruth Wilson Gilmore, on the other hand, speaks of infrastructure of feeling in the context of the Black Radical Tradition to point to the ways ideology and actions that feelings enable or constrain become material. For her, the infrastructure of feeling is a "consciousness-foundation, sturdy but not static, that underlies our capacity to select, to recognize viscerally (no less than prudently) immanent possibility as we select and reselect liberatory lineages—in a lifetime . . . as well as between and across generations" (Gilmore, *Abolition Geography*, 490).

31 Todorova, *Imagining Utopia*, 172; Sharma and Tygstrup, *Structures of Feeling*, 2.

32 Todorova, *Imagining Utopia*, 174.

33 Federici, "Feminism," 289.

34 Quotation from Federici, "Feminism," 289.

Bibliography

Abram, Sandi. "Na koži pisana Jugoslavija: Tetovaže iz Jugoslavenske narodne armije i naracije s poviješću oslikanog tijela" [Yugoslavia written on the skin: Tattoos from the Yugoslav People's Army and narratives of the body inscribed with history]. *Etnološka tribina* 36, no. 43 (2013): 65–80.

Ahlbäck, Anders. *Manhood and the Making of the Military: Conscription, Military Service and Masculinity in Finland, 1917–39*. Farnham, UK: Ashgate, 2016.

Akrivou, Kleio, and Lorenzo Todorow Di San Giorgio. "A Dialogical Conception of Habitus: Allowing Human Freedom and Restoring the Social Basis of Learning." *Frontiers in Human Neuroscience* 8 (2014): 1–4.

Al-Qazzaz, Ayad. "Army and Society in Israel." *Pacific Sociological Review* 16, no. 2 (1973): 143–65.

Andersson, Kjerstin. "Constructing Young Masculinity: A Case Study of Heroic Discourse on Violence." *Discourse and Society* 19, no. 2 (2008): 139–61.

Appadurai, Arjun. "The Colonial Backdrop." *Afterimage* 24 (1997): 4–7.

Archer, Rory, Igor Duda, and Paul Stubbs, eds. *Social Inequalities and Discontents in Yugoslavia*. London: Routledge, 2016.

Arns, Inke, and Sylvia Sasse. "Subversive Affirmation: On Mimesis as a Strategy of Resistance." In *NSK from Kapital to Capital*, edited by Zdenka Badovinac, Eda Čufer, and Anthony Gardner, 266–76. Ljubljana: Moderna Galerija; Cambridge, MA: MIT Press, 2015.

Arsenijević, Damir. *Forgotten Future: The Politics of Poetry in Bosnia and Herzegovina*. Baden-Baden: Nomos Verlaggesellschaft, 2010.

Arsenijević, Damir. "A Politics of Memory and Knowledge Production in Bosnia and Herzegovina: The Case for Studije Jugoslavije." In *Conflict and Memory: Bridging*

Past and Future in (South East) Europe, edited by Wolfgang Petritsch and Vedran Dzihic, 215–23. Baden-Baden: Nomos Verlaggesellschaft, 2010.

Avšič, Jaka. "O poveljevalnem jeziku NOB Slovenije" [On the language of command in the national liberation struggle of Slovenia]. *Jezik in slovstvo* 4 (1969): 97–103.

Avšič, Jaka. "Pismo zvezni ustavni komisiji" [A letter to the federal constitutive commission]. *Časopis za kritiko znanosti* 91/92 (1986): 23–41.

Avšič, Jaka. "Za enakopravnost slovenskega jezika" [For the equality of the Slovenian language]. *Jezik in slovstvo* 3 (1967): 96–97.

Baer, Ulrich. *Spectral Evidence: The Photography of Trauma*. Cambridge, MA: MIT Press, 2002.

Batinić, Jelena. *Women and Yugoslav Partisans: A History of World War II Resistance*. Cambridge: Cambridge University Press, 2015.

Bebler, Anton. "Political Pluralism and the Yugoslav Professional Military." In *The Tragedy of Yugoslavia: The Failure of Democratic Transformation*, edited by Jim Seroka and Vukašin Pavlović, 105–40. London: Routledge, 1992.

Bebler, Anton. "Socialist Countries of Eastern Europe: The Old Orders Crumble." In *The New Conscientious Objection: From Sacred to Secular Resistance*, edited by Charles Moskos and John Whiteclay Chambers II, 167–74. Oxford: Oxford University Press, 1993.

Bell, Catherine. *Ritual Theory, Ritual Practice*. Oxford: Oxford University Press, 1992.

Benjamin, Walter. *The Arcades Project*, translated by Howard Elland and Kevin McLaughlin. Cambridge, MA: Belknap Press of Harvard University Press, 2002.

Berdahl, Daphne. "Goodbye, Lenin! Aufwiedersehen GDR: On the Social Life of Socialism." In *Post-Communist Nostalgia*, edited by Maria Todorova and Zsuzsa Gille, 177–89. Oxford: Berghahn Books, 2010.

Bernstein, Basil. *Class, Codes, and Control*. Vol. I, *Theoretical Studies towards a Sociology of Language*. London: Routledge, 2003.

Bertsch, Gary K. "Ethnicity and Politics in Socialist Yugoslavia." *Annals of the American Academy of Political and Social Science* 433 (1977): 88–99.

Bhabha, Homi. "Of Mimicry and Man: The Ambivalence of Colonial Discourse." *October* 28 (1984): 125–33.

Bieber, Florian. "The Role of the Yugoslav People's Army in the Dissolution of Yugoslavia: The Army without a State." In *State Collapse in South-Eastern Europe: New Perspectives on Yugoslavia's Disintegration*, edited by Lenard J. Cohen and Jasna Dragović-Soso, 301–32. West Lafayette, IN: Purdue University Press, 2008.

Bilić, Bojan, ed. *LGBT Activism and Europeanisation in the Post-Yugoslav Space: On the Rainbow Way to Europe*. London: Palgrave Macmillan, 2016.

Bjelajac, Mile. *Jugoslovensko iskustvo sa multietničkom armijom 1918–1991* [Yugoslav experience with a multiethnic army 1918–1991]. Belgrade: Udruženje za društvenu istoriju, 1999.

Blackman, Lisa. "Habit and Affect: Revitalizing a Forgotten History." *Body and Society* 19, nos. 2/3 (2013): 186–216.

Blackmar, Elizabeth. "Modernist Ruins." *American Quarterly* 53, no. 2 (2001): 324–39.

Blitz, Brad K. "Statelessness and the Social (De)Construction of Citizenship." *Journal of Human Rights* 5 (2006): 453–79.

Bloch, Ernst. *The Principle of Hope*, vol. 1, translated by Neville Plaice, Stephan Plaice, and Paul Knight. Cambridge, MA: MIT Press, 1986.

Bloch, Maurice. "Symbols, Song, Dance and Features of Articulation: Is Religion an Extreme Form of Traditional Authority?" *European Journal of Sociology* 15, no. 1 (1974): 54–81.

Bonfiglioli. Chiara. "Post-Socialist Deindustrialisation and its Gendered Structure of Feeling: The Devaluation of Women's Work in the Croatian Garment Industry." *Labor History* 61 (2020): 36–47.

Bonfiglioli, Chiara. *Women and Industry in the Balkans: The Rise and Fall of the Yugoslav Textile Sector*. London: I. B. Tauris, 2020.

Bourdieu, Pierre. *The Logic of Practice*, translated by Richard Nice. Stanford, CA: Stanford University Press, 1990.

Bourdieu, Pierre. *The Social Structures of the Economy*, translated by Chris Turner. Cambridge: Polity Press, 2005.

Boyer, Dominic, and Alexei Yurchak. "American Stiob: Or, What Late-Socialist Aesthetics of Parody Reveal about Contemporary Political Culture in the West." *Cultural Anthropology* 25, no. 2 (2010): 179–221.

Brinkema, Eugenie. *The Forms of the Affects*. Durham, NC: Duke University Press, 2014.

Brocks, Christine. *Die bunte Welt des Krieges: Bildpostkarten aus dem Ersten Weltkrieg 1914–1918* [The colorful world of the war: Postcards from World War I, 1914–1918]. Essen: Klartext, 2008.

Buden, Boris. "Children of Post-Communism." In *Welcome to the Desert of Post-Socialism: Radical Politics after Yugoslavia*, edited by Srećko Horvat and Igor Štiks, 123–39. London: Verso, 2015.

Buden, Boris. *Zone des Übergangs: Vom Ende der Postkommunismus* [Transition zone: About the end of post-communism]. Frankfurt am Main: Suhrkamp, 2009.

Bugarski, Ranko. *Jezik u društvenoj krizi* [Language in social crisis]. Belgrade: Čigoja štampa, 1996.

Butler, Judith. *Gender Trouble: Feminism and the Subversion of Identity*. New York: Routledge, 1990.

Cahn, Naomi R., and Fionnuala D. Ni Aolain. "Gender, Masculinities, and Transition in Conflicted Societies." *New England Law Review* 44, no.1 (2010): 101–23.

Candiotto, Laura, and Roberta Dreon. "Affective Scaffoldings as Habits: A Pragmatist Approach." *Frontiers in Psychology* 12 (2021): 1–14.

Carrier, James G. "People Who Can Be Friends: Selves and Social Relationships." In *The Anthropology of Friendship*, edited by Sandra Bell and Simon Coleman, 21–38. Oxford: Berg, 1999.

Coates, Jennifer. *Men Talk: Stories in the Making of Masculinities*. Malden, MA: Blackwell Publishing, 2003.

Cole, Laurence. *Military Culture and Popular Patriotism in Late Imperial Austria*. Oxford: Oxford University Press, 2014.

Cvetkovich, Ann. *An Archive of Feelings*. Durham, NC: Duke University Press, 2003.

Das, Santanu. "'Kiss Me, Hardy': Intimacy, Gender and Gesture in First World War Trench Literature." *Modernism/Modernity* 9 (2002): 51–74.

Deák, István. *Beyond Nationalism: A Social and Political History of the Habsburg Officer Corps, 1848–1918*. Oxford: Oxford University Press, 1992.

Deakin, Frederick William. *The Embattled Mountain*. London: Oxford University Press, 1971.

Dedić, Nikola. "Yugoslavia in Post-Yugoslav Artistic Practices: Or, Art as . . ." In *Post-Yugoslav Constellations: Archive, Memory, and Trauma in Contemporary Bosnian, Croatian, and Serbian Literature and Culture*, edited by Vlad Beronja and Stijn Vervaet, 169–90. Berlin: De Gruyter, 2016.

De Kosnik, Abigail. *Rogue Archives: Digital Cultural Memory and Media Fandom*. Cambridge, MA: MIT Press, 2016.

Derrida, Jacques. "Archive Fever: A Freudian Impression." *Diacritics* 25, no. 2 (1995): 9–63.

Dimitrijević, Bojan. *Jugoslavenska narodna armija u Hrvatskoj i Sloveniji 1945–1968* [The Yugoslav People's Army in Croatia and Slovenia 1945–1968]. Zagreb: Despot Infinitus, 2017.

Dimitrijević, Branislav. "In-Between Utopia and Nostalgia, or How the Worker Became Invisible on the Path from Shock-Worker to Consumer." In *Nostalgia on the Move*, edited by Mirjana Slavković and Marija Đorgović, 30–41. Belgrade: Museum of Yugoslavia, 2017.

Dota, Franko. "Javna i politička povijest muške homoseksualnosti u socijalističkoj Hrvatskoj (1945–1989)" [Public and political history of male homosexuality in socialist Croatia (1945–1989)]. PhD diss., University of Zagreb, 2017.

Dragojević, Mila. *Amoral Communities: Collective Crimes in the Time of War*. Ithaca, NY: Cornell University Press, 2019.

Droit, R. P., and T. Ferenczi. "The Left Hand and the Right Hand of the State." Interview with Pierre Bourdieu. *Variant*, no. 32 (2008). https://www.variant.org.uk/32texts/bourdieu32.html.

Dukovski, Darko. *Povijest Pule* [History of Pula]. Pula: Nova Istra, 2011.

Dumančić, Marko. "He Who Does Not Serve Is Not Fit for a Wife: The Problems of Military Service and Late Socialist Masculinity in 1980s Yugoslavia." *The Soviet and Post-Soviet Review* 50 (2023): 91–118.

Duplančić, Goran. *Vojna* [The war]. Zagreb: Barbatus, 2021.

Đurić, Dubravka. "Radical Poetic Practices: Concrete and Visual Poetry in the Avant-garde and Neo-avant-garde." In *Impossible Histories: Historical avant-gardes, Neo-avant-gardes and Post-avant-gardes in Yugoslavia, 1918–1991*, edited by Dubravka Đurić and Miško Šuvaković, 64–95. Cambridge, MA: MIT Press, 2003.

Dzenovska, Dace. "Emptiness: Capitalism without People in the Latvian Countryside." *American Ethnologist* 47, no. 1 (2020): 10–26.

Edensor, Tim. *Industrial Ruins: Spaces, Aesthetics and Materiality*. Oxford: Berg, 2005.

Eichler, Maya. *Militarizing Men: Gender, Conscription, and War in Post-Soviet Russia*. Stanford, CA: Stanford University Press, 2012.

El-Shaarawi, Nadia, and Maple Razsa. "Movements upon Movements: Refugee and Activist Struggles to Open the Balkan Route to Europe." *History and Anthropology* 30, no. 1 (2019): 91–112.

Falski, Maciej. "Who Has the Right to Decide? Pula and the Problem of Demilitarized Urban Zone." *Philological Studies—Literary Research* 12, no. 9 (2019): 135–48.

Federici, Silvia. "Feminism and the Politics of the Commons in an Era of Primitive Accumulation." In *Uses of a Whirlwind: Movement, Movements, and Contemporary Radical Currents in the United States*, edited by Craig Hughes, Stevie Peace, and Kevin Van Meter, 283–93. Oakland, CA: AK Press, 2010.

Feldman, Allen. "Memory Theaters, Virtual Witnessing, and the Trauma-Aesthetic." *Biography* 27, no. 1 (2004): 163–202.

Feuchtwang, Stephan. "Ritual and Memory." In *Memory: Histories, Theories, Debates*, edited by Susannah Radstone and Bill Schwartz, 281–98. New York: Fordham University Press, 2010.

Foucault, Michel. "Body/Power." In *Power/Knowledge: Selected Interviews and Other Writings 1972–1977*, edited by Colin Gordon, 55–62. New York: Pantheon, 1980.

Foucault, Michel. "The Subject and Power." In *Michel Foucault: Beyond Structuralism and Hermeneutics*, edited by Hubert L. Dreyfus and Paul Rabinow, 2nd ed., 208–26. Chicago: University of Chicago Press, 1983.

Fraser, Erica L. *Military Masculinity and Postwar Recovery in the Soviet Union*. Toronto: University of Toronto Press, 2019.

Gal, Susan. "A Semiotics of the Public/Private Distinction." *differences* 13, no. 1 (2002): 77–95.

Galjer, Jasna, and Sanja Lončar. "Socially Engaged Architecture of the 1950s and Its Transformations: The Example of Zagreb's Workers' University." *Etnološka tribina* 42 (2019): 194–222.

Galton, Francis. *Inquiries into Human Faculty and Its Development*. London: Macmillan, 1883.

Garb, Maja, and Ljubica Jelušič. "The Cultural Gap between the Military and the Parent Society in Slovenia." *Contributions to Conflict Management, Peace Economics and Development* 2 (2005): 171–92.

Gatalo, Veselin. *Slika sa uspomenom* [A photo with memory]. Sarajevo: Mauna-Fe, 2009.

GDJNA (Galerija Doma Jugoslovenske narodne armije). *Vojnici—likovni umetnici 1966* [Soldiers—figurative artists 1966], exhibition catalog. Belgrade: Galerija Doma Jugoslovenske narodne armije, 1966.

GDJNA. *Vojnici—likovni umetnici 1968* [Soldiers—figurative artists 1968], exhibition catalog. Belgrade: Galerija Doma Jugoslovenske narodne armije, 1968.

GDJNA. *Vojnici—likovni umetnici 1972* [Soldiers—figurative artists 1972], exhibition catalog. Belgrade: Galerija Doma Jugoslovenske narodne armije, 1972.

GDJNA. *Vojnici—likovni umetnici 1974* [Soldiers—figurative artists 1974], exhibition catalog. Belgrade: Galerija Doma Jugoslovenske narodne armije, 1974.

Georgiescu, Diana. "Between Trauma and Nostalgia. The Intellectual Ethos and Generational Dynamics of Memory in Postsocialist Romania." *Südosteuropa* 64, no. 3 (2016): 284–306.

Ghodsee, Kristen. "Tale of 'Two Totalitarianisms': The Crisis of Capitalism and the Historical Memory of Communism." *History of the Present* 4, no. 2 (2014): 115–42.

Gilmore, Ruth Wilson. *Abolition Geography: Essays towards Liberation*. London: Verso, 2022.

Ginzburg, Carlo. "Microhistory: Two or Three Things That I Know about It," translated by John and Anne C. Tadeschi. *Critical Inquiry* 20, no. 1 (1993): 10–35.

Goffman, Erving. *Asylums: Essays on the Social Situation of Mental Patients and Other Inmates*. Garden City, NY: Anchor Books, 1961.

Gombač, Boris M. *Na drugi strani: Odbor staršev za varstvo in vrnitev slovenskih vojakov ob slovenski samosvojitvi leta 1991* [On the other side: The Committee of Parents for the Protection and Return of Slovene Soldiers in the period of Slovenia's gaining independence in 1991]. Ljubljana: Založba ZRC, 2005.

Gordon, Avery. *Ghostly Matters: Haunting and the Sociological Imagination*. Minneapolis: University of Minnesota Press, 2008.

Grandits, Hannes. "Dynamics of Socialist Nation-Building: The Short-Lived Programme of Promoting a Yugoslav National Identity and Some Comparative Perspectives." *Dve domovini* 27 (2008): 15–28.

Grlić, Rajko, and Ante Tomić. *Karaula: scenarij* [Border post: A screenplay]. Zaprešić: Fraktura, 2006.

Gržinić, Marina. "Štravs' Photographic Incarnations." In *Jane Štravs: Photographic Incarnations*, 7–9. Ljubljana: Založba ZRC, 2003.

Hadžić, Miroslav. "The Army's Use of Trauma." In *Road to War in Serbia: Trauma and Catharsis*, edited by Nebojša Popov, 509–34. Budapest: Central European University Press, 2000.

Hadžić, Miroslav. *Sudbina partijske vojske* [Destiny of a party army]. Belgrade: Samizdat B92, 2001.

Hajiyski, Ivan. "Psihologiya na voennata disciplina" [Psychology of military discipline]. In *Optimistichna teoriya na nashiya narod* [An optimistic theory of our nation]. Sofia: Otechestvo, 1970.

Halilovich, Hariz. *Kako opisati Srebrenicu/Writing after Srebrenica*. Sarajevo: Buybook, 2017.

Halilovich, Hariz. "Reclaiming Erased Lives: Archives, Records and Memories in Post-War Bosnia." *Archival Science* 14, nos. 3/4 (2014): 231–47.

Hallama, Peter. "Men and Masculinities under Socialism: Toward a Social and Cultural History." *Aspasia* 15 (2021): 1–20.

Hamber, Brandon. "Masculinity and Transitional Justice: An Exploratory Essay." *International Journal of Transitional Justice* 1, no. 3 (2007): 375–90.

Hayes, Particia, and Iona Gilburt. "Other Lives of the Image." *Kronos* 46 (2020): 10–28.

Herzog, Dagmar, ed. *Brutality and Desire: War and Sexuality in Europe's Twentieth Century*. Basingstoke: Palgrave Macmillan, 2009.

Hirsch, Marianne. *Family Frames: Photography, Narrative, and Postmemory*. Cambridge, MA: Harvard University Press, 2002.

Hofman, Ana. "Disobedient: Activist Choirs, Radical Amateurism, and the Politics of the Past after Yugoslavia." *Ethnomusicology* 64, no. 1 (2020): 89–109.

Horvat, Srećko, and Igor Štiks, eds. *Welcome to the Desert of Post-Socialism: Radical Politics after Yugoslavia*. London: Verso, 2015.

Hunt, Nancy Rose. "Afterlives: A Trajectory and the Curatorial Turn." *Allegra Lab*, May, 2020. https://allegralaboratory.net/afterlives-a-trajectory-and-the-curatorial-turn/.

Hunt, Nancy Rose. *A Nervous State: Violence, Remedies, and Reverie in Colonial Congo*. Durham, NC: Duke University Press, 2016.

Ibson, John. *Picturing Men: A Century of Male Relationships in Everyday American Photography*. Chicago: University of Chicago Press, 2006.

Ignjatijević, Marija, Bojan Elek, and Marija Pavlović. *Naoružavanjem protiv bele kuge, kriminala i korupcije: Stavovi građana o bezbednosti* [Fighting depopulation, crime, and corruption by arming: Citizens' attitudes toward security]. Belgrade: Beogradski centar za bezbednosnu politiku, 2020. https://bezbednost.org/wp -content/uploads/2020/11/naoruzanje-03.pdf.

Ingesson, Tony. "Conscription, Citizenship, and Democracy." *Oxford Research Encyclopedia of Politics*, Oxford: Oxford University Press, 2010. https://oxfordre.com/politics /view/10.1093/acrefore/9780190228637.001.0001/acrefore-9780190228637-e-1909.

Isakjee, Arshad, Thom Davies, Jelena Obradović-Wochnik, and Karolína Augustová. "Liberal Violence and the Racial Borders of the European Union." *Antipode* 52, no. 6 (2020): 1751–73.

Ivančić, Viktor, Hrvolje Polan, and Nemanja Stjepanović. *Killing Culture*. Cologne: Forum ZFD, 2019.

Jackson, David. *Unmasking Masculinity*. London: Unwin Hyman, 1990.

Jakovljević, Branislav. *Alienation Effects: Performance and Self-Management in Yugoslavia, 1945–1991*. Ann Arbor: University of Michigan Press, 2016.

Jameson, Fredric. "An American Utopia." In *An American Utopia: Dual Power and the Universal Army*, edited by Slavoj Žižek, 1–96. London: Verso, 2016.

Jan, Radoslav. "O problemima kulturnog života u Sloveniji" [About problems of cultural life in Slovenia]. In *Kulturni život u JNA*, edited by Voja Vukićević, 100–107. Belgrade: Politička uprava Državnog sekretarijata za narodnu odbranu, 1971.

Janjatović, Petar. *Ilustrovana YU rock enciklopedija: 1960–1997* [Illustrated YU rock encyclopedia]. Belgrade: Geopoetika, 1998.

Jansen, Stef. "Of Wolves and Men: Postwar Reconciliation and the Gender of Inter-National Encounters." *Focaal* 57 (2010): 33–49.

Jelača, Dijana, Maša Kolanović, and Danijela Lugarić, eds. *The Cultural Life of Capitalism in Yugoslavia: (Post)Socialism and Its Other*. Basingstoke: Palgrave Macmillan, 2017.

Jones, Ellen. *Red Army and Society: A Sociology of the Soviet Military*. Boston: Allen and Unwin, 1985.

Jullien, François. *On the Universal, the Uniform, the Common and Dialogue between Cultures*, translated by Michael Richardson and Krzysztof Fijalkowski. Cambridge: Polity Press, 2014.

Kalinin, Il'ya. "'Ugnetennye dolzhny govorit' (massovyi prizyv v literaturu i formirovanie Sovetskogo sub'ekta, 1920e–nachalo 1930kh godov)" [Subalterns must speak: On the mass call to join the literary circles, and the formation of Soviet subject from the 1920s to the early 1930s]. In *Praktiki vnutrennei kolonizatsii v kul'turnoi istorii Rossii* [Practices of internal colonization in the cultural history of Russia], edited by Alexander Etkind, Il'ya Kukulin, and Dmitry Ufel'man, 587–663. Moscow: Novoe Literaturnoe Obozrenie, 2012.

Kardov, Kruno, Lidija Knežević, and Nives Rogoznica, eds. *Kome pripadaju bivše vojne nekretnine? Iskustva prenamjene u Hrvatskoj* [To whom belong former military objects? Experiences of repurposing in Croatia]. Zagreb: Centar za mirovne studije—Zavod za sociologiju Filozofskog fakulteta u Zagrebu, 2014.

Kingston, Mark. "Subversive Friendships: Foucault on Homosexuality and Social Experimentation." *Foucault Studies* 7 (2009): 7–17.

Kirn, Gal. *The Partisan Counter-Archive: Retracing the Ruptures of Art and Memory in the Yugoslav People's Liberation Struggle*. Berlin: De Gruyter, 2020.

Kirn, Gal. *Partisan Ruptures: Self-Management, Market Reform, and the Spectre of Socialist Yugoslavia*. London: Pluto Press, 2019.

Knežević, Anto. "Inhabitants of the Proud Bosnia: The Identity of the European Native Muslims." *Islamic Studies* 40, no. 1 (2001): 133–49.

Koleva, Daniela. *Biografija i normalnost* [Biography and normality]. Sofia: LiK, 2002.

Komelj, Miklavž. "The Function of the Signifier 'Totalitarianism' in the Constitution of the 'East Art' Field." In *Retracing Images: Visual Culture after Yugoslavia*, edited by Daniel Šuber and Slobodan Karamanić, 55–79. Leiden: Brill 2012.

Korošec, Tomo, et al. *Vojaški slovar* [Military dictionary]. Ljubljana: Partizanska knjiga, 1977.

Koselleck, Reinhart. *Futures Past: On the Semantics of Historical Time*. New York: Columbia University Press, 2004.

Kratz, Corinne. *The Ones That Are Wanted: Communication and the Politics of Representation in a Photographic Exhibition*. Berkeley: University of California Press, 2002.

Krebs, Ronald R. *Fighting for Rights: Military Service and the Politics of Citizenship*. Ithaca, NY: Cornell University Press, 2011.

Kruglova, Anna. "Social Theory and Everyday Marxists: Russian Perspectives on Epistemology and Ethics." *Comparative Studies in Society and History* 59, no. 4 (2017): 759–85.

Krylova, Anna. *Soviet Women in Combat: A History of Violence on the Eastern Front*. Cambridge: Cambridge University Press, 2010.

Kulić, Vladimir. "Orientalizing Socialism: Architecture, Media, and the Representations of Eastern Europe." *Architectural Histories* 6, no. 1 (2018). https://journal.eahn.org /article/id/7546/.

Kurtović, Larisa. "An Archive to Build a Future: The Recovery and Rediscovery of the History of Socialist Associations in Contemporary Bosnia-Herzegovina." *History and Anthropology* 30, no. 1 (2019): 20–46.

Lasch, Cristopher. *The True and Only Heaven: Progress and Its Critics*. New York: Norton, 1991.

Le Normand, Brigitte. *Citizens without Borders: Yugoslavia and Its Migrant Workers in Western Europe*. Toronto: Toronto University Press, 2021.

Lindenberger, Thomas. "Eigen-Sinn, Domination and No Resistance." *Zeitgeschichte Digital*, 2015. https://docupedia.de/zg/Lindenberger_eigensinn_v1_en_2015.

Lowenthal, David. *The Past Is a Foreign Country*. Cambridge: Cambridge University Press, 1985.

Luerhman, Sonja. *Secularism Soviet Style: Teaching Atheism and Religion in a Volga Republic*. Bloomington: Indiana University Press, 2011.

MacDougall, David. *The Corporeal Image: Film, Ethnography, and the Senses*. Princeton, NJ: Princeton University Press, 2006.

MacLeish, Kenneth T. *Making War at Fort Hood: Life and Uncertainty in a Military Community*. Princeton, NJ: Princeton University Press, 2013.

Mandić, Dušan. "A Short Discourse on Painting." In *Vojak D. M. (Private D. M.): Die Welt ist schön/Svet je lep/The World Is Beautiful*, 141–43. Ljubljana: Mestna galerija Ljubljana, 2014.

Marković, Zvezdan. *Jugoslovanska narodna armada 1945–1991* [The Yugoslav People's Army 1945-1991]. Ljubljana: Založba Defensor, 2007.

Martin, Brian Joseph. *Napoleonic Friendship: Military Fraternity, Intimacy, and Sexuality in Nineteenth-Century France*. Hanover, NH: University Press of New England, 2011.

Mazzarella, William. "Totalitarian Tears: Does the Crowd Really Mean It?" *Cultural Anthropology* 30, no. 1 (2015): 91–112.

Mbembe, Achille. "The Power of the Archive and Its Limits." In *Refiguring the Archive*, edited by C. Hamilton, V. Harris, J. Taylor, M. Pickover, G. Reid, and R. Saleh, 19–27. Dordrecht: Springer, 2002.

Mbembe, Achille. "Provisional Notes on the Postcolony." *Africa* 62, no. 1 (1992): 3–37.

MCO (Medija centar "Odbrana"). *Umetnička zbirka Doma vojske Srbije* [Art collection of the Central Military Club of the Serbian Army], edited by Jelena Knežević and Vesna Mijatović Vujić. Belgrade: Medija centar "Odbrana," 2017.

Mikulan, Krunoslav, and Emil Smutni. *Partizanska vojska i Jugoslovenska armija 1941–1953* [The Partisan army and Yugoslav army 1941-1953]. Zagreb: Despot Infinitus, 2016.

Miletić, Branko B. "Predvojnička obuka u Jugoslaviji 1948-1958" [Premilitary training in Yugoslavia 1948-1958]. *Istorija 20. veka* 40, no. 1 (2022): 129–48.

Milićević, Aleksandra. "Joining the War: Masculinity, Nationalism and War Participation in the Balkans War of Secession, 1991–1995." *Nationalities Papers* 34, no. 3 (2006): 267–87.

Milivojević, Marko. "The Yugoslav People's Army: The Political Dimension." *Bradford Studies on Yugoslavia*, no. 13 (1988).

Miljački, Ana. "Once Upon a Time in Yugoslavia." *Avery Review* 35 (2018). http://www .averyreview.com/issues/35/once-upon-a-time.

Milojević, Ivana. "Transforming Violent Masculinities in Serbia and Beyond." In *Peace Psychology in the Balkans: Dealing with a Violent Past while Building Peace*, edited by Olivera Simić, Zala Volčič, and Catherine R. Philpot, 57–73. New York: Springer, 2012.

Milošević, Zoran. "Prilog proučavanju vojnog pitanja u slovenačkom programu civilnog društva" [A contribution to the research on the military questions in the Slovene civil society program]. *Politička misao* 25, no. 4 (1988): 94–104.

Moll, Nicolas. "A Positive Hero for Everyone? The Memorialization of Srđan Aleksić in Post-Yugoslav Countries." *Contemporary Southeastern Europe* 3, no. 1 (2016). https://unipub.uni-graz.at//cse/periodical/titleinfo/1887073.

Moran, Mary H. "Gender, Militarism, and Peace-Building: Projects of the Postconflict Moment." *Annual Review of Anthropology* 39 (2010): 261–74.

Mouzelis, Nicos P. "On Total Institutions." *Sociology* 5, no. 1 (1971): 113–20.

Naylor, Kenneth. "The Sociolinguistic Situation in Yugoslavia, with Special Emphasis on Serbo-Croatian." In *Language Planning in Yugoslavia*, edited by Ranko Bugarski and Celia Hawkesworth, 80–92. Columbus, OH: Slavica, 1992.

Nenadović, Aleksandar. *Razgovori s Kočom* [Conversations with Koča]. Zagreb: Globus, 1989.

Niarchos, Catherine. "Women, War, and Rape: Challenges Facing the International Tribunal for the Former Yugoslavia." *Human Rights Quarterly* 17, no. 4 (1995): 649–90.

Niebuhr, Robert. "Death of the Yugoslav People's Army and the Wars of Succession." *Polemos* 7, nos. 1/2 (2004): 91–106.

Onyeoziri, Gloria Nne. *Shaken Wisdom: Irony and Meaning in Postcolonial African Fiction*. Charlottesville: University of Virginia Press, 2011.

Oružane snage Socijalističke federativne republike Jugoslavije [The armed forces of the Socialist Federative Republic of Yugoslavia]. Belgrade: Novinsko-izdavačka ustanova Narodna armija, n.d.

Palčok, Zoran. "Uloga aktivne kulturne djelatnosti u procesu prilagođavanja društvenoj sredini" [The role of cultural activities in the process of adaptation to the social setting]. In *Kulturni život u JNA* [Cultural life in the JNA], edited by Voja Vukićević, 108–18. Belgrade: Politička uprava Državnog sekretarijata za narodnu odbranu, 1971.

Pankhurst, Donna. "Post-War Backlash Violence against Women: What Can 'Masculinity' Explain?" In *Gendered Peace: Women's Struggles for Post-War Justice and Reconciliation*, edited by Donna Pankhurst, 293–320. London: Routledge, 2010.

Pantelić, Ivana. "Yugoslav Female Partisans in World War II." *Cahiers Balkaniques* 41 (2013): 239–50.

Patterson, Patrick H. *Bought and Sold: Living and Losing the Good Life in Socialist Yugoslavia*. Ithaca, NY: Cornell University Press, 2011.

Pedwell. Carolyn. *Revolutionary Routines: The Habits of Social Transformation*. Montreal: McGill-Queen's University Press, 2021.

Petrović, Tanja. "Mourning the Lost Modernity: Industrial Labor, Europe, and (Post) Yugoslav Post-Socialism." In *Mirroring Europe: Ideas of Europe and Europeanization in Balkan Societies*, edited by Tanja Petrović, 91–113. Leiden: Brill, 2014.

Petrović, Tanja. "Nostalgia for the JNA? Remembering the Army in the Former Yugoslavia." In *Post-Communist Nostalgia*, edited by Maria Todorova and Zsuzsa Gille, 61–81. Oxford: Berghahn Books, 2010.

Petrović, Tanja. "Officers without an Army: Memories of Socialism and Everyday Strategies in Post-Socialist Slovenia." In *Remembering Utopia: The Culture of Everyday Life in Socialist Yugoslavia*, edited by Breda Luthar and Maruša Pušnik, 93–118. Washington, DC: New Academia, 2010.

Petrović, Tanja. "Towards an Affective History of Yugoslavia." *Filozofija i društvo* 27, no. 3 (2016): 504–20.

Petrović, Tanja. "When We Were Europe: Socialist Workers in Serbia and Their Nostalgic Narratives—the Case of the Cable Factory Workers in Jagodina." In *Remembering Communism: Genres of Representation*, edited by Maria Todorova, 127–53. New York: Social Science Research Council, 2010.

Petrović, Tanja. *Yuropa: Jugoslovensko nasleđe i politike budućnosti u postjugoslovenskim društvima* [Yuropa: Yugoslav legacy and the politics of the future in post-Yugoslav societies]. Belgrade: Fabrika knjiga, 2015.

Pine, Frances. "Inside and Outside the Language of Kinship: Public and Private Conceptions of Sociality." In *Reconnecting State and Kinship*, edited by Tatjana Thelen and Erdmute Alber, 87–107. Philadelphia: University of Pennsylvania Press, 2018.

Plato. *The Republic*, edited by G. R. F. Ferrari, translated by Tom Griffith. Cambridge: Cambridge University Press, 2000.

Podlesnik, Mateja. "Die verkehrte Welt/The Topsy-Turvy World." In *Vojak D. M. (Private D. M.): Die Welt ist schön/Svet je lep/The World Is Beautiful*, 13–20. Ljubljana: Mestna galerija Ljubljana, 2014.

Požgaj-Hadži, Vesna. "Language Policy and Linguistic Reality in Former Yugoslavia and Its Successor States." *Interfaculty* 5 (2014): 49–91.

Radišić, Đorđe. *Vojaki—likovni umetniki* [Soldiers—figurative artists], exhibition catalog. Ljubljana: Mestna Galerija, 1973.

Radovanović, Milorad. *Planiranje jezika i drugi spisi* [Language planning and other works]. Novi Sad: Izdavačka knjižarnica Zorana Stojanovića, 2004.

Rajković, Ivan. "Future Snatchers and Their Tactics." *Etnološka tribina* 50, no. 43 (2020): 20–23.

Rexepi, Piro. "Arab Others at European Borders: Racializing Refugees along the Balkan Route." *Ethnic and Racial Studies* 41, no. 12 (2018): 2215–34.

Richter, Gerhard. *Afterness: Figures of Following in Modern Thought and Aesthetics.* New York: Columbia University Press, 2011.

Rusinow, Dennison. "The Yugoslav Idea before Yugoslavia." In *Yugoslavism: Histories of a Failed Idea, 1918–1992*, edited by Dejan Djokić, 11–26. London: Hurst, 2003.

Samuel, Raphael. *Theatres of Memory: Past and Present in Contemporary Culture.* London: Verso, 1994.

Scarboro, Cristofer. "Living after the Fall: Contingent Biographies in Post-Socialist Europe." *Südosteuropa* 64, no. 3 (2016): 277–83.

Schroer-Hippel, Miriam. *Gewaltfreie Männlichkeitsideale: Psychologische Perspektiven auf zivilgesellschaftliche Friedensarbeit* [Nonviolent ideals of masculinity: Psychological perspectives on civil society work for peace]. Berlin: Springer, 2017.

Schwenkel, Christina. *Building Socialism: The Afterlife of East German Architecture in Urban Vietnam.* Durham, NC: Duke University Press, 2020.

Scott, David. *Omens of Adversity: Tragedy, Time, Memory, Justice.* Durham, NC: Duke University Press, 2014.

Sekula, Allan. "The Body and the Archive." *October* 39 (1986): 3–64.

Sharma, Devika, and Frederik Tygstrup, eds. *Structures of Feeling: Affectivity and the Study of Culture.* Berlin: Walter de Gruyter, 2015.

Shevchenko, Olga. *Crisis and the Everyday in Post-Socialist Moscow.* Bloomington: Indiana University Press, 2009.

Sivakumaran, Sandesh. "Sexual Violence against Men in Armed Conflict." *European Journal of International Law* 18, no. 2 (2007): 253–76.

Slavković, Mirjana, and Marija Đorgović, eds. *Nostalgia on the Move.* Belgrade: Museum of Yugoslavia, 2017.

Smith, Tom. *Comrades in Arms: Military Masculinities in East German Culture.* Oxford: Berghahn Books, 2020.

Søndergaard, Dorte Marie. "Poststructuralist Approaches to Empirical Analysis." *International Journal of Qualitative Studies in Education* 15 (2002): 187–204.

Sontag, Susan. *On Photography.* New York: Farrar, Straus and Giroux, 1977.

Spaskovska, Ljubica. "The 'Heteroglossia' of Loss: Memory, Forgetting and (Post)-Yugoslav Citizenship." In *Cultures and Politics of Remembrance: Southeast European and Balkan Perspectives*, edited by Naum Trajanovski, Petar Todorov, Biljana Volchevska, and Ljupcho S. Risteski, 35–40. Skopje: Forum ZFD, 2021.

Spiegelman, Art. *Maus: Zgodba o preživetju, II: In tu so se začele moje težave* [*Maus II, a Survivor's Tale: And Here My Troubles Began*]. Ljubljana: Založba ZRC, 2003.

Stergar, Rok, and Tamara Scheer. "Ethnic Boxes: The Unintended Consequences of Habsburg Bureaucratic Classification." *Nationalities Papers* 46, no. 4 (2018): 575–91.

Štiks, Igor. "Activist Aesthetics in the Post-Socialist Balkans: Resistance, Rebellion, Emancipation." *Third Text* 34, nos. 4/5 (2020): 461–79.

Stilinović, Mladen, Bieke Cattoor, and Bruno De Meulder. "Mapping the Realms of the Soldiers: Cartographies of Military Landscapes in Skopje and Bitola." Paper presented at the conference Virtual City and Territory, Rome, October 2013. https://upcommons.upc.edu/handle/2099/16387.

Stoler, Ann Laura. "Introduction." In *Imperial Debris: On Ruins and Ruination*, edited by Ann Laura Stoler, 1–35. Durham, NC: Duke University Press, 2013.

Stover, William J. "The Armed Forces and Nation Building: Revolutionary Socialist Theory and Praxis in China." *Journal of Contemporary Asia* 6, no. 3 (1976): 323–33.

Strangleman, Tim. "Deindustrialisation and the Historical Sociological Imagination: Making Sense of Work and Industrial Change." *Sociology* 51, no. 2 (2017): 466–82.

Štravs, Jane. *Photographic Incarnations*. Ljubljana: Založba ZRC, 2003.

Stubbs, Paul. "The Emancipatory Afterlives of Non-Aligned Internationalism." *Rosa Luxemburg Stiftung*, January 2020. https://www.rosalux.de/en/publication/id/41631/the-emancipatory-afterlives-of-non-aligned-internationalism.

Supek, Rudi. "Sociološki značaj amaterizma" [The sociological importance of amateurism]. *Kultura* 26 (1974): 8–16.

Sztandara, Magdalena. "Expired Places and Forgotten People: Spatial and Temporal Practices of Military Homeless People in Serbia." *Time and Society* 28, no. 2 (2019): 521–42.

Tagg, John. *The Burden of Representation: Essays on Photographies and Histories*. Amherst: University of Massachusetts Press, 1988.

Taylor, Karin, and Hannes Grandits. "Tourism and the Making of Socialist Yugoslavia." In *Yugoslavia's Sunny Side: A History of Tourism in Socialism (1950s–1980s)*, edited by Hannes Grandits and Karin Taylor, 1–30. Budapest: Central European University Press, 2010.

Theidon, Kimberly. "Reconstructing Masculinities: The Disarmament, Demobilization, and Reintegration of Former Combatants in Colombia." *Human Rights Quarterly* 31, no. 1 (2009): 1–34.

Thompson, Edward Palmer. *The Railway: An Adventure in Construction*. London: Yugoslav-British Association, 1947.

Tikhomirov, Alexey. "The Grammar of Trust and Distrust under State Socialism after Stalin: An Introduction." *Journal of Modern European History* 15, no. 3 (2017): 313–29.

Todorova, Maria. *Imagining Utopia: The Lost World of Socialists at Europe's Margins, 1870s–1920s*. London: I. B. Tauris, 2020.

Tomić, Ante. *Ništa nas ne smije iznenaditi: roman* [Nothing should surprise us: A novel]. Zaprešić: Fraktura, 2003.

Trachtenberg, Alan. *Reading American Photographs*. New York: Hill and Wang, 1989.

Ugrešić, Dubravka. "An Archaeology of Resistance." In *The Age of Skin: Essays*. Translated by Ellen Elias-Bursać, 221–36. Rochester, NY: Open Letter Books, 2020.

Van Dijck, José. *Mediated Memories: Personal Cultural Memory in the Digital Age*. Stanford, CA: Stanford University Press, 2007.

Velikonja, Mitja. *Titostalgia: A Study of Nostalgia for Josip Broz*. Ljubljana: Peace Institute, 2008.

Verdery, Katherine. "Socialist Societies: Anthropological Aspects." *International Encyclopedia of the Social and Behavioral Sciences*, 2nd edition, vol. 22 (2015), 849–53.

Vratuša, Anton, et al., eds. *Enciklopedija samoupravljanja* [Encyclopedia of self-management]. Belgrade: Savremena administracija, Izdavački centar Komunist, 1979.

Vučetić, Radina. *Nevidljivi neprijatelj: Variola vera 1972* [An invisible enemy: Variola Vera 1972]. Belgrade: Službeni glasnik, 2022.

Vukićević, Voja. "Koherentnost nacionalnih kultura u kulturnom životu JNA" [The coherence of national cultures in the cultural life of the JNA]. In *Kulturni život u JNA* [Cultural life of the JNA], edited by Voja Vukićević, 93–99. Belgrade: Politička uprava Državnog sekretarijata za narodnu odbranu, 1971.

Vukušić, Iva. *Serbian Paramilitaries and the Breakup of Yugoslavia: State Connections and Patterns of Violence*. London: Routledge, 2022.

Wedeen, Lisa. *Ambiguities of Domination: Politics, Rhetoric, and Symbols in Contemporary Syria*. Chicago: University of Chicago Press, 1999.

Weidman, Amanda. "Anthropology and Voice." *Annual Review of Anthropology* 43 (2014): 37–51.

Wetherell, Margaret. *Affect and Emotion: A New Social Science Understanding*. London: Sage, 2012.

White, Luise. "Civic Virtue, Young Men, and the Family: Conscription in Rhodesia, 1974–1980." *International Journal of African Historical Studies* 37, no. 1 (2004): 103–21.

Williams, Raymond. *Marxism and Literature*. Oxford: Oxford University Press, 1985.

Willis, Deborah. "A Search for Self: The Photograph and Black Family Life." In *The Familial Gaze*, edited by Marianne Hirsch, 107–23. Hanover, NH: University Press of New England, 1999.

Wilmer, Franke. *The Social Construction of Men, the State, and War: Identity, Conflict, and Violence in the Former Yugoslavia*. London: Routledge, 2002.

Yurchak, Alexei. *Everything Was Forever until It Was No More: The Last Soviet Generation*. Princeton, NJ: Princeton University Press, 2006.

Yurchak, Alexei. "Soviet Hegemony of Form: Everything Was Forever, until It Was No More." *Comparative Studies in Society and History* 45, no. 3 (2003): 480–510.

Zagorac, Đuro. *Jovanka*. Belgrade: AIZ Dosije, 1990.

Žarkov, Dubravka. *The Body of War: Media, Ethnicity, and Gender in the Break-Up of Yugoslavia*. Durham, NC: Duke University Press, 2007.

Žerdin, Ali. *Generali brez kape: Čas Odbora za varstvo človekovih pravic* [Generals without caps: Time of the Committee for the Defense of Human Rights]. Ljubljana: Krtina, 2007.

Žilnik, Želimir, and Boris Buden. *Uvod u prošlost* [Introduction to the past]. Novi Sad: Kuda, 2013.

Zimmermann, Warren. *Origins of a Catastrophe: Yugoslavia and Its Destroyers—America's Last Ambassador Tells What Happened and Why*. New York: Times Books, 1996.

Index

civilians, 79, 82–85, 90, 103, 127, 205n16; clothes, 84, 124, 150, 158, 178; life, 66, 69, 78; self, 77, 87; society, 58

civil service, 25

civil war, 4, 62

class, 28, 52, 55–60, 103, 117, 190–93; background, 7, 40–41; barriers, 30; boundaries, 40, 56, 192; difference, 49, 55; divisions, 12, 40, 60, 215n27; identity, 19, 35, 57, 190; struggle, 22; working, 49

classlessness, 60, 203n57

Coates, Jennifer, 32

Cold War, 120, 214n11

collectivity, 7, 10, 12, 20, 29–30, 38, 58, 120, 192

college, 4, 40. 69, 77, 164. *See also* education; university

colonialism, 1, 11

comic books, 49

commands, 47–48, 64–65, 68, 72

commemoration, 99, 143–44, 210n27

common ground, 17–18, 164

communism, 46–47, 58, 61–63, 155–56

Communist Party of Yugoslavia, 24–25, 204n6

community, 52, 185, 192; affective, 12; amoral, 122; ethnic, 1, 24, 38, 122; international, 1; political, 185, 188; religious, 24; rural, 45

comradeship, 7, 12, 21, 29, 35, 170

Comrades/Jarani, 162, 182

concentration camp, 132, 135; Nazi, 109, 197n47; Trnopolje, Bosnia and Herzegovina, 17, 132

confinement, 4, 6, 13, 34, 56–57, 72, 75, 92, 150, 159, 163, 167, 176, 179, 191

conflict, 3, 28–29, 39, 49, 69, 138, 147, 188–89; ethnic, 26; Kosovo, 134, 174

conscientious objection, 13, 25, 59, 120, 196n22, 199n10

conscription, 4, 14, 39–40, 43, 50, 186–87, 203n45; mandatory, 35, 41, 50; universal, 24–25, 38–39, 41, 58, 82. *See also* draft

conservativism, 26, 61, 190

continuity, 5, 8, 33–34, 148, 162, 181

control, 13, 15, 63, 71, 97, 102, 104, 106–7, 119, 124, 154, 156, 158–59, 191

cooking, 16, 42, 70, 86–87

Coordinative Commission for Realization of the Constitution, 46

Ćosić, Svetlana, 45

cosmopolitanism, 39–40

COURAGE (Cultural Opposition—Understanding the Cultural Heritage of Dissent in the Former Socialist Countries), 197n47

COVID-19, 20, 185

criminality, 46–47, 71, 141

Croatian Democratic Union, 213n12

Croats, 34, 122; and nationhood, 23; socialists, 178

cultural centers, 7, 25, 56, 82–83, 89, 132, 215n27

cultural production, 7, 37

culture, 10, 39, 154–55; American, 170; alternative, 159; high, 32; national, 25; popular, 4, 26–27, 30, 32–33, 113; punk, 138; socialist, 32

curfew, 166

Cvetkovich, Ann, 10

cynicism, 11, 29–30, 196n32. See also *stiob*

Cyrillic, 136, 140, 182

Đakovica, Kosovo, 185

Đakovo, Croatia, 175

Dalmatia, Croatia, 183, 199n11

Deakin, William, 204n2

death, 34, 117, 129, 144, 151, 169, 177, 180. *See also* killing; violence

dedications, 8, 169

dehumanization, 77

democratic principles, 28, 188

desensitization, 74

despair, 69, 130

destruction, 5, 13, 19, 34–35, 122, 139, 142–45, 174–75, 177, 182, 188

detachment, 12, 37–40, 49, 60, 67, 77, 107, 138, 159, 163–64

Dežulović, Boris, 144

dialect, 45, 47, 52, 93, 177; Serbian, 177. *See also* language

Die Welt ist schön: Private D. M., 91, 101–2, 157–59

difference: class, 49, 55; educational, 55–56; erasure of, 18, 19, 85–86, 102–3; ethnic, 49, 55, 127; language, 165

Dimitrijević, Dejan, 50, 52, 55, 165, 177–80

disaffection, 74

disaster aid, 41, 43–44, 103, 120

discipline, 6–7, 18, 25, 28, 33, 61–63, 69, 76, 85, 97, 124, 163, 186, 190, 204n7

discontinuity, 181, 190

discotheque, 83

discourse, 11–13, 16, 21, 49, 51, 75, 102–3, 143, 155–56; academic, 26; authoritative, 11–12, 21, 197n38; hegemonic, 156; ideological, 99, 155; political, 26; public, 143; ritualized, 102–3

diversity, 47–49, 53–55, 57–58, 164; cultural, 40; linguistic, 49; radical, 18, 30, 75

division, 12, 113, 175; class, 12, 40, 60, 215n27; educational, 35; ethnic 12, 35, 60; gender, 12; linguistic, 60; social, 35, 40

DNA identification, 146–47

Doboj, Bosnia and Herzegovina, 151

documentary film, 90, 134, 151, 162, 205n5

dom vojske. See cultural centers

www.ingramcontent.com/pod-product-compliance
Lightning Source LLC
Chambersburg PA
CBHW071737270326
41928CB00013B/2707